London calling Italy

Manchester University Press

STUDIES IN POPULAR CULTURE
General editor: Professor Jeffrey Richards

Already published

Dancing in the English style: consumption, Americanisation, and national identity in Britain, 1918–50   Allison Abra

Christmas in nineteenth-century England   Neil Armstrong

Healthy living in the Alps: the origins of winter tourism in Switzerland, 1860–1914   Susan Barton

Working-class organisations and popular tourism, 1840–1970   Susan Barton

Leisure, citizenship and working-class men in Britain, 1850–1945   Brad Beaven

Leisure and cultural conflict in twentieth-century Britain   Brett Bebber (ed.)

Leisure cultures in urban Europe, c.1700–1870: a transnational perspective   Peter Borsay and Jan Hein Furnée (eds)

British railway enthusiasm   Ian Carter

Railways and culture in Britain   Ian Carter

Time, work and leisure: life changes in England since 1700   Hugh Cunningham

Darts in England, 1900–39: a social history   Patrick Chaplin

Holiday camps in twentieth-century Britain: packaging pleasure   Sandra Trudgen Dawson

History on British television: constructing nation, nationality and collective memory   Robert Dillon

The food companions: cinema and consumption in wartime Britain, 1939–45   Richard Farmer

Songs of protest, songs of love: popular ballads in eighteenth-century Britain   Robin Ganev

Heroes and happy endings: class, gender, and nation in popular film and fiction in interwar Britain   Christine Grandy

Women drinking out in Britain since the early twentieth century   David W. Gutzke

The BBC and national identity in Britain, 1922–53   Thomas Hajkowski

From silent screen to multi-screen: a history of cinema exhibition in Britain since 1896   Stuart Hanson

Dangerous amusements: Leisure, the young working class and urban space in Britain, c. 1870–1939   Laura Harrison

Juke box Britain: Americanisation and youth culture, 1945–60   Adrian Horn

Popular culture in London, c. 1890–1918: the transformation of entertainment   Andrew Horrall

Inventing the cave man: from Darwin to the Flintstones   Andrew Horrall

Popular culture and working-class taste in Britain, 1930–39: a round of cheap diversions?   Robert James

The experience of suburban modernity: how private transport changed interwar London   John M. Law

Worlds of social dancing: Dance floor encounters and the global rise of couple dancing, c. 1910–40   Klaus Nathaus and James Nott (eds)

Amateur film: meaning and practice, 1927-1977   Heather Norris Nicholson

Films and British national identity: from Dickens to *Dad's Army*   Jeffrey Richards

Cinema and radio in Britain and America, 1920–60   Jeffrey Richards

Looking North: Northern England and the national imagination   Dave Russell

The British seaside holiday: holidays and resorts in the twentieth century   John K. Walton

Politics, performance and popular culture in the nineteenth century   Peter Yeandle, Katherine Newe and Jeffrey Richards

London calling Italy

BBC broadcasts during the Second World War

Ester Lo Biundo

MANCHESTER UNIVERSITY PRESS

Copyright © Ester Lo Biundo 2022

The right of Ester Lo Biundo to be identified as the author of this work has been asserted by them in accordance with the Copyright, Designs and Patents Act 1988.

All translations of BBC material are the author's own and have not been checked by the BBC.

Published by Manchester University Press
Oxford Road, Manchester M13 9PL

www.manchesteruniversitypress.co.uk

British Library Cataloguing-in-Publication Data
A catalogue record for this book is available from the British Library

ISBN 978 1 5261 6481 0 hardback
ISBN 978 1 5261 9080 2 paperback

First published 2022
Paperback published 2025

The publisher has no responsibility for the persistence or accuracy of URLs for any external or third-party internet websites referred to in this book, and does not guarantee that any content on such websites is, or will remain, accurate or appropriate.

EU authorised representative for GPSR:
Easy Access System Europe – Mustamäe tee 50,
10621 Tallinn, Estonia
gpsr.requests@easproject.com

Typeset
by New Best-set Typesetters Ltd

STUDIES IN POPULAR CULTURE

There has in recent years been an explosion of interest in culture and cultural studies. The impetus has come from two directions and out of two different traditions. On the one hand, cultural history has grown out of social history to become a distinct and identifiable school of historical investigation. On the other hand, cultural studies has grown out of English literature and has concerned itself to a large extent with contemporary issues. Nevertheless, there is a shared project, its aim, to elucidate the meanings and values implicit and explicit in the art, literature, learning, institutions and everyday behaviour within a given society. Both the cultural historian and the cultural studies scholar seek to explore the ways in which a culture is imagined, represented and received, how it interacts with social processes, how it contributes to individual and collective identities and world views, to stability and change, to social, political and economic activities and programmes. This series aims to provide an arena for the cross-fertilisation of the discipline, so that the work of the cultural historian can take advantage of the most useful and illuminating of the theoretical developments and the cultural studies scholars can extend the purely historical underpinnings of their investigations. The ultimate objective of the series is to provide a range of books which will explain in a readable and accessible way where we are now socially and culturally and how we got to where we are. This should enable people to be better informed, promote an interdisciplinary approach to cultural issues and encourage deeper thought about the issues, attitudes and institutions of popular culture.

Jeffrey Richards

To Christopher Duggan, a kind historian who believed in the younger generations

Contents

Acknowledgements	*page* viii
List of abbreviations	x
General editor's foreword	xi
Introduction: why Radio London?	1
1 Radio at war	19
2 The Italian Service	38
3 Exiles: biographies, memories and experiences of the Italian anti-fascist broadcasters	53
4 The Italian broadcasters and the British Foreign Office	80
5 The enemy: Ente Italiano per le Audizioni Radiofoniche (EIAR)	98
6 Occupation/liberation	132
7 Who tuned in to the BBC? The Italian Service: its target audiences and listeners	156
Conclusion: Radio Londra between myth and reality	191
Bibliography	196
Index	203

Acknowledgements

Behind every book there is a human being with a personal story. A story made up of moves to different houses, cities and countries; many jobs; professional encounters; friends both old and new. My story is full of joyful and terrible chapters. Every single chapter has contributed to giving me strength and courage. If I were to acknowledge all the people who have been part of both my professional and personal life since I embarked on this research project, I would have to write a second manuscript, but I will try to accomplish this mission in a few paragraphs.

My first thought goes to Christopher Duggan. Christopher was the reason why I started my journey at the University of Reading. Many years ago, when I met him in his office, he encouraged me to apply for research funding. I was new to the UK and he helped me navigate the world of British academe. His guidance has been terribly missed, but I strongly believe that his legacy will continue to live in every individual with a genuine passion for history.

I was very lucky to receive the advice of Matthew Worley, John Foot, Hilary Footitt and Philip Cooke, who gave me very constructive feedback on this manuscript during my years at the University of Reading.

I would not have been able to write this book without the financial support of the AHRC (Arts and Humanities Research Council) and the University of Reading. I am extremely grateful to Matthew Worley and the history department for granting me access to a library account when I was no longer a member of the University of Reading.

Special thanks go to Claudia Baldoli, John Dickie, Mirco Dondi, David Hendy, Salvatore Lupo, Marzia Maccaferri, Andrea Mammone, Arturo Marzano, Richard Overy, Manoela Patti, Simon Potter, Linda Risso, Lucio Sponza, Simona Tobia, Alban Webb and all the academics who have offered some of their time to discuss my professional and research projects while I was working on this book.

It was a pleasure to meet Danny Nissim, son of the BBC broadcaster Elio Nissim. Danny generously provided me with interesting material for my research and offered his help for future public engagement projects. The photo of the cover of this book belongs to his personal collection.

Giorgio Peresso told me of the existence of some key archival documents among the records of the British Labour Party in Manchester.

The Kluge Center of the Library of Congress welcomed me into a vibrant and friendly environment during my AHRC fellowship in Washington, DC.

Another thought goes to the members of staff of the BBC Written Archives Centre, the National Archives, the British Library, the People's History Museum and all the institutions and universities I visited for archival research and conferences. The opportunity of presenting my research at international conferences and expanding my networks helped me grow as an academic.

The chats and pints I shared with other early career researchers made me feel part of an international community. I was delighted to meet Esther, Michela, Neha, Usha, Julia, Adnan, Ya-Ting, Stefania P., Maria R., George, Armen, Anna B. R., and all the research fellows of the Library of Congress.

It was a great privilege to be able to rely on old and new friends like Francesca, Maria Chiara, Valentina, Alberto C., Castrenze, Silvia, Giuseppe, Martina, Stefania, Lia, Marzia, Gabriella, Annalisa D., Pauline, Alessandro, Annamaria, Sara and Giulia O.

The biggest thanks go my family, to those who are here and to my parents who are no longer with us. I am especially grateful to Manuel, Sergio and Bruna for their support and encouragement.

Abbreviations

BBC	British Broadcasting Corporation (formerly Company)
BBC WAC	BBC Written Archives Centre
DNPA, ENP	Danny Nissim Personal Archive, Elio Nissim Papers
EIAR	Ente Italiano per le Audizioni Radiofoniche
FAM, SNSP	Fondo Arnoldo Momigliano, Scuola Normale Superiore di Pisa
FUC, CSPG	Fondo Umberto Calosso, Centro Studi Piero Gobetti
IS	Italian Service
ISH, PTP	Institute for Social History, Paolo Treves Papers
FFT FPT	Fondazione Filippo Turati, Fondo Paolo Treves
FO	Foreign Office
IBU	International Broadcasting Union
JRL	John Rylands Library
MGA	*Manchester Guardian* Archive
MI5	Military Intelligence 5
NAO	National Archives
OVRA	Opera Volontaria di Repressione Antifascista
PHM, IDLP, WGP	People's History Museum, International Division, Labour Party, William Gillies Papers
PWB	Psychological Warfare Branch
PWE	Political Warfare Executive
RSI	Repubblica Sociale Italiana

General editor's foreword

The Second World War was a wireless war. People tuned into the radio for news and entertainment but governments turned to it as a vehicle for propaganda both on the Home Front and for allies and enemies overseas. The BBC Italian Service was one of the foreign services established during the Second World War following Italy's entry into the war on the side of Germany. Ester Lo Biundo's book is the first full-length study in English to focus squarely on the history of the Italian Service as she seeks to answer three principal questions: to what extent Italian exiles working for the BBC were allowed to operate independently of the British Foreign Office; what the broadcasts said to win over the Italian population, particularly after the Italian surrender to the allies in 1943; and how the broadcasts were received by the Italian population.

Drawing on a wide variety of sources, including the memoirs of Italian broadcasters working for the BBC, the written transcripts of the broadcasts, BBC audience surveys and letters from Italian listeners to the BBC, she traces the delicate balancing act that had to be performed by the Corporation, which was the voice simultaneously of an occupier and a liberator from Nazi domination. The prime directive behind the propaganda was to make a distinction between Italians and fascists. Italian civilians and even Italian soldiers were invariably portrayed as the victims of an irresponsible regime and a treacherous ally. Broadcasts were to stress what the British and Italian people had in common. The success of Radio London lay in the effective deployment of stereotypes of British and Italian life and habits, the celebration of Italy's cultural heritage and the transmission of messages from Italian prisoners in British prisoner-of-war camps. The book successfully extends our understanding of the nature, function and limitations of propaganda.

Jeffrey Richards

Introduction: why Radio London?

According to an anecdote reported by Asa Briggs, when the Allies landed in Sicily in July 1943, some strange graffiti on the walls of Sicilian cities and towns were found by the Anglo-American soldiers who were occupying the island. One of these graffiti was dedicated to the most famous broadcaster of the BBC Italian Service, and read '*Viva il Colonnello Stevens*' ('Hooray for Colonel Stevens').[1] The truth of this anecdote is difficult, if not impossible, to verify. However, its existence explains much about the popularity of Radio Londra, as the BBC was known in Italy.

The BBC Italian Service was one of the foreign services established during the Second World War. The first broadcast in Italian dated back to September 1938, when Chamberlain's speech on the Munich crisis was translated and broadcast in France, Germany and Italy. However, it was only in 1940, after Italy entered the war on the side of Germany, that the Italian Service was properly established.

The Italian Service's broadcasts constitute one of the myths of Italian cultural heritage of the Second World War.[2] I use the word myth in this book to refer to events, facts and phenomena that are only partially true. As I will explain, false or non-verifiable information about the BBC circulated in Italy during the conflict. Yet false rumours about the BBC Italian Service are extremely valuable since they reveal a great deal about the impact that the British broadcasts had on the lives of Italian civilians. The myth of Radio Londra can be attributed to both the memories of the Italian exiles working at the BBC and the reception of the programmes in Italy at the time. It is undeniable that BBC programmes supported the Italian population during the war. However, it should be noted that these programmes were perceived by a portion of Italian society as 'the voice of freedom', despite Radio London being the station of an enemy country. The memories of the coded messages broadcast to the partisans during the

Italian resistance to Nazi Germany are particularly vivid for those who experienced the war and for subsequent generations who heard about the station from their elderly relatives or friends. The same can be said of the gatherings of people who secretly listened to British news bulletins in the basements of many houses.[3] Almost eighty years after the end of the conflict, Radio Londra is still remembered as the genuine voice of anti-fascism. A simple online search shows that British radio is commonly associated with the Italian Resistance, since positive information on the BBC can often be found on local websites of the Associazione Nazionale Partigiani d'Italia (National Association of Italian Partisans, ANPI).[4] Just to provide another example, a card game called *Radio Londra. Ora e sempre Resistenza* can be found among the results of a Google search. The game, devised by the Frenchman Charles Chevallier, can be played by three to six people. The players include a broadcaster who reads out a special coded message, some partisans and a member of the *Wehrmacht*. The partisans and the member of the *Wehrmacht* have to interpret the message correctly in order to win the game.[5]

There are several legends about the Second World War in Italy, as often happens in the history of traumatic events. Among these was the story of Pippo, the small Allied aircraft which, many civilians believed, flew over Italy every night to check on the population and ensure that the curfew laws were respected. Pippo had various names and features in different areas of Italy. Called Pippo in the Northern Salò Republic and Ciccio o'ferroviere (Ciccio the railwayman) in the South, this almost anthropomorphic plane was the embodiment of the difficulties Italians faced due to the war and the fascist regime. Pippo was also the symbolic representation of the ambivalent role of the Allies, who were sending friendly messages to the Italians while at the same time bombing their cities.[6] The legend of Pippo was particularly popular in the north of the country.

Another widespread tale, more common in the south of Italy, related to the Allied landings in Sicily. According to the story, during Operation Husky Anglo-American tanks and aircraft bore flags with the printed initials of Lucky Luciano. These flags were interpreted as proof of the vital help given to the Allies by the famous Sicilian mafioso who had emigrated to the United States. Moreover, the flags showed evidence of collaboration between the Anglo-American authorities and the Sicilian mafia. Both stories, though undoubtedly fascinating, have been discredited by historians and archival evidence.[7] To some extent, the myth of Radio Londra in Italy is similar to these stories.

On the British side, the BBC programmes in Italian, as well as in other foreign languages, were very important because they helped to export the British model to other countries, not only during the Second World War, but also during the Cold War. As noted by Alban Webb, the post-war period was a turning point in the history of the BBC, since 'it opened a window on the world while at the same time introducing audiences abroad to British culture, politics and institutions'.[8]

Despite the key role played by Radio London's broadcasts both in Italy and Britain, we cannot rely on satisfactory scholarly work on the BBC Italian Service. Radio London's campaigns are often mentioned in publications on the conflict, especially in monographs about Anglo-American war propaganda, the Allied Italian campaign and the Italian Resistance.[9] However, none of these studies focuses specifically on the history of the BBC Italian Service and its programmes.

The only really comprehensive work on the topic before 2014 was an inventory curated by Maura Piccialuti Caprioli in collaboration with historian Claudio Pavone.[10] The inventory, published in 1976 by the Italian Ministero per i Beni Culturali e Ambientali, has made the Italian Service's archives more accessible. It encompasses details of the documents held at the BBC Written Archives Centre in Caversham, Berkshire as well as other useful sources for researching Radio London. While Piccialuti Caprioli's work provides an insight into the history of the Italian section of Radio London and its protagonists, her aim was not to write an exhaustive history of the BBC Italian Service. The author's scope was rather to create a catalogue for researchers and to promote research on the subject.

Piccialuti Caprioli's inventory was the starting point of a research project I undertook nearly ten years ago for a Master's thesis. The results of this study developed into a book entitled *London Calling Italy: La propaganda di Radio Londra nel 1943*, published in 2014.[11] Its scope was to understand how the station prepared the Italian population for the Allied landing in Sicily in July 1943 and for Italy's consequent unconditional surrender. The book addresses issues such as the political influence of the British Foreign Office on the BBC, as well as the role of the Italian anti-fascist exiles working for the corporation. In doing so, it analysed the content of the programmes broadcast in 1943 and attempted to paint a portrait of the listeners in Italy.

The aim of this work is to continue the research I started in *London calling Italy* by studying the programmes broadcast during the Allied Italian campaign in 1943–45, and to support the discoveries I have already made with further documentation and literature. However, this monograph is more international in scope and aims to contribute to the rewriting of the history of the BBC from a foreign angle.

After explaining why it is relevant to undertake research on Radio Londra, the next section will place this book in the context of scholarly publications about the BBC.

The BBC foreign services: a brief review of the literature

Writing an exhaustive literature review about the BBC is not a mission that any academic can accomplish in one single monograph. The variety of approaches, disciplines, years investigated, type of media (radio, podcasts, TV, streaming platforms) and geographical areas examined makes it impossible to adopt a holistic approach to the study of the corporation. The diversity of past and present research groups and projects focusing on either the BBC itself or radio broadcasts more generally provides evidence of this complexity. Recent examples include the Connecting the Wireless World project (Leverhulme), led by Professor Simon Potter of the University of Bristol; the Transnational Radio Encounters: Mediations of Nationality, Identity and Community through Radio project (HERA), led by Professor Golo Föllmer of the Martin Luther University of Halle-Wittenberg; the ongoing Connected Histories of the BBC project (AHRC), led by Professor David Hendy (University of Sussex); the Entangled Media History network, bringing together historians of European media; groups of international academics working on BBC broadcasts in foreign languages; and literary scholars researching the relationship between radio and modernism.[12] For the purpose of this brief literature review I will mention only a few key publications that allow us to understand how the focus of research on the BBC has switched from Britain to foreign countries, whereas the next section about transnationalism will engage with the work of some of the groups and scholars just mentioned.

The use of radio as a medium for addressing ordinary people was arguably one of the main innovations introduced into political warfare during the Second World War. The extensive use of transnational broadcasts to destroy the morale of civilians living in enemy countries and provide alternative views on the conflict led to a parallel 'war of words' fought over the airwaves as tanks, aircraft and warships were battling on the traditional military fronts.[13]

As the outcomes of a research project called Languages at War have shown, foreign languages play an important role in conflicts. They allow communications and cultural exchanges between armies and civilians, interrogators and prisoners of war, and facilitate the work of intelligence and propaganda officers seeking information on their enemies.[14] This reasoning also applies to the airwaves, since it was thanks to translators, foreign broadcasters and multilingual journalists that civilians could listen to foreign programmes and news bulletins for the first time during the Second World War. The BBC's European and Overseas branches were set up to counter enemy propaganda. Their activities would continue after the conflict and would contribute to exporting British history, traditions, culture and lifestyle to other countries.

From the first years of the conflict, it became evident that the use of radio sets had opened new frontiers in the fields of political warfare and cultural entertainment, as some monographs published at the beginning of the 1940s in different countries demonstrate.[15] Despite this awareness, research into BBC radio propaganda in foreign languages during the Second World War progressed slowly until relatively recently.

Moreover, most of the early literature on the role of the BBC during the conflict tends to approach the subject from a British perspective. These contributions include the publications of former members of the corporation as well as former officials of British organisations in charge of propaganda.[16]

The first academic monograph on BBC radio broadcasts during the conflict dates back to 1970. The work in question is *The War of Words*, written by historian Asa Briggs, the third volume of his ambitious project, the *History of Broadcasting in the United Kingdom*.[17] Briggs does refer to the European sections of the BBC; however, as he states, the topic was too vast to be comprehensively treated in one single monograph. The history of the individual foreign branches is, therefore, neglected in his book.

The twenty-first century inaugurated a phase of renewed interest in the history of the BBC during the Second World War, as shown by several publications on the theme of radio and propaganda.[18] Since 2012, British historians have researched BBC broadcasting to other English-speaking countries and analysed the way in which the corporation attempted to create a sense of 'Britishness' among citizens of the Commonwealth.[19] They have also started to rewrite the history of the BBC from a more international perspective and questioned the idea of the corporation as a reliable and objective source of information, often present in the early publications about British national radio.[20]

The switch in perspectives among BBC scholars is further confirmed by some more recent publications on specific BBC foreign services.[21] Nevertheless, as stated in a 2015 volume that can be regarded as the first publication bringing together researchers on individual BBC foreign services, 'there are still surprisingly few historical studies of individual BBC foreign-language services attempting to synthesise the history of transnational broadcasting with British government policy prior to, and during, the Second World War'.[22]

In line with this ongoing research, my work on the Italian Service offers a transnational reading of Radio Londra during the Second World War. In particular, it intends to contribute to a history of the BBC from a foreign perspective by analysing the political and cultural role of radio in Italy while concurrently broadening the existing knowledge on British political warfare towards Italy. This will help us understand how the BBC's transnational broadcasts during the Second World War contributed to both the creation of a British multicultural society and an European identity and popular culture.

Going transnational: research approaches to a new–old medium

The establishment of national radio stations in the UK and Italy as well as in other countries in the early 1920s introduced a new medium whose potential, as we will see in Chapters 1 and 5, was carefully evaluated by international organisations and exchanges.

Since the increasing popularity of television in the second half of the twentieth century, radio can no longer be regarded as a new medium. Traditional broadcasts and actual radio sets are being replaced by podcasts and digital platforms where we can listen to programmes aired by both national and independent radio stations.

And yet, as David Hendy remarked in the early 2000s in the introduction to his *Radio in the Global Age*, radio does not seem to have lost its key role in creating a special bond between broadcasters and listeners:

> We talk of radio's ability to keep us company, even to draw us into new relationships, by building up a sense of intimacy with broadcasters and fellow listeners (Douglas 1999). We talk about its ability to be a wider window on the world, to mark out a discursive space where people's voices can be heard and a debate sustained in a way that makes the world and all the people in it somehow more tangible, more real (Scannel 1996). We even talk of its powers of emancipation – a cheap and technically easy medium to master, allowing people otherwise excluded from the mainstream media a voice and a role, a real chance of interpreting the world for themselves (O'Connor 1990; Lloréns; Hocheimer 1993).[23]

Nor, continues Hendy, has radio been completely replaced by television. While we mainly watch television at home, we can listen to the radio in all kinds of circumstances such as in our cars or on our personal devices as we walk in the street. Moreover, since radio is a more affordable medium than television and does not always need electricity, it is still popular in the developing world.[24] These reflections, written more than twenty years ago, can still be applied today.

In fact, radio and its contemporary surrogates are still at the very centre of academic debate. One of the research networks that has played a leading role in these discussions is the Entangled Media Histories group, established in 2013 and bringing together European media historians. In particular, the EMHIS group has offered new methodological insights by giving the study of radio a transnational and transmedial focus.[25] According to some group members, 'while media history has often been studied as the history of one specific medium in one specific national context, the transnational and transmedial dimensions activated by concepts such as entangled media history opens up past communication patterns, practices and phenomena, and lift their complexity, interrelatedness and variability'.[26] As the same group suggests, to successfully find entanglements in media history, it is key to network with scholars researching radio from a variety of geographical perspectives and disciplines. In other words, collective research projects involving several academics might be more effective than individual projects.[27]

Defining what 'transnational' means and how the word differs from 'international', it is key to both the entangled media history debate and this book.

> While 'international' may refer to some kind of formal connection between two (or more) entities (e.g. nations/national states or state broadcasters) with the boundaries of nation-states very much in focus, 'transnational' implies the existence of phenomena which are located in a heterogeneous spatio-temporal framework (of concepts, agencies and objects) that transgresses or operates irrespective of formal nation-state boundaries and which therefore cannot necessarily or unambiguously be identified with one or other nation or nation-state.[28]

The word 'transnational', therefore, refers to mutual exchanges and influence that cannot be confined to national territories. Similarly, Nelson Costa Ribeiro and Stephanie Seul point out that 'the BBC foreign-language services ... are "national media with a transnational mission" that aim "to reach an audience outside the national territory"'.[29] This is also the case of the BBC Italian Service, at the centre of this book.

But the word 'transnational', as Alec Badenoch and Golo Föllmer show in a recent volume on 'transnationalizing radio research', two decades ago the meaning of the term 'transnational' was already being discussed by academics. And yet there is still space for research into transnational phenomena in the context of radio broadcasting. Radio can be studied from a transnational perspective in many ways:

> As a mode of cultural production based on both sound and language that can strengthen local bonds within transnational communities; as a transnational institution (even when rooted in a nation or local community) generating transnational communities of practice and standardizing transnational sounds.[30]

In the field of radio studies, as claimed by Badenoch and Föllmer in the same volume, thinking transnationally means reflecting on what kind of content travels globally and what kind of audiences global radio broadcasts reach. It also means to go beyond 'the entities often considered "natural" units of analysis (the city, the nation, the continent, the globe)' and think in terms of 'structures, processes or experiences'.[31] The examples of transnational phenomena in radio include, among others, broadcasting and listening to foreign radio programmes; and sharing the methodologies and outcomes of audience research and surveys carried out by national radio stations.[32] These two aspects of transnational broadcasting will be investigated in

Chapters 5 and 7, where we analyse the relationships between the audiences of the BBC and the Ente Italiano per le Audizioni Radiofoniche (EIAR) and the BBC Italian Service, respectively.

While finding the way in which the structures and processes of transnational history work can be challenging, one way of approaching this issue when studying radio broadcasts consists of narrowing the empirical focus down and analysing what happens in individual buildings such as Bush House, home to the BBC World Service from the Second World War until relatively recent years, and the diasporic communities working at the BBC.[33] Chapters 4 and 5 will analyse the role of Italian exiles at the BBC Italian Service and the exchanges of letters between staff of the BBC and the EIAR.

Some reflections on the BBC Italian Service's collection

If doing justice to the transnational dimension of radio broadcasts during the Second World War is a difficult but necessary task, understanding radio collections is another challenge for media scholars.

Several academics have reflected on the effective approaches and methodologies when working with audio or audiovisual collections.[31] However, the challenges faced by researchers when studying radio archives may differ considerably according to the purposes of the research, disciplines, periods of time investigated and, as always in archival research, the state of conservation of the papers and records.

In the case of radio material from the first decades of the history of radio and the Second World War, collections might not be comprehensive for several reasons, including partial destruction by bombing, lack of awareness of the importance of radio transcripts as a source of information on cultural propaganda and diplomacy during the war, and underestimation of the impact that radio broadcasts to foreign countries would continue to have at the end of the conflict.

Even when we do have access to radio transcripts, it is often difficult – if not impossible – to find traces of how a particular programme series or individual broadcast was created. Referring to the BBC Home Service, Siân Nicholas has noticed that:

> Historians of broadcasting – or at least, of the BBC – are privileged to have the creative process archived in sometimes extraordinarily minute detail thanks to the BBC's obsessive institutional record-keeping practices, a comparative advantage in the archival record that partly accounts for the relative neglect of British commercial broadcasting in the historiography until very recently.[32]

While this might be true for the BBC Home Service, this is not the case of the Italian Service during the Second World War, for which there is rarely evidence of the entire creative process that led to the launch of a new programme. However, if we talk about listeners and audience research, Nicholas's theories can be partly applied to the BBC Italian Service's archive and the wartime as well.

> As for the history of the media audience(s), documentary evidence ranges from newspaper circulation figures (always unreliable sources of information about newspaper readership), to cinema box office records and receipts and BBC audience research, all requiring to be supplemented by opinion polls, advertising surveys, social research studies, diaries and memoirs, and a huge but disparate and miscellaneous range of surviving cultural ephemera, each with its own methodological challenges.[33]

The BBC Italian Service's documents include both BBC audience surveys conducted with the help of British informants who lived in Italy, and letters sent by listeners of the Italian programmes to the BBC, as we will see in Chapter 7.

In terms of analysis of the BBC's political and cultural agenda for Italy, the collection of Italian Service radio transcripts, held at the BBC Written Archives Centre in Caversham, almost comprehensively covers the entire period of the war. To be able to read the transcripts of Radio London's daily broadcasts allows for a more systematic analysis of the narrative strategies adopted during the conflict, an acknowledgement of how these changed in different moments of the war and an understanding of what decisions were made about the programmes' features, depending on the requirements of wartime.

The majority of the audio recordings, however, have been destroyed or lost.[34] As noted by Piccialuti Caprioli, the absence of the audio recordings of the BBC programmes in Italian makes it impossible to verify whether a particular programme was actually broadcast or whether changes in the text were made while it was aired.[35] However, this is not a huge obstacle to researching the Italian Service's radio transcripts. Even if some of the texts were not actually broadcast, we can still get an overall idea of the themes and political scope of British radio propaganda to Italy.

As for the interpretation of the audio elements of the texts, many radio transcripts in Italian include notes taken by the broadcasters, with underlined words, letters or adverbs suggesting the tone in which a particular sentence was supposed to be read. Moreover, several transcripts also contain references to songs, as well as words indicating special sound effects used in the programmes. These elements cannot substitute for an actual audio recording, but they can make it easier to interpret the text.[36]

The difficulties encountered by researchers working on texts intended to be read aloud are well described by Alessandro Portelli in his *The Death of Luigi Trastulli and other Stories: Form and Meaning in Oral History*:

> The tone and volume range and rhythm of popular speech carry implicit meaning and social connotations which are not reproducible in writing – unless, and then in inadequate and hardly accessible form, as musical notation ... In order to make the transcript readable, it is usually necessary to insert punctuation marks, which are always the more-or-less arbitrary addition of the transcriber. Punctuation indicates pauses according to grammatical rules: each mark has a conventional place, meaning, and length.[37]

The author, who has worked extensively on oral history, is here referring to the transcription process of an interview. And yet his reasoning also applies to the text of radio programmes. In the case of radio transcripts, the situation is exactly the opposite because the texts of the programmes were written first and broadcast afterwards. However, Portelli's analysis gives us an insight into the ways in which a radio text differs from a newspaper article or other forms of written propaganda.

Radio scholar and producer Siobhán McHugh, who specialises in oral history in the context of radio documentaries, has made similar deductions, which are also relevant to the act of reading a transcript as opposed to listening to the recording.

> Oral historians who work from a printed transcript miss out on the performance; their experience is as close to the real interview as reading Hamlet compares to seeing a fine actor play Hamlet ... Put simply, the affective power of sound and voice, combined with the intimacy of the listening process, means we can be moved by listening to oral history; this, in turn, affects how we absorb and retain its content, as well as how we judge that content.[38]

Even though these methodological issues cannot give us a full and proper appreciation of content that was supposed to be listened to rather than read, a close study of the transcripts from the BBC Italian Service, combined with an analysis of British government sources and listeners' letters, allows us to understand the cultural, political and emotional impact that Radio Londra had on its audiences.

The next section will explain in more detail what methodology was used to analyse the archival sources consulted for this book and will provide some historical information for a better contextualisation of the programmes.

Research questions, key sources and methodology

While placing the role of the BBC Italian Service in an international and transnational context, the book also sheds light on British political warfare by answering three main research questions: to what extent were the Italian exiles working at the BBC allowed to operate independently from the British

Foreign Office; what did the broadcasts say during the most delicate phases of the Allied Italian campaign in order to engage with as many Italians as possible; and how were the programmes received by Italian civilians?

Some of the themes discussed by BBC broadcasters before Italy's unconditional surrender, at the centre of my previous book, remained crucial during the years of the Anglo-American occupation. This was the case with the food question, the dropping of bombs and the representation of Germany as an unreliable Italian ally. However, the Italian political and military scenario changed completely in the period of time investigated in this book and new archival research conducted in Italy and the UK has brought new sources to light.

Before July 1943, the Allies were still the enemies of Italy. A few months before, at the Casablanca Conference in January, Operation Husky had been planned; the Allied forces would land in Sicily on 10 July 1943.[39] In order to secure a favourable reception by the Italian population it was necessary to convince the Italians to get rid of the fascist regime. Moreover, the Allies needed to present themselves as guarantors of better living conditions.[40]

After the Allied landings in July 1943, the consequent fall of Mussolini's government and the unconditional surrender of Italy in September, the Anglo-Americans were no longer Italy's official enemies. Italy was now divided into two parts: the South, administered by the Allied Military Government of the Occupied Territories (AMGOT) and the North, occupied by the Germans and governed by the new fascist Repubblica Sociale Italiana (RSI). Moreover, the Allied troops were now supported by the Italian army in the southern part of the country and the partisan Resistance to Nazi Germany in the north. In these delicate years of the conflict it was fundamental for the Allies to demonstrate that the AMGOT administration was preferable for the Italians. It was also vital to secure the collaboration of civilians – or at least the non-obstruction of the Allied military operations.

Twenty years of fascism and three years of war had destroyed the morale of many Italians who were hoping for a swift end to the conflict. These Italians welcomed the Allies as long-awaited liberators.[41] Yet the Anglo-American troops were still conquering Italy by force of arms and their soldiers committing crimes against civilians, as often happens during military conflicts. Moreover, after the fall of the fascist regime and the Italian surrender, freedom of expression was gradually restored. In other words, Radio London was no longer one of the rare alternative voices in Italy. As a consequence, the Italian Service lost some of its popularity among Italian listeners.[42] For the period between September 1943 and April 1945, it is therefore essential to comprehend how the BBC coped with its ambivalent role as the voice of an occupier and liberator from the Nazi yoke at the same time. This duplicity will be the leitmotif of this work.

While examining the BBC's role in this historical context, my research contributes to broadening the existing knowledge on the Italian branch of the BBC. However, its aim is not to produce a comprehensive institutional history of the BBC Italian Service; the process by which information about the conflict was circulated between the British institutions in charge of propaganda and the BBC Italian Service is not researched. Rather, the perspectives of both the British authorities and the BBC's Italian broadcasters and listeners will be investigated in order to find traces of the ambivalent relationship between Radio Londra and Italy.

It is only by applying transnational lenses to the study of the BBC Italian Service that we can understand why Radio London became one of the myths of Italian cultural heritage of the Second World War. This kind of research can only be carried out by considering concurrently the points of view of the occupier/liberator on the one hand, and the occupied on the other. The point of view of the Italian population, in its turn, can only be understood by analysing the actual programmes and their reception.

From a political point of view, the book concentrates on two main issues: the extent to which the BBC Italian Service was influenced by the British government and the degree of independence experienced by Italian anti-fascist exiles working for the station. Publications on radio propaganda during the Second World War might provide a partial answer to the first issue for the European Service, but in order to discover more about the Italian branch, the programmes will be compared with existing literature on the Allies and Italy during the conflict.

As to the Italian exiles working for the BBC, Piccialuti Caprioli does refer to tensions between members of the Free Italy Movement, an association of Italian exiles that curated some programmes for the radio, and the BBC authorities. Nevertheless, this aspect is not analysed in depth in her inventory.[43] While the memoirs published by some radio broadcasters at the end of the war refer to a completely independent and positive experience at the BBC, some British Foreign Office documents at the National Archives at Kew demonstrate that the Italians were not free to work on the political content of the programmes without the supervision of the Political Warfare Executive (PWE).[44] Further evidence of this situation is provided in the personal papers of Umberto Calosso, an anti-fascist from Piedmont, famous for his intransigent political positions.[45]

Some historians have already investigated the Italians who emigrated to Britain before and during the war and their internment in British prisoner-of-war camps.[46] Building on their work, this book intends to find further instances of friction between Italian employees and members of the BBC and provide details of their political position in Britain (Chapter 4). In particular, their relationships with both the British Labour Party and the Foreign Office will be examined.

Also, in this case, the documents held at Kew allow for further answers regarding the issue of the political independence of Italian Socialists both at the BBC and in Britain more generally. An example of these include the reports of some Italian employees on their treatment received while interned in British prisoner-of-war camps and letters in which some exiles asked to be allowed to return to Italy after the Allied landings. Labour Party records at the People's History Museum in Manchester are another source of information on the political role of the Italian broadcasters, since they include correspondence between the party and the BBC.

In terms of cultural arguments and the programmes' target audiences, the radio transcripts themselves reveal a great deal about the ways in which the different elements of Italian society were represented. BBC propaganda did not only address politicised people and intellectuals. A number of programmes targeted ordinary Italian men and women, to undermine their consent to Mussolini's dictatorship before July 1943 and to incite anti-German feelings in the country as well as to encourage actions and forms of resistance against the German occupiers.[47] To mention a few groups: women, soldiers, workers, the upper classes and ex-fascists were at the centre of the BBC's attention. In order to become popular, the themes and formats of the programmes had to appeal to a wide range of citizens. Broadcasts on the 'fears and hopes of the Italians', to borrow Di Nolfo's expression,[48] as well as on their roles as mothers, fathers and ordinary people suffering under wartime conditions, were therefore very common in the BBC schedule. As this study will show, an effective use of stereotypes about British and Italian habits, references to Italian cultural traditions, and the transmission of music and messages from Italian prisoners interned in British camps were important elements in the success of Radio London in Italy.

It is almost impossible to make reliable estimations as to the number of Italian listeners to the BBC for several reasons. Before the gradual Anglo-American conquest of the Italian mainland, listening to foreign radio stations was forbidden in fascist Italy. An obvious consequence was that the fans of Radio London did not publicise their appreciation of the British broadcasts and shared this information only with a few trusted people. Second, the absence of advanced methods for studying the audience and the habit of listening to the radio in groups make it difficult to deduce possible percentages of listeners from the numbers who owned radio sets. Nevertheless, various sources confirm that Radio London did obtain the trust of at least a portion of Italian society. These sources include the already mentioned letters, sent by many Italians to the BBC Italian Service, clandestine pamphlets and printed material found in the British archives, surveys conducted by the BBC and documents from the fascist police attesting to the contraveners who listened to foreign radio stations regardless of the censorship laws.

This work is divided into seven chapters. Chapter 1 provides an insight into the innovations introduced by transnational radio broadcasts during the Second World War. It also focuses on the development of the BBC European Services as well as on the institutions in charge of war propaganda on behalf of the British Foreign Office. Chapter 2 investigates the establishment of the Italian Service. The first section concentrates on the careers of Cecil Jackson Squire Sprigge and Cecil Frederick Whittal, the two editors of the service, and Colonel Harold Raphael Stevens, the most popular BBC broadcaster in Italy. The second section offers an overview of themes, titles and directives for the BBC programming in Italian. Chapter 3 is dedicated to the biographies of the Italian exiles working at the BBC as well as to their memories of exile in Britain. It also addresses the issue of the absence of freedom of expression in fascist Italy that led to their expatriation. Chapter 4 studies the relationship between the Italian broadcasters, the British Foreign Office and the Labour Party. It concentrates particularly on the political role of Italian refugees in Britain, their internment in British camps, and the issues they experienced when trying to return to Italy after the Allied landings in Sicily. Chapters 5, 6 and 7 analyse a selection of radio transcripts from the Italian Service. In particular, Chapter 5 shows how Radio London responded to the attacks from fascist propaganda and how the Nazi-fascist enemy was represented in the British programmes. In Chapter 6 the narrative strategies adopted by the BBC during the occupation/liberation of Italy are investigated. The chapter addresses themes such as the unconditional surrender of Italy, the issues experienced by civilians due to the war and the partisan Resistance to the Nazis.[49] Finally, Chapter 7 is dedicated to the BBC's target audiences and the reactions of Italian listeners. The analysis of the programmes and their reception will allow us to comprehend why a positive portrait of the BBC has prevailed in spite of the ambiguous relationships between the corporation and Italian broadcasters and civilians.

Notes

1 Asa Briggs, *The War of Words* (Oxford: Oxford University Press, 1970), p. 396. Briggs says that the anecdote is taken from Ivone Kirkpatrick, *Mussolini: Study of a Demagogue* (London, Odhams, 1964). The episode is also reported in Hilary Footitt and Simona Tobia, *War Talk: Foreign Languages and the British War Effort in Europe, 1940–47* (Basingstoke: Palgrave Macmillan, 2013), p. 82.
2 It is not a coincidence that Gianni Isola wrote a short article on *Radio Londra* as part of a volume on the symbols and myths of Italian history after unification: Gianni Isola, 'Radio Londra', in Mario Isnenghi (ed.), *I luoghi della memoria: simboli e miti dell'Italia unita* (Rome: Laterza, 1998). However, the author

does not use primary sources and does not explain how the BBC Italian Service became a myth.
3 Among the memoirs referring to the BBC programmes: Antonio Zanella (ed.), *Sentivamo radio Londra: l'odissea di due fratelli ampezzani in Bulgaria, nel corso della seconda guerra mondiale, dal diario di Oreste Ghedina* (Cortina d'Ampezzo: Cooperativa di Cortina, 1992).
4 Some examples include: 'Le radio proibite dal fascismo: Radio Londra', http://anpi-lissone.over-blog.com/article-le-radio-proibite-dal-fascismo-radio-londra-37122724.html, 2009, accessed 29 May 2017; 'Radio Londra. 1939–1945', www.anpi.it/libri/76/radio-londra-1939–1945, 2011, accessed 29 May 2017; 'BBC: Radio Londra 1941–42', http://anpi-lissone.over-blog.com/article-37158365.html, 2009, accessed 29 May 2017.
5 Dario De Toffoli, 'Giochi: il festival a Modena tra Turing e Radio Londra', www.ilfattoquotidiano.it/2014/04/09/giochi-il-festival-a-modena-tra-turing-e-radio-londra/945492/, 2014, accessed 29 May 2017.
6 Claudia Baldoli and Andrew Knapp, *Forgotten Blitzes: France and Italy under Allied Air Attack, 1940–1945* (London: Continuum, 2012), pp. 209–210.
7 Among the historians who brought into question the story of the collaboration between Lucky Luciano and the Allies during Operation Husky: Salvatore Lupo, *The Two Mafias: A Transatlantic History, 1888–2008* (Basingstoke: Palgrave Macmillan, 2015).
8 Alban Webb, *London Calling: Britain, the BBC World Service and the Cold War* (London: Bloomsbury, 2014), pp. 2–3.
9 Among these, Lamberto Mercuri, *Guerra psicologica: la propaganda anglo-americana in Italia, 1942–1946* (Rome: Archivio Trimestrale, 1983); David Ellwood, *Italy 1943–45* (Leicester: Leicester University Press, 1985). Claudio Pavone, *A Civil War: A History of the Italian Resistance*, trans. Peter Levy and David Broder (London: Verso, 2014); Filippo Focardi, *Il cattivo tedesco e il bravo italiano: la rimozione delle colpe della seconda guerra mondiale* (Rome: Laterza, 2013).
10 Maura Piccialuti Caprioli (ed.), *Radio Londra 1940–45: inventario delle trasmissioni per l'Italia* (Rome: Ministero per i Beni Culturali e Ambientali, 1976). A few years later Piccialuti Caprioli published a short version of her inventory: Maura Piccialuti Caprioli, *Radio Londra 1939–45* (Rome: Laterza, 1979).
11 Ester Lo Biundo, *London Calling Italy: La propaganda di Radio Londra nel 1943* (Milan: Edizioni Unicopli, 2014).
12 Examples of works on radio modernism include: Aasiya Lodhi and Amanda Wrigley (eds), *Radio Modernisms: Features, Cultures and the BBC* (London: Routledge, 2020) (based on the papers given at a conference organised by the British Library in 2016); Ian Whittington, *Writing the Radio War: Literature, Politics, and the BBC, 1939–1945* (Edinburgh, Edinburgh University Press, 2018); Emily Bloom, *The Wireless Past: Anglo-Irish Writers and the BBC, 1931–1968* (Oxford, Oxford University Press, 2016).
13 The expression 'war of words' was used by Asa Briggs to refer to radio propaganda in the Second World War. Briggs, *War of Words*.

14 Hilary Footitt and Michael Kelly, *Languages at War: Policies and Practices of Language Contacts in Conflict* (Basingstoke: Palgrave Macmillan, 2012); Footitt and Tobia, *War Talk*.
15 These include Otto Friedmann, *Broadcasting for Democracy* (London: Allen & Unwin, 1942); Charles A. Rigby, *The War on the Short Waves* (London: Lloyd Cole, 1944); Charles Rolo, *Radio Goes to War* (London: Faber & Faber, 1943). The three monographs have different focuses. Friedmann concentrates on the persuasive methods used by Nazi Germany, Rigby looks at the technical and practical innovations introduced by radio, and Rolo discusses its role as a new weapon of war. What connects them is the awareness of the huge impact that radio was to have on international political propaganda and mass communication.
16 R.H. Bruce Lockhart, *Comes the Reckoning* (London: Putnam, 1947); David Garnett, *The Secret History of PWE: The Political Warfare Executive, 1939–1945* (London, St Ermin's, 2002); Gerard Mansell, *Let Truth be Told: 50 Years of BBC External Broadcasting* (London: Weidenfeld & Nicolson, 1982). Lockhart and Garnett focus on the influence exerted by the PWE on the BBC on behalf of the Foreign Office. The perspective of BBC insiders is extremely valuable, since it offers information not necessarily available in the archives. Moreover, it gives an insight into the complex relations between BBC officials and institutions in charge of propaganda. Nevertheless, these works do mirror the point of view of Britain, since the perspectives of the receiving countries and the foreign broadcasters working at the BBC are not investigated.
17 Briggs, *War of Words*. The book focuses on the BBC Home and European Services and the influence of the government on radio. The majority of archival sources on which it is based are intelligence papers and reports written by BBC monitors.
18 Michael Stenton, *Radio London and Resistance in Occupied Europe* (Oxford: Oxford University Press, 2000); Gerd Horten, *Radio Goes to War: The Cultural Politics of Propaganda during World War II* (Berkeley, University of California Press, 2001); Richard Havers, *Here is the News: The BBC and the Second World War* (Stroud, Sutton, 2007). Michael Stenton studies the BBC's role in supporting the Resistance in Nazi-occupied countries. The sources used by the author are government documents from the National Archives in Kew Gardens. The book investigates the radio propaganda towards France, Denmark, Poland and Yugoslavia. However, the focus is mainly on British political warfare and does not investigate the impacts of the programmes on these countries' populations, or the contribution of foreign broadcasters to British propaganda.
19 Simon Potter, *Broadcasting Empire: The BBC and the British World, 1922–1970* (Oxford: Oxford University Press, 2012).
20 Simon Potter, *Wireless Internationalism and Distant Learning: Britain, Propaganda, and the Invention of Global Radio, 1920–1939* (Oxford, Oxford University Press, 2020); Webb, *London Calling*; Marie Gillespie and Alban Webb (eds), *Diasporas and Diplomacy: Cosmopolitan Contact Zones at the BBC World Service (1932–2012)* (London: Routledge, 2013).
21 Here some examples are: Aurelie Luneau, *Radio Londres: les voix de la liberté, 1940–1944* (Paris, Perrin, 2005); Aurelie Luneau, *Je vous écris de France: lettres*

inédites à la BBC, 1940–1944 (Paris, L'Iconoclaste, 2014). On the letters sent by the listeners of the Italian Service to BBC in 1943 see Lo Biundo, *London Calling Italy*, pp. 51–58. Claire Launchbury, *Music, Poetry, Propaganda: Constructing French Cultural Soundscapes at the BBC During the Second World War* (Berne, Peter Lang, 2012). Nelson Costa Ribeiro, *BBC Broadcasts to Portugal in World War II: How Radio Was Used as a Weapon of War* (Lewiston, NY: Edwin Mellen, 2011).

22 Nelson Costa Ribeiro and Stephanie Seul (eds), 'Revisiting Transnational Broadcasting: The BBC's Foreign-Language Services During the Second World War', *Media History*, 21:4 (2015), 369.
23 David Hendy, *Radio in the Global Age* (Malden, MA: Polity Press, 2000).
24 Hendy, *Radio in the Global Age*.
25 Michelle Hilmes, 'Entangled Media Histories: A Response', *Media History*, 23:1 (2017), 142–144; 142.
26 Christoph Hilgert, Marie Cronqvist and Hugh Chignell, 'Tracing Entanglements in Media History', *Media History*, 26:1 (2020), 1–5; 1.
27 Marie Cronqvist and Christoph Hilgert, 'Entangled Media Histories: Response to the Responses', *Media History*, 23:1 (2017), 148–149.
28 Marie Cronqvist and Christoph Hilgert, 'Entangled Media Histories: The Value of Transnational and Transmedial Approaches in Media Historiography', *Media History*, 23:1 (2017), 130–141; 132.
29 Costa Ribeiro and Seul, 'Revisiting Transnational Broadcasting', 366.
30 Golo Föllmer and Alexander Badenoch (eds), *Transnationalizing Radio Research: New Approaches to an Old Medium* (Bielefeld: transcript Verlag, 2018), p. 16.
31 Among these studies Giovanni De Luna, *L'occhio e l'orecchio dello storico: le fonti audiovisive nella ricerca e nella didattica della storia* (Scandicci: La Nuova Italia, 1993); Luisa Passerini, 'L'archivio sonoro', *Rivista di Storia Contemporanea*, 3 (1987), 438–441.
32 Siân Nicholas, 'Media History or Media Histories? Re-addressing the history of the mass media in inter-war Britain', *Media History*, 18:3–4 (2012), 379–394, 382.
33 Nicholas, 'Media History or Media Histories?', 382.
34 The few surviving audio recordings can be requested and listened to at the British Library.
35 Piccialuti Caprioli, *Radio Londra 1940–45*, p. xxvi.
36 Lo Biundo, *London Calling Italy*, pp. 62–63.
37 Alessandro Portelli, *The Death of Luigi Trastulli and Other Stories: Form and Meaning in Oral History* (Albany, State: University of New York Press, 1991), pp. 47–48.
38 Siobhán McHugh, 'The Affective Power of Sound: Oral History on Radio', *Oral History Review*, 39:2 (2019), 187–206; 188–9, 195.
39 On Operation Husky see Francis Henry Hinsley, *British Intelligence in the Second World War* (London: HMSO, 1993); S.W.C. Pack, *Operation Husky: The Allied Invasion of Sicily* (Newton Abbot: David & Charles, 1977). On the Italian Service's programmes before Operation Husky see also Ester Lo Biundo, 'The War of Nerves: Le Trasmissioni di Radio Londra da El Alamein

all'Operazione Husky', *Meridiana: Rivista di Storia e Scienze Sociali*, 82, *Sicilia 1943* (2015), 13–35.
40 Lo Biundo, *London Calling Italy*. See also Lo Biundo, 'Voices of Occupiers/Liberators', 60–73.
41 On the dual role of the Allies as both occupiers and liberators of Italy see: Ellwood, *Italy 1943–45*; Tommaso Piffer, *Gli Alleati e la Resistenza italiana* (Bologna: Il Mulino, 2010); Isobel Williams, *Allies and Italians Under Occupation: Sicily and Southern Italy 1943–45* (Basingtoke: Palgrave Macmillan, 2013); Gabriella Gribaudi, *Guerra totale: tra bombe alleate e violenze naziste: Napoli e il fronte meridionale, 1940–44* (Turin: Bollati Boringhieri, 2005).
42 Piccialuti Caprioli, *Radio Londra 1940–45*, pp. xcviii–cx
43 Piccialuti Caprioli, *Radio Londra 1940–45*, pp. xcviii–cx.
44 Lo Biundo, *London Calling Italy*.
45 Lo Biundo, *London Calling Italy*, pp. 116–123.
46 Lucio Sponza, *Divided Loyalties: Italians in Britain During the Second World War* (Berne: Peter Lang, 2000); Alfio Bernabei, *Esuli ed emigrati italiani nel Regno Unito, 1920–40* (Milan: Mursia, 1997); Pietro Sebastiani, *Laburisti inglesi e socialisti italiani: dalla ricostruzione del PSI (UP) alla scissione di palazzo Barberini, da Transport House a Downing street, 1943–47* (Rome: FIAP, 1983).
47 The use of the word 'consent' to refer to the fascist regime has been at the centre of several debates among historians of fascism. In the words of Giulia Albanese and Roberta Pergher, 'the degree of coercion and the forceful suppression of dissent make it very hard to ascertain opinions, attitudes and individuals' scope for choice' (Giulia Albanese and Roberta Pergher, *In the Society of Fascists: Acclamation, Acquiescence, and Agency in Mussolini's Italy* (Basingstoke: Palgrave Macmillan, 2012), p. 4. See their volume for an overview of this debate. See also Sanpasquale Santomassimo, 'Consenso', in Vittoria De Grazia and Sergio Luzzatto (eds), *Dizionario del fascismo* (Turin: Einaudi, 2010). In the context of this research on British radio propaganda it is legitimate to use the word consent. As relatively recent research has shown, the fascist regime established associations and *fasci* in Britain. These associations had subscribers and supporters despite the fact that Britain was a democratic country. See Claudia Baldoli, *Exporting Fascism: Italian Fascists and Britain's Italians in the 1930s* (Oxford: Berg, 2003); Francesca Cavarocchi, *Avanguardie dello spirito: il fascismo e la propaganda culturale all'estero* (Rome: Carocci, 2010). Moreover, as this work will show, the BBC employed exiles whose political beliefs were ambiguous and ex-fascist sympathisers as well as anti-fascist refugees. It is therefore not surprising that in the eyes of the British authorities Italian society was divided into fascist and anti-fascist.
48 Ennio Di Nolfo, *Le paure e le speranze degli italiani: 1943–53* (Milan: Mondadori, 1986).
49 Similar reflections have been made in Ester Lo Biundo, 'Voices of Occupiers/Liberators'.

1

Radio at war

The aim of this chapter is to provide an introduction to the key issues and themes relating to political warfare during the Second World War on a global scale; and to offer an institutional context for a deeper understanding of the BBC Italian Service, its programmes and reception. The chapter will detail how the birth of a mass society and the technological progress of the twentieth century influenced political warfare, when ordinary men and women became the key target audiences of the propaganda of many countries involved in the conflict.

The first part of the chapter will focus on the variety of approaches adopted by different countries to undermine their enemies as well as on the introduction of two transnational tools of propaganda: radio and leaflets. Radio broadcasts and leaflets dropped by enemy aeroplanes allowed civilians to experience a more direct form of interaction with the enemy. As a consequence, workers, peasants, housewives and those with little education could no longer be ignored by government institutions in charge of propaganda.

The second part will concentrate on the birth of the BBC and the contribution of the war to its development as a leading international radio broadcaster.[1] In particular, it will explain how the BBC's transition from private company to public corporation led to British radio taking on a public educational role. This educational function was also a feature of the foreign branches established during the conflict, including the Italian Service. As the next chapters will show, also in the case of the Italian Service, ordinary Italian men and women were the key target audience.

The 'fourth front' during the Second World War: international propaganda

The introduction of political propaganda to support military conflicts is not a peculiarity of the Second World War. Campaigns to persuade civilians of the legitimacy of wars and political decisions had been conducted for centuries and in various forms by governments around the world prior to 1939. What characterises the 'short twentieth century',[2] and above all the Second World War, is the wide-scale use of propaganda and its impact on the populations of many countries.[3] The industrial and technological progress at the beginning of the century led to the birth of mass society as well as to the introduction of new media (such as cinema and radio) that could communicate with ordinary people. At the end of the twentieth century the global political scenario was also very different, since the world was no longer Eurocentric. As a consequence, national economies and the politics of territorial states became more complex due to transnational and global activities.[4] By the 1990s, important aspects of people's private lives, as well as international politics and economics, had changed considerably, 'mainly by the unimaginable acceleration of communication and transport'.[5]

In this regard the Second World War was a turning point, since it changed political and economic relations between different parts of the globe as well as internal politics in several countries. In many cases people would have to wait until the end of the war to access basic rights such as the vote and education. This was the case for Italian and French women, who only obtained the right to vote in 1946. Moreover, it was only in 1946 that the Italian referendum of 2 June marked the transition from the monarchy to a republic. This gradual process of democratisation and the inclusion of new social classes in the political life of many countries also affected political warfare.

As noted by Nelson Costa Ribeiro and Stephanie Seul, 'there can be no doubt that the media have played a significant part in establishing new diplomatic practices'.[6] While before the First World War diplomatic relations were mainly conducted in secret by governments and diplomats, 'the technological inventions of global communication during the late nineteenth and early twentieth centuries – wireless telegraphy, radio, television – greatly expanded the scope of communicating across borders'.[7] In particular, the two authors continue in the same article, radio is the ideal medium for propaganda, since its reception is difficult to control.

But in order to familiarise ourselves with the nature of propaganda in the context of BBC transnational broadcasts, it is necessary to understand what the British government and the BBC meant by 'propaganda'. After the First World War, the term assumed a negative connotation and both the BBC and British governmental environments started questioning whether it was appropriate for a democracy to disseminate propaganda.[8]

As Simon Potter claims, 'this reflected a belief that propaganda was both unsavoury and un-British'.[9] While in the 1930s propaganda was mainly regarded as brainwashing, many civil servants in the Foreign Office explicitly used the word 'propaganda' to refer to BBC news bulletins and programmes.[10] During the Second World War the term was widespread among British government officers and it was not unusual to hear it in public discourse when talking about British national and foreign information policy.[11]

The importance of propaganda during the Second World War is further confirmed by the historiography of the twentieth century. It is not a coincidence that between the end of the 1970s and the beginning of the 1980s historians from different nationalities such as Charles Cruickshank and Lamberto Mercuri used, respectively, the expressions 'fourth arm' and 'psychological war' in relation to the Second World War.[12] The propaganda 'front', which was now contributing to war efforts alongside the more traditional military fronts, became so specialised as to require specific institutions and bodies to organise the campaigns. Examples of these include the American Office of Strategic Services (1942) and the Office of War Information (1942); the British Political Warfare Executive, led by Bruce Lockhart and established in 1941 to unify all propaganda activities under the control of one institution; the British Special Operations Executive (1940) that specialised in intelligence operations; and the Psychological Warfare Branch (1943), a joint Anglo-American institution responsible for propaganda in the occupied territories. Other institutions we should mention are the Italian Ministero della Cultura Popolare (known as MinCulPop, 1937), and the German Ministry for Popular Enlightenment and Propaganda (1933) under the direction of the Nazi propagandist Josef Goebbels. However, there is a crucial difference between the latter and the Anglo-American institutions mentioned above. While these had been set up at the beginning or during the conflict specifically for war purposes, the Italian and German organisations had been founded prior to the 1940s to build bases for totalitarian regimes. When countries such as Italy, Germany and the USSR went to war, the members of their societies were unused to pluralism and freedom of expression. All these institutions had been founded for the same purpose: dishonouring the enemy and supporting the home front on behalf of their government, but the approaches adopted by each country varied considerably according to the different ideologies and forms of government. There is, however, common ground. While during the First World War intellectuals and politicians were still the main audiences who needed to be addressed in order to obtain political consent, in 1939–45 ordinary men and women were at the centre of the propaganda of many countries.

The propaganda of the Third Reich was based on the assumption that the masses could be persuaded only by addressing their emotions, rather than their intelligence. Moreover, as Hitler wrote in *Mein Kampf*, the human psyche would not be convinced by weak concepts or images.[13] This belief is mirrored, for example, by the aggressiveness of Hitler's voice in his speeches.

The visual aspects of Nazi propaganda further confirm this: posters showing physical atrocities, skulls and death symbols, or children brutally being taken away from their mothers were extremely common in the representations of the enemy by the Nazi regime. The exaltation of youth, power, technology, speed and strength, typical of fascist Futurism and propaganda, is the other side of the coin. A brave fascist would not be afraid of showing his bravery by using violence for the sake of his regime. Mussolini and Hitler were portrayed as heroes capable of all kinds of valiant feats. At the same time, both dictators have been depicted as representing the common people. In fascist Italy, it was not rare to see images of Mussolini holding children or listening to radio broadcasts on popular topics such as family and childhood.[14]

In contrast, despite its participation in the war and its expansionist policy in East Europe, the Soviet Union's propaganda was based on the promotion of peace. Even though the USSR described the First World War as the horrific consequence of capitalism, after Operation Barbarossa in 1941 – as the German attack of the Polish territories occupied by the Soviet Union was called – the argument changed slightly. The conflict was now presented as desirable, as 'it would weaken capitalism more than communism'.[15]

Attacks on the capitalistic policies of Western countries were also very common in the propaganda of the Japanese military empire. After the Japanese invasion of China in 1931, it became a high priority for Japan to describe itself as the guarantor of the old Asian traditions against corrupt Western countries. This 'mission' was used to justify Japanese territorial annexations. This portrait was also exploited to discredit the image of Japan's most detested enemy in the Second World War, the United States.[16]

During its years of isolationism, the United States showed no interest in developing any form of war propaganda. This situation changed during the year of the Japanese attack of Pearl Harbor in December 1941 and the consequent participation of the Americans in the conflict. In July 1941, at the request of President Roosevelt, Colonel Donovan, the future head of the Office of Strategic Services, set up the first department of American political warfare. American public opinion, as the political history of the United States had demonstrated since the previous century, was particularly responsive. It was therefore necessary to develop forms of propaganda that could penetrate society as broadly as possible. Cinema was a particularly powerful area of American propaganda; Hollywood films released during the conflict contributed to the war effort by promoting pro-Jewish and pro-Allied messages. Nevertheless, such a crucial sector of the American economy also had to consider its profits. The political content was therefore delivered through traditional film formats such as romances, musicals and thrillers.[17]

As for Britain, the Second World War contributed considerably to the development of state propaganda. To use Michael Balfour's words, after

1939 'the world grew more dangerous, and it was conceded that "propaganda" there must be and the pursuit of other unfair advantages'.[18]

The aspect that probably distinguished most British propaganda was the emphasis on civilians and the efforts that every single person had to make for the sake of the country. Every citizen could contribute to the cause of Britain. The campaigns to encourage women to volunteer for the war were representative in this regard: posters showing women wearing uniforms or working in factories and farms were very common.[19] The famous slogan 'we can take it' referred to the problem of the safety of civilians. The reason the British 'could take it' was that all the necessary measures to protect the population had been implemented, or so the government claimed. From posters to radio programmes, all forms of propaganda in Britain pointed out how many air-raid shelters and gas masks had been provided, how food rationing was satisfying people's needs despite the shortage of essential goods, and how many children had been evacuated to unknown and safe destinations.[20] These themes were also at the centre of the BBC's radio broadcasts for Italians, as Chapters 5, 6 and 7 will show.

Crossing national borders and domestic walls: transnational broadcasts and leaflets

The birth of new institutions that shaped the content and approaches of propaganda is not the only peculiarity of the 1939–45 conflict. The main innovations introduced by the 'fourth front' in the Second World War were arguably the use of radio and leaflets. The telegraph, the forerunner of radio, had already been used to send military messages. As for leaflets, while the first attempts at using them date back to the beginning of the twentieth century, the massive improvements in airfields considerably increased the extent of their use as well as their effectiveness. As the head of the PWE, Bruce Lockhart, stated in *Comes the Reckoning*, radio and leaflets were the principal instruments employed by British political warfare to destroy enemy morale:

> Our two main tasks, which had been approved by the Foreign Office and Chiefs of Staff, were clear enough. They were to undermine and to destroy the morale of the enemy and to sustain and foster the spirit of resistance in enemy-occupied countries. The principal instruments of our propaganda or of our political warfare as it was now beginning to be called were radio and leaflets.[21]

The introduction of these two instruments of communication revolutionised the concept of war propaganda. It was now possible to cross the territorial borders that separated national states, and to establish contact with common people in the ordinary moments of their everyday lives. Literature, the press and the cinema had been used in the past to support wars, which were mainly waged with tanks and cannons, but the opportunity to speak directly to foreign civilians turned radio and leaflets into equally effective 'weapons'. In the case of leaflets, there was an even stronger connection with traditional weapons, since leaflets and bombs were dropped from the same British planes. As a consequence, RAF Bomber Command and the PWE needed to coordinate their activities and operate together to 'build up the morale' of the civilians in conquered countries, and 'break up the morale' among enemy populations.[22]

Another peculiarity of leaflets and radio was that people did not necessarily have to go and search for information to access it. Any man or woman could accidentally come across a leaflet dropped from an enemy plane or, in some countries, listen to national radio from a public transmitter while shopping, walking in the street or going to the post office. Moreover, unlike newspapers, radio messages could also reach the ears of distracted listeners who happened to be close to a public radio transmitter.[23] This was especially true for countries such as Germany and Italy, whose governments had invested a great deal in radio as an instrument for building consent for the Nazi and fascist governments.

In the case of Italy, as Chapter 5 will explain, the fascist government distributed radio transmitters to schools and rural areas.[24] In this regard, in 1933 the Ente Radio Rurale was set up with the aim of distributing such radio transmitters throughout the countryside. Moreover, some public transmitters were built in places where peasants met during breaks from work. As we will see in the chapter about the EIAR and the BBC, the high cost of radio transmitters and Italian cultural backwardness did not allow the fascist government to obtain the results it wanted from the investments in radio.[25] However, the existence of such public radio transmitters implied that even people who could not afford to buy a radio could listen to radio programmes while working or studying at school.

Radio also abolished the traditional separation between private and public spaces by crossing domestic walls as well as national borders. By simply tuning in to a radio station, people who were wealthy enough to buy a radio could bring the outside world into their living rooms. Updates on the latest political debates or war events could be easily accessed without leaving the house.[26]

Another crucial change that radio brought to the propaganda 'front' was the involvement of voices and the sense of hearing as important elements in the communication process. In this regard, Marshall McLuhan has used the expression 'tribal drum' to refer to radio. According to the Canadian sociologist, such a 'drum' possesses a special persuasive power, which is not necessarily linked to the particular message delivered. It depends, rather, on the nature of the medium itself. In other words, the sound of a voice and the impossibility of seeing the body from which that voice comes were more effective than visual messages. Charismatic personalities such as Hitler, claims McLuhan, would not have obtained the same popularity on television.[27]

However, the most important change introduced by radio during the Second World War, as mentioned, was the opportunity to speak to the civilians of enemy countries through transnational radio programmes and news.

> La voce amplificata non è più quella del potere, bensì quella degli avversari: l'informazione diffusa non è più quella di stato, ma si è in presenza di una vera e propria controinformazione; la radio non è più uno strumento per esaltare e innalzare Führer, duci e presidenti, bensì per minarne il consenso, l'autorità, l'immagine.[28]

> The amplified voice no longer belongs to the people in power, but to their enemies: the information disseminated is no longer that of the state, but proper counter-information; radio is no longer a tool to exalt and give praise to the Führer and presidents, but to undermine their consensus, authority and image.

The transformation of radio into a weapon of war led to the creation of special sections and departments in pre-existing national radio, charged with shaping broadcasts for the enemy countries. As Gerard Mansell has commented in *Let Truth be Told*, 'as soon as the potential for reaching audiences beyond national frontiers in their own language was appreciated, efforts were made at an international level to lay down rules about what was and what was not permissible'.[29] The awareness of the impact that international radio broadcasts could have on foreign audiences encouraged debates on the topic within the International Broadcasting Union (IBU), which was founded with the help of the first director-general of the BBC, John Reith. The IBU, based in Geneva alongside many international interwar institutions, 'provided the key forum in which European and other broadcasters could discuss their common concerns and develop new means of practical cooperation'.[30] However, the increasing number of broadcasts in the 1930s with an aggressive and nationalist approach led to negotiations and international broadcasting agreements. As a consequence, the League of Nations set up its own radio station (Radio Nations) with the aim of both playing a leading role in the discussion of these agreements and promoting international cooperation.[31]

The League of Nations contributed to setting the boundaries between what radio stations were allowed to broadcast and what was considered 'inadmissible propaganda'. In 1936 a special League of Nations conference was held in Geneva, where delegates established that broadcasts inciting the population of any territory to act in ways that did not respect the internal security of their countries should be banned. Moreover, aggressive propaganda and incitements to war and insurrections were forbidden.

The next sections will explain how the Home and European Services of the BBC were set up and developed between the two world wars.

The British Broadcasting Corporation: from private company to public corporation

The development of radio between the 1920s and 1930s was extraordinarily rapid. As noted by David Hendy, at first, it was simply a hobby of a small number of individuals called 'radio amateurs', but in nearly two decades listening to wireless broadcasts became a common habit.

> These were the 'wireless amateurs' who sprang up on both sides of the first decade of the twentieth century and the early 1920s: individuals who had realized that, whatever the commercial or military operators had envisaged about the privacy of their messages, signals radiated freely through the air, and could be hauled in from the electromagnetic realm by whoever was motivated enough to build simple receiving equipment in their homes or garden sheds. This was, albeit briefly, a thriving subculture.[32]

As we are aware, the person to whom the birth of wireless telegraph is generally attributed is Guglielmo Marconi. And yet according to Hendy, this role is actually largely undeserved, since a key role was also played by the British physicist Oliver Lodge, who demonstrated that Morse-code signals could be transmitted through the ether by electromagnetic waves.[33] In 1896 Marconi arrived in Britain to exhibit his invention and one year later the Marconi Company was founded, whereas the Wireless Society of London was not established until 1913.[34]

It was from a Marconi station at Writtle in Essex that, on 14 February 1922, the first regular broadcast service in Britain was set up. Another station began broadcasting in London in the following May. The first regular programmes from this station were aired in November 1922, though the company did not receive a licence from the Post Office until January 1923.

The company was first directed by John Reith, who worked as head of the BBC until the first years of the Second World War. According to Reith's daughter, Marista Leisham, the controversial relations between John Reith and Winston Churchill, as well as the beginning of the conflict, might be among the reasons why the former left the corporation.[35] The lack of attention paid by Churchill to the BBC in his six-volume history of the Second World War can be attributed to the same reason.[36]

John Reith was offered a job as General Manager a few weeks after the start of the BBC broadcasts. In only a year he became Managing Director and gained the trust of both BBC members and listeners. 'By the end of 1923 in most people's eyes he was the BBC.'[37] Reith had clear ideas about the way to lead the BBC as well as about the function a national radio broadcaster should have. As he wrote in the introduction to his *Broadcasting Over Britain*, radio broadcasts should both entertain and educate:

> The keen interest in broadcasting is due in large measure to the essential directness of the service, in whatever line it might be. Till the advent of this universal and extraordinarily cheap medium of communication, a very large proportion of the people were shut off from first-hand knowledge of the events which make history.[38]

Later in the same introduction Reith explained what an accurate definition of the word 'entertainment' should include. While 'to entertain' meant to occupy some spare time in an enjoyable way, it would be too simplistic to think that 'this is only to be effected by the broadcasting of jazz bands and popular music, or of sketches by humourists'.[39] As the word 're-create' shows, Reith claimed, enjoyment could also be associated with the creation of new knowledge. For Reith, radio broadcasts allowed for the provision of both pleasure and intellectual stimulation.

Reith was also the man who guided the BBC in its transition from a commercial company to an established national institution. At the very beginning of its history, the British Broadcasting Company consisted of some private companies that specialised in the production of radio transmitters and founded a consortium. The consortium's funding was based on a tax paid by purchasers of radio sets as well as on a subscription fee to allow them to listen to the radio programmes. Membership of the British Broadcasting Company was open to any manufacturer who wanted to be part of it. Therefore, the BBC claimed in those years, the company could not be called a monopoly, since its members were not only large radio firms supplying huge amounts of capital, but also included smaller manufacturers as well.[40] In 1927 the BBC began to be supported by public funds and was renamed the British Broadcasting Corporation. The gradual transformation of the BBC into a public corporation was obtained through negotiations run by two special enquiry committees called Sykes and Crawford. A key role was also played by two other commissions called Selsdon and Ullswater. In particular, the Crawford Commission confirmed that the BBC would be controlled by the Post Office and that its annual economic reports would be monitored by parliament. The BBC would also maintain a neutral political position towards any political party. The Ullswater Report stated that the BBC should broadcast programmes in foreign languages to ensure Britain influenced global affairs.⁴¹ The commission decided that the government could take control of radio broadcasts in cases of national emergency.⁴²

Among the factors that led to a public corporation was the idea that a private radio company would prioritise profit and commercial interests by investing in low-quality programmes. Furthermore, there was an increasing awareness in British government environments of the advantages offered by broadcasting. This awareness was associated with a protectionist policy on matters of radio frequency. The transition from a commercial company to a national radio broadcaster led to the BBC having an educational role, and this was evidently in line with Reith's idea of what radio should be. While 1927 was the official year from which the BBC was publicly funded, December 1932 marked its symbolic passage to the new public function of the corporation, when King George V sent his Christmas wishes to the British population through the BBC's microphones. The Second World War was another turning point, inaugurating the transmission of programmes for workers and the army.⁴³ Between 1939 and 1945 the BBC would play an indispensable part in the average Briton's life.⁴⁴

In 1932 the British Broadcasting Corporation set up its Empire Service to broadcast to all the territories of the British Commonwealth. While John Reith declared that the BBC should be regarded as a more reliable institution than the British government itself, the programmes of the Empire Service were the expression of the British imperialistic attitude towards the other parts of the Commonwealth.⁴⁵ The Empire Service 'sought to promote enthusiasm at home for Britain's imperial role, and to link Britons in these islands with a wider British diaspora in the "white settler dominions" of Canada, Australia, New Zealand, and South Africa'.⁴⁶ Similarly, the foreign branches established at the outbreak of the Second World War aimed at promoting enthusiasm for the Allied cause. Moreover, there was another similarity between the BBC Empire and European Services. The broadcasts of the Empire Service allowed the corporation to develop some expertise in the field of international propaganda.⁴⁷ This expertise was used to launch the BBC programmes in foreign languages.

While early publications about the BBC argue that the corporation was mainly acting independently from the British government, recent historiography offers a slightly different perspective:

> A close reading of material at the BBC Written Archives and the UK National archives shows that both Briggs and Mansell significantly underplayed the intimacy of the relationship between the BBC and the British government. Between 1937 and 1939 the BBC conceded a significant role to the British state in directing its overseas services. W. J. West's exaggerated and unevidenced claim that, from 1938, 'the BBC foreign language services were under almost total direct control of the Foreign Office' is a misleading simplification. Nevertheless,

claims that the BBC retained its 'independence' in international broadcasting during this period can only be sustained if we accept a very narrow definition of what independence entailed.[48]

The years in which each foreign service was established provide some evidence of the connection between the BBC and British international politics. The first news bulletins and programmes in a foreign language were broadcast in the Middle East. This is not a coincidence, considering that fascist radio propaganda was already operating in the area. Fascist programmes were trying to build an image of Mussolini as a protector of Islam.[49] On the request of the Foreign Office, the BBC started broadcasting in Arabic, since 'the stream of anti-British vituperation in Arabic pouring into the Middle East from a transmitter at Bari needed answering'.[50] Foreign Office authorities had at first thought to start up a station themselves. However, after realising that they did not have the necessary skills, they decided to ask the BBC.[51]

Broadcasts in foreign languages: the European Service

The first BBC broadcasts in European languages date back to September 1938 when Chamberlain's speech on the Munich crisis was translated and broadcast in France, Germany and Italy. Initially the transmission of bulletins in French, German and Italian was supposed to last until the crisis had passed. However, after almost a month, the BBC and the Foreign Office agreed that the new service should be maintained and broadcast on a regular basis.[52] These programmes were followed by broadcasts for Cyprus and Malta.

The number of languages covered by the BBC increased considerably year on year. In 1939 the BBC broadcast in nine foreign languages including Arabic, Spanish and Portuguese. In the same year the BBC was subjected to several enemy bombings. As a consequence, in 1940 the European Service of the BBC was transferred from Broadcasting House to Bush House and other buildings. The European Service operated safely from Bush House despite the explosion of another V-1 flying bomb next to one of the building's entrances.[53] As the Italian broadcaster of the BBC, Elio Nissim, recalls in some unpublished notes about the war, prior to becoming home to the BBC foreign services, Bush House contained many offices and was mainly visited by businessmen. The outbreak of the war, however, turned it into a sort of Babel tower, where many different voices could be heard. Thanks to these international voices, the BBC European Service expanded quite rapidly, despite the difficulties caused by the conflict.

In 1943 the BBC was broadcasting in over 45 different languages. By the end of the conflict the hours of foreign broadcasts were more akin to those of domestic transmissions.[54]

The choice of each new language during the late 1930s and early 1940s was dictated by political, economic and strategic necessities; the radio transmissions were meant to compensate for the loss of Britain's influence in the world in the diplomatic, economic and military sphere by rallying the sympathy of foreign publics for the British cause.[55]

The territories covered by British broadcasts included Europe, the Middle East, Latin America, the Soviet Union, Persia, India and Japan. At the beginning there was almost no evidence that these programmes were being heard by the people for whom they were intended because little correspondence was received. Moreover, there were many complaints about the quality of microphone delivery and translations.[56]

Apart from the Italian Service, among the most successful branches of the European Service were the French and German Services. However, there was a crucial difference between the French and the German Service: while the majority of staff members of the former were French, at the German Service native speakers were employed only as translators.[57]

Recent studies of other BBC foreign services during the Second World War have shown that there was a contrast between Britain's self-portrait as the guarantor of 'truth' and 'objectivity' and that the British radio station often omitted unwelcome facts in the interest of the British government.[58] Just to provide an example, the BBC German Service never expressed any 'sympathy on behalf of Jews as a propaganda line'.[59] The same applies to the Portuguese Service that avoided broadcasting any programme that could potentially threaten the Salazar regime. 'The British Embassy in Lisbon frequently advised that the BBC should avoid items that would annoy the Lisbon regime, namely communism, democracy and social disturbances in Portugal.'[60]

As I claim in this book, this was also the case for the BBC Italian Service. As a comparison between the PWE directives for 1943 and the programmes in Italian shows, the content of the broadcasts for Italy mirror the BBC directives.[61] Moreover, while the Italian exiles were allowed to curate the cultural aspects of their programmes, there seemed to be a stronger control from the PWE on political issues. This was especially true in those cases where delicate issues were involved, such as the unconditional surrender of Italy or the political reconstruction of the country.[62]

As the BBC was expanding, it began to be associated with a symbol that made it recognisable in every European country: the 'V' for victory. This letter was the initial of the word 'victory' not only in English, but also in other European languages including Flemish, French and Italian. The symbol had been already used in Poland and Czechoslovakia to express dissent towards the German occupiers. Civilians from these countries were no longer allowed to use or show objects that expressed their national identities.

Hence, Polish and Czech citizens started using the V symbol as a tool of resistance to the Nazi yoke. For example, they would fold their banknotes into a V-shape when buying something in a shop.[63] Soon the V symbol was transcribed into sound and was expressed with the Morse signal (... -), which was actually the rhythmic theme of numerous pieces of music, including the opening notes of Beethoven's Fifth Symphony. [64] On the night of 27 June 1941, Colonel Britton from the French Service introduced the V sound to his audience. The V campaign was welcomed with great enthusiasm:

> Not only were the theme of the Fifth Symphony and the Morse signal abundantly used, but the feature demonstrated in a striking manner how everything in the daily life of a French village or town could be made into a V: the schoolmistress calling her children by clapping her hands in V rhythm; trains rattling through the night; dogs barking and cocks crowing at dawn; customers calling for the waiter in the village café; the blacksmith hammering on his anvil – all created a V symphony worthy of the best sound effects of a Réné Clair film.[65]

The rapid expansion of the BBC European Services, as well as the lack of cooperation between the British institutions in charge of propaganda, necessitated the creation of a body to coordinate Britain's political warfare towards enemy countries. In 1938, before the outbreak of war, a Department for Enemy Propaganda was established. This department was based at Electra House and its scope was to help the British Foreign Office with the propaganda aimed at Germany. The Political Intelligence Department would monitor its operations. In 1940, the Ministry of Economic Warfare became involved in propaganda activities and cooperated with another new institution called the Special Operations Executive. All these bodies made the organisation of propaganda activities very complex, since there was plenty of space for divergence between the Ministry of Information, the Ministry of Economic Warfare, the Foreign Office and the Political Intelligence Department.[66]

In August 1941, after several discussions and debates, Churchill signed a new agreement about propaganda. The three main personalities involved in propaganda activities would meet on a regular basis under the chairmanship of the Foreign Office representative, Bruce Lockhart. These people were the Foreign Secretary, Anthony Eden; the Minister of Economic Warfare, Hugh Dalton and Brendan Bracken, who was responsible in parliament for all the broadcasts. After a few months, in 1942, the Political Warfare Executive was formally constituted and included Rex Leeper, head of the Foreign Office's Political Intelligence Department, and Brigadier Dallas Brooks, head of the Military Wing of the Department for Enemy Propaganda. Bruce Lockhart kept his leading role and became Director-General of the PWE. The BBC's activities began to be coordinated by this institution when Ivone Kirkpatrick, a Foreign Adviser at the BBC, was invited to join the PWE.[67]

The BBC European Services and the PWE would be based in the same building, Bush House.

The tasks of the PWE included preventing the economic exploitation of the countries invaded by Nazi Germany; encouraging the formation of resistance movements; destroying the morale of the German occupying forces; and educating 'the various sections of the population on the parts they should play during liberation'.[68]

Apart from having a controller, the BBC European Services were also monitored by an assistant controller, whose role was to coordinate the activities of the Information Service. The secretary of the Information Service was in charge of collecting the news to translate into the language of the country where they would be broadcast, as well as of deciding on the structure of the bulletins. Another vital role was played by the four main information agencies of the time – Reuters, the Associated Press, the Exchange Telegraph and the British United Press – that collected the main news from foreign countries.[69]

Foreign press and radio broadcasts were a crucial source of information. It was necessary to know the enemy in order to effectively counter-attack its propaganda effectively. In 1939 the BBC Monitoring Service was set up with the purpose of 'spying' on the enemy and reporting on the content of radio programmes and the press. In particular, the scope of this body was to monitor especially those states in which, due to strict censorship measures, British journalists could not operate. Extracts from the most relevant articles would then be sent to the various branches of the European Service and would be read out in the programmes. The person who selected the extracts to distribute to the various services was called the 'copy taster'.

All the material collected would be used for other, unconventional forms of propaganda: 'black' propaganda. This consisted of programmes broadcast by the BBC to enemy countries, under the guise of being transmitted by local authorities. An Italian or German citizen could be listening to a programme from London without realising that there was no Nazi or Fascist propagandist at the microphone. This kind of programme required a very sophisticated knowledge of the enemy. Fascist Italy was obviously on the list of the countries to observe.[70] In order to be believable, the rhetoric and the style of 'black' propaganda had to be scrupulously reproduced in every single detail. Such an ambitious enterprise clearly needed continuous investigation into the production of foreign propaganda. Espionage, letters to neutral territories and the testimony of war prisoners were other commonly used sources of information on the enemy.[71] In 1941 Sefton Delmer, an employee of the German Service, started working for the Psychological Warfare Department as a 'black' propagandist. Since the British campaigns in German territories had proved unsuccessful, the British authorities resorted to this clandestine form of propaganda. Witnesses to Delmer's collaboration with the British parallel 'black' propaganda confirm that German spies were often consulted in order to obtain crucial information to use in the programmes.[72]

Yet the operation of communicating with foreigners living in enemy territories was not an easy job. It was not only a matter of making the programmes understandable from a linguistic point of view. The issue was rather finding the right ways to approach different cultures. For this reason, the contribution of foreigners living in Britain was valuable. Among these, as we will see in Chapter 3, were exiles who had been forced to leave their countries due to the censorship measures imposed by political regimes or by the German occupying forces, people whose lives were at risk in their cities of origin, due to their political opposition. The exiles, as well as the other foreigners, were aware of the best methods and arguments to engage with their compatriots and were therefore able to adapt programmes to the cultural backgrounds of each social class.[73] To gain the trust of civilians it was essential to pay attention to what was important to them in their daily life. In other words, their lifestyle, their way of socialising and interacting, their preferences about food, fashion and their habits, as well as their emotions and feelings about the war – all needed to be known. As a Foreign Office document quoted by Cruickshank states:

> The propagandist had to know intimately the country and the people whom he was addressing – so intimately that when he spoke to them or drafted a leaflet for them not a single false note would creep in. He had to be familiar with their state of mind week by week – 'what the housewife says waiting in a food queue; what workmen talk about in a factory; what the farmer feels about the government; what a street in the capital looks like; what shopkeepers and tradesmen think about the business outlook; what the ordinary man is saying about the business outlook; what the ordinary man is saying about air raids'.[74]

The analysis of the transcripts of the Italian Service in this book will show how these reflections were applied to Radio London's programming for Italian civilians.

This chapter has investigated the innovations introduced by transnational radio broadcasts in the field of political warfare during the Second World War. These changes have arguably contributed to a more significant involvement of ordinary people on the international political scene. For the first time, citizens of the entire world could have a direct access to foreign sources of information. The outbreak of the Second World War contributed to the growth of the BBC. It was to counter enemy countries that the BBC began broadcasting in other languages. This led to more general changes in political warfare since, in order to speak effectively to foreign civilians, it was crucial to have a deep and accurate knowledge of their language and culture. As a result, specific institutions in charge of spying on enemy propaganda were created. The development of the BBC European Services also provided the opportunity for cultural exchanges and collaborations between the British and foreigners living in Britain, as the case of the Italian Service will show. The success of the BBC's foreign programmes would not have been possible without this cooperation.

The next two chapters will explore the establishment of the Italian Service and the biographies of Italian exiles working at the BBC.

Notes

1. Although new research on the cultural and diplomatic role of the BBC Empire and World Service has been published and used in this and other chapters of this book, this section will also refer to the work of Asa Briggs, David Garnett and Gerard Mansell, since the purpose is to situate the BBC as an institution. While my research focuses on the cultural and political role of the Italian Service, an overview of the institutional history of the BBC will offer the context for a deeper understanding of the programmes and their scope.
2. Eric Hobsbawm, *The Age of Extremes: The Short Twentieth Century, 1914–1991* (London: Abacus, 1995).
3. Similar reflections are at the centre of the analyses of my entry, 'Information, Censorship and Propaganda', in Jean-François Muracciole and Guillaume Piketty (eds), *Encyclopédie de la seconde guerre mondiale* (Paris: Robert Laffont–Ministère de la défense, 2015).
4. Hobsbawm, *Age of Extremes*, p. 14.
5. Hobsbawm, *Age of Extremes*, p. 15.
6. Costa Ribeiro and Seul, 'Revisiting Transnational Broadcasting', p. 365.
7. Costa Ribeiro and Seul, 'Revisiting Transnational Broadcasting', p. 365.
8. Costa Ribeiro and Seul, 'Revisiting Transnational Broadcasting', p. 367.
9. Potter, *Wireless Internationalism and Distant Listening*, p. 12.
10. Potter, *Wireless Internationalism and Distant Listening*, p. 13.
11. Costa Ribeiro and Seul, 'Revisiting Transnational Broadcasting', p. 366.
12. Charles Cruickshank, *The Fourth Arm: Psychological Warfare 1938–1945* (London: Davis-Poynter, 1977); Mercuri, *Guerra Psicologica*.
13. Anthony Rhodes, *Propaganda. The Art of Persuasion: World War II* (London: Angus & Robertson, 1976), p. 12. Although this dates from 1976, it remains an interesting attempt to provide a general overview of worldwide propaganda during the Second World War by taking into account different media. Particularly interesting is the attention to visual aspects of propaganda.
14. Rhodes, *Propaganda*, p. 71.
15. Rhodes, *Propaganda*, p. 216.
16. Rhodes, *Propaganda*, pp. 243–244.

17 Rhodes, *Propaganda*, pp. 150–152; 144.
18 Michael Balfour, *Propaganda in War, 1939–1945: Organisations, Policies and Publics in Britain and Germany* (London: Routledge & Kegan Paul, 1979), p. 3.
19 Fashion was often used as a propaganda tool to engage with women. On fashion in Britain during the Second World War and the 'Make Do and Mend' campaign, see Julie Summers, *Fashion on the Ration: Style in the Second World War* (London: Profile Books, 2015). The book was published in partnership with the Imperial War Museums on the occasion of an exhibition, held in 2015 called *Fashion on the Ration: 1940s Street Style*.
20 These themes were at the centre of the programmes of the Italian Service in 1943 and continued to be crucial in the years of the Allied occupation. See Lo Biundo, *London Calling Italy*. On the measures taken to protect civilians and artworks both in Britain and other European countries see Claudia Baldoli, Andrew Knapp and Richard Overy (eds), *Bombing States and Peoples in Western Europe, 1940–45* (London: Continuum, 2011).
21 Lockhart, *Comes the Reckoning*, p. 125.
22 Richard Overy, 'Making and Breaking Morale: British Political Warfare and Bomber Command in the Second World War', *Twentieth Century British History*, 26:3 (2015), 370–399.
23 Enrico Menduni, *I linguaggi della radio e della televisione: teorie, tecniche, formati* (Rome: Laterza, 2006), p. 57.
24 Philip Cannistraro, *La fabbrica del consenso: Fascismo e mass media* (Rome: Laterza, 1975), pp. 234–36.
25 Alberto Monticone, *Il Fascismo al microfono: radio e politica in Italia (1924–45)* (Rome: Studium, 1978), p. 48.
26 Enrico Menduni (ed.), *La radio: percorsi e territori di un medium mobile e interattivo* (Bologna: Baskerville, 2002), pp. 31–32.
27 Marshall McLuhan, 'Radio: the Tribal Drum', *AV Communication Review*, 12 (1964), 133–45.
28 Enrico Novelli, 'Politica e propaganda alla radio', in Enrico Menduni (ed.), *La radio*, p. 286; author's translation.
29 Mansell, *Let Truth be Told*, p. 40.
30 Potter, *Wireless Internationalism and Distant Listening*, p. 3.
31 Potter, *Wireless Internationalism and Distant Listening*.
32 David Hendy, *Public Service Broadcasting* (Basingstoke: Palgrave Macmillan, 2013), p. 10. On radio amateurs see Maria Rikitianskaia, 'A Transnational Approach to Radio Amateurism in the 1910s', in Föllmer and Badenoch, *Transnationalizing Radio Research*.
33 Hendy, *Public Service Broadcasting*.
34 Asa Briggs, *The Birth of Broadcasting* (Oxford: Oxford University Press, 1961), p. 19.
35 Marista Leishman, *My Father: Reith of the BBC* (Edinburgh: Saint Andrew, 2006).
36 Briggs, *War of Words*.

37 Briggs, *Birth of Broadcasting*, p. 123.
38 John Reith, *Broadcast Over Britain* (London: Hodder & Stoughton, 1924), p. 15.
39 Reith, *Broadcast Over Britain*, p. 18.
40 Briggs, *Birth of Broadcasting*, pp. 3–20, 123.
41 Potter, *Wireless Internationalism and Distant Listening*, pp. 96–97.
42 Matthew Hibberd, *Il grande viaggio della BBC: Storia del servizio pubblico britannico dagli anni venti all'era digitale* (Rome: Rai-ERI, 2005).
43 Hibberd, *Il grande viaggio della BBC*, p. 60.
44 Balfour, *Propaganda in War*, pp. 80–88.
45 Piccialuti Caprioli, *Radio Londra 1939–45*, p. 7. On the Empire Service and its evolution see also Potter, *Broadcasting Empire*.
46 Potter, *Broadcasting Empire*, p. 1.
47 Julian Hale, *Radio Power: Propaganda and International Broadcasting* (London: Elek, 1975). Hale's book is particularly interesting for the focus on the political role of international radio broadcasts. Hale identifies the origins of the political usage of radio in some messages broadcast by Lenin during the October revolution in 1917. The first message announced the overthrow of Kerensky's government and the formation of the new Soviet government. This broadcast was international and addressed potential revolutionaries in Europe and Russia. The book is particularly interesting for its attention on radio as a tool to create an international political community and the intercontinental approach, since the author does not take into account only European countries. The book focuses instead on several countries including Germany, Soviet Union, United States, the Middle East, East of Suez and Latin America.
48 Potter, *Wireless Internationalism and Distant Listening*, p. 12.
49 British Broadcasting Corporation (BBC), *Ecco Radio Londra* (Wembley: 1945), pp. 4–6.
50 Mansell, *Let Truth be Told*, p. 88.
51 On Radio Bari see Arturo Marzano, *Onde fasciste: La propaganda araba di Radio Bari (1934–43)* (Rome: Carocci, 2015); Danny Nissim's Private Archive, Elio Nissim's Papers (hereafter DNPA, ENP), Scripts of Elio Nissim, Ricordi di Bush House, Articolo Primo.
52 Mansell, *Let Truth be Told*, p. 58.
53 Stenton, *Radio London and Resistance*, p. 22.
54 Webb, *London Calling*, p. 2.
55 Costa Ribeiro and Seul, *Revisiting Transnational Broadcasting*, 368.
56 'History of the BBC. Overseas programming', www.bbc.co.uk/historyofthebbc/research/general/overseas, accessed 30 May 2017.
57 Piccialuti Caprioli, *Radio Londra 1939–45*.
58 Stephanie Seul, '"Plain, unvarnished news"? The BBC German Service and Chamberlain's propaganda campaign directed at Nazi Germany, 1938–1940', *Media History*, 21:4 (2015), 379.
59 Stephanie Seul, ' "For a German Audience We Do Not Use Appeals for Sympathy on Behalf of Jews as a Propaganda Line": the BBC German Service and the

Holocaust', in Simon Eliot and Marc Wiggam (eds), *Allied Communication to the Public during the Second World War: National and Transnational Networks* (London: Bloomsbury, 2020).
60 Nelson Ribeiro, 'BBC Portuguese Service during World War II. Praising Salazar while defending the Allies', *Media History*, 21:4 (2015), 397–411; 408.
61 Lo Biundo, *London Calling Italy*.
62 Lo Biundo, *London Calling Italy*. See also Lo Biundo, *Voices of Occupiers/Liberators*.
63 Rolo, *Radio Goes to War*, p. 135.
64 Rolo, *Radio Goes to War*, p. 139. See also Walter Cavalieri, *Tre punti e una linea* (L'Aquila: Consiglio regionale d'Abruzzo, 2007).
65 Rolo, *Radio Goes to War*, p. 139.
66 Briggs, *War of Words*, p. 32.
67 Briggs, *War of Words*, p. 33.
68 Garnett, *Secret History of PWE*, p. 169.
69 BBC, *Ecco Radio Londra*.
70 On black propaganda see: Alejandro Pizarroso Quintero, *Stampa, radio e propaganda: gli alleati in Italia, 1943–1946* (Milan: Franco Angeli, 1989); Sefton Delmer, *Black Boomerang: An Autobiography* (London: Secker & Warburg, 1962).
71 Pizarroso Quintero, *Stampa, radio e propaganda*, 17.
72 Delmer, *Black Boomerang*, 23–42.
73 Lo Biundo, *London Calling Italy*.
74 Cruickshank, *Fourth Arm*, 59. The document is in FO 898/30 and is dated 11 August 1940.

2

The Italian Service

After exploring the birth and evolution of the BBC as a whole and the changes to international political warfare initiated by the outbreak of the Second World War, this chapter will concentrate on the Italian Service.

The first section will explain when the service was set up, who the first people involved in the project were and what political line was followed when preparing the programmes.

The second part will provide an overview of titles and programme themes. This section will also refer to translation issues experienced during the early months of the service as well as to the use of music as a tool to successfully engage with the Italian population.

The third and last section will analyse some PWE guidelines for the BBC Italian Service to show how a typical directive from the Foreign Office was structured.

Again, in this case, ordinary Italians were at the centre of the BBC's interest. This will be further confirmed in Chapters 5, 6 and 7, when programme extracts will be analysed.

The dual nature of the BBC Italian Service will also emerge from this chapter. While elaborating ideas to entertain and inform Italians, the propagandists were ultimately aiming at Italy's defeat. As explained in the introduction, the various ways in which this ambiguity took place will be investigated in the following chapters.

Parla Londra!

PARLA LONDRA ...
Quante volte in questi anni, quando eravate ancora sotto il giogo fascista, avrete sentito queste parole: 'PARLA LONDRA!' Parole che non vi avranno

però forse dato l'idea di tutto il lavoro febbrile di preparazione della BBC, delle improvvisazioni impostele dalla guerra, di tutta la sua immensa macchina amministrativa, giornalistica, tecnica. Quanti di voi avranno immaginato i tecnici delle trasmissioni trasmittenti, quelli del suono, i redattori, i traduttori, gli annunciatori, i corrispondenti di guerra, i musicisti, gli scrittori di commenti di tutte le nazionalità, che lavorano per la BBC.

... Ed oggi, dopo tutti questi anni durante i quali ha parlato ai suoi innumerevoli ascoltatori italiani, oggi Radio Londra vorrebbe dar loro un'idea della sua immensa organizzazione, inglese, europea, mondiale, fare un breve cenno storico della Sezione Italiana, aiutarli a trovare, fra le sue trasmissioni, le onde desiderate.

Non è certo possibile rispondere in questa pubblicazione a tutte le domande che molti si saranno posti ascoltando Radio Londra, quando la Radio era l'unico legame che univa i paesi liberi e i popoli oppressi. Ma la BBC sarà sempre lieta di rispondere alle vostre domande circa le sue trasmissioni. Se volete dunque scrivere a Radio Londra, indirizzate: BBC, – Londra W. I.[1]

THIS IS LONDON CALLING ...
How many times in the last few years, when you were still under the fascist yoke, did you hear these words? 'LONDON CALLING!' Perhaps these words did not really give you an insight into the hectic groundwork going on at the BBC, its day-to-day improvisations imposed by the war, its huge administrative, journalistic and technical machine. We are sure that many of you have tried to figure out who these broadcasting and sound technicians, editors, translators, announcers, war correspondents, and scriptwriters of all nationalities working for the BBC are ...

... And today, after all these years of talking to its numerous Italian listeners, Radio Londra would like to give them an idea of its complex English, European and world organisation, to talk briefly about the history of the Italian Service, to help them tune in to their favourite BBC Italian programmes.

Of course, this publication cannot answer all the questions that many people might have wanted to ask when listening to Radio Londra, when radio was the only means of contact between free countries and oppressed people. But the BBC will be always happy to answer all your questions about its broadcasts. Therefore, if you want to write to Radio Londra, you can use this address: BBC, – London W. I.

These are the opening words of a pamphlet published on 2 May 1945, at the end of the Italian campaign. On 25 April, only seven days before the publication of this pamphlet, Milan had been liberated from German troops. The efforts of the Italian partisans and the Allied troops over the previous two years had finally resulted in the long-awaited victory.

After almost seven years of programmes for Italy, the voices and names of the BBC broadcasters were now familiar to many Italians. However, details of how Radio London had set up its foreign services and organised its daily schedule were still unknown to the Italian and European audiences.

Hence the BBC, as suggested by the title of its pamphlet *Ecco Radio Londra* (Here is Radio London), disclosed all this secret information that could not be revealed during the conflict.

The first broadcast in Italian, as previously mentioned, was Chamberlain's speech on the Munich crisis. This first transmission to Italy would be followed by regular news bulletins in Italian. However, Radio Londra would not be properly established until 1940, when Italy's entrance into the war appeared likely.[2]

As stated by historian Lucio Sponza, the first directives on propaganda towards Italy dated back to September 1940.[3] According to the directives, it was crucial to encourage anti-war feeling among Italians. It was also important to deliver the message that the war would last a long time. In particular, there were four main points to be covered by the British campaigns: British propaganda needed to be anti-regime, anti-Germany, pro-Britain and pro-Church. Italians ought not be attacked directly, rather their problems needed to be attributed to fascism and its unreliable ally. It was also vital to focus on the similarities between Britain and Italy to make the Italians realise that the two countries had many things in common. In addition, it was important to exploit the widespread Italian attachment to religious values to discredit Nazi Germany by emphasising that Hitler's paganism would undermine the role of the Pope and the Catholic Church in Europe. While preparing propaganda in Italian it was necessary to bear in mind that after almost twenty years of fascist propaganda, Italians were desperately looking for balanced and objective information. Moreover, Italians had a great sense of humour and an emotional outlook; it was necessary to take these attitudes into account in seeking the most appropriate way to approach them.[4]

When the PWE started preparing propaganda in Italian, the situation was moving in Britain's favour; Italians were tired of the fascist regime and saw British radio as a more reliable source of information than Radio Rome.[5] The first Assistant Editor of the BBC Italian Service was Cecil Jackson Squire Sprigge (1896–1956), a former journalist at the *Manchester Guardian* (1923–39) and a specialist in foreign affairs.[6] Sprigge was contacted in 1922 by C.P. Scott from the *Manchester Guardian* regarding a post mainly concerned with foreign affairs, involving occasional journeys to other countries in Europe and some secretarial work. Sprigge was offered a permanent post the following March.[7]

In January 1925, Scott wrote to Sprigge to inform him that the Italian situation was becoming complex. Therefore, the *Manchester Guardian* needed a correspondent in Rome to monitor the Italian situation. Given his expertise on the country, Sprigge seemed to be the ideal candidate for the position.

My dear Sprigge,
The Italian situation has become so difficult and important and may at any time become more so that we have decided to have a correspondent of our own at Rome. I don't know how far you are tied to your present job or whether you would consider an appointment of this kind, but I thought I would put the matter before you before taking any other steps. The salary would probably be £600 with an additional £100 for entertaining and minor day to day expenses.[8]

This job was followed, at the end of the 1920s, by another engagement as war correspondent in Berlin. Sprigge's German experience lasted until January 1928, when the *Manchester Guardian* offered him a job as City Editor.[9] Early in 1939, Sprigge was invited by Sir Campbell Stuart to take charge of British propaganda towards Italy in case of war.[10]

In June 1940, when Italy entered the war, Cecil Sprigge was working at the Italian section of the Ministry of Information, as any 'lover of Italy would be', in the words of his wife, Sylvia Saunders.[11] He would soon be offered a job as BBC European News Talks Assistant in the Overseas Department:

Dear Sir,
We are considering employing Mr. C. J. S. Sprigge as a European News Talks Assistant in our Overseas department, and he has given us your name as a reference. We should be very glad to know whether you consider him a suitable person for employment in our staff, and to have any other information about him that you care to give us.[12]

Sprigge was not initially interested in working for the Ministry of Information. Prior to being offered the BBC position, the journalist had tried to return to the *Manchester Guardian*. After receiving a negative answer from the newspaper, he decided to accept the job as European News Talks Assistant.[13] In July 1941, his wife Sylvia was also hired by the BBC as sub-editor in the European News Department.[14]

After two years of work on Italian radio propaganda, Sprigge decided to leave the BBC. His role as Assistant European Editor for the Italian Service would be taken by Cecil Frederick Whittal, who joined the station in February 1941.[15] In 1943, Whittal was upgraded to become Italian Editor, staying in this role until July 1945. His contribution to the Italian Service's activities during the conflict was greatly appreciated by the corporation, as shown in some correspondence between him and other members of the BBC at the end of his engagement:

Dear Whittal,
May I take this opportunity ... of thanking you for the personal contribution you have made to the work of the European Division during the vital years of war. In the past year we have all had it confirmed from territories as they

have been liberated that our work has not only been of direct assistance to the Allied military effort, but has evoked a warm and appreciative response from countries to which broadcasting gave us access during the German occupation.

I wish you all possible success in your future work and I hope that you will always have happy memories of your time with us here.[16]

Whittal was born in Sri Lanka and had a background in foreign languages and cultures. He had studied Oriental Languages, Persian and Arabic at Lancing College and Balliol between 1921 and 1925.[17] After finishing his studies at Oxford, Whittal started working as a journalist. Between 1925 and 1926 he ran the *Church of England Newspaper*. In 1926, he became a sub-editor on the *Morning Post*. Like his predecessor Sprigge, Whittal had worked for Reuters (1927–32) prior to being hired by the BBC. In 1932 he moved to Italy, where he continued to work for Reuters as its Rome correspondent. With the exception of a period in 1934 when he worked in Paris, Whittal remained in the Italian capital until 1938.[18] Before the outbreak of the war he worked at Electra House and at the Ministry of Information.

One of the most popular broadcasters of the BBC's Italian section was Colonel Harold Raphael Stevens. Stevens was also known as 'Colonnello Buonasera' because he began and ended his talks by greeting his listeners with the word *buonasera* (good evening) and, as his title suggests, he had a past career in the British army. Stevens was of Italian origin and had lived in Rome. His relatives, who were wine traders, had moved to Naples during Admiral Nelson's era. By the end of the conflict, Stevens had become an icon for many Italians, who sent him several letters expressing their gratitude. Stevens was popular with many Italians because he embodied the idea of the average British man; generally, his British accent and moderate words were appreciated.[19]

Despite his popularity, he was not the author of his programmes. Stevens's ghost writer was a journalist from Trieste called Aldo Cassuto, who specialised in economics and finance. Cassuto was in Britain as a political refugee and was hired by the BBC in the spring of 1939.[20] The fact that Stevens did not write his talks does not imply that his role at the Italian Service was marginal; he was one of the first broadcasters the British authorities involved in the launch of Italian programmes.

Stevens was contacted for the first time in November 1939 by the Programme Division while he was working at the Ministry of Home Security. The Programme Division had heard from Military Intelligence 7 (MI7), that Stevens was interested in helping the BBC to broadcast commentaries on the war in Italian.[21]

In consultation with the War Office and other interested authorities we have decided that the inclusion of regular news commentaries (as distinct from occasional news-talks) in our daily Italian service is an urgent necessity, and we hope to embark at a very early date on a comprehensive plan of action ... If a proposal of this kind would appeal to you, we should be extremely grateful if you could come to London to discuss possibilities, and to meet one or two of those who are concerned in this project ... One advantage of your coming to London, if the idea appeals to you, is that we could try your voice at the microphone, this being an essential preliminary to well laid plans.[22]

On 15 December 1939, Stevens received an official letter of appointment as Italian News Commentator in the Overseas News Department:

The work will consist in obtaining material for writing and delivering over the microphone commentaries in Italian on current events from the British point of view. You will be responsible under the direction of designated officials of the Corporation and in consultation with officials of Government departments concerned, for the collection and preparation of your own material, the work to be carried out to the satisfaction of the Corporation ... You will not, without the previous written consent of the Corporation, publicly write or speak about the Corporation or its affairs during the continuance of this engagement. Furthermore, you will not either during or after the determination of this engagement disclose to any person, in any circumstances whatsoever, any information processes or secret matters relative to the business or affairs of the Corporation which may have come to your knowledge during the period of this engagement.[23]

After a trial period, his engagement was confirmed in January 1940.[24] With the exception of a short period in 1941 during which Stevens was appointed by the PWE, he worked for the Italian Service until December 1945.

Another person who was involved in the Italian Service's project from its early days was Anthony Lawrence. Lawrence was born in London of Italian parents. He had obtained a degree in Italian and French from the University of Cambridge in 1937. According to Sponza, Lawrence played a leading role at the BBC and it was he who put together the Italian Service.[25]

Between 1939 and 1942, numerous translators and announcers joined the Italian Service.[26] They all worked under the direction of its editor, Geoffrey Dennis, whose role consisted of checking all the programme texts and ensuring that both content and form met the BBC's requirements. Among these employees were a number of Italian anti-fascist exiles who had emigrated to Britain. These included Paolo and Piero Treves, sons of the socialist Claudio; the literary critic Uberto Limentani; the university professor Umberto Calosso; the lawyer and journalist Elio Nissim; the historian Arnaldo Momigliano and the journalist Ruggero Orlando. Their biographies and careers at BBC will be investigated in the next chapter.

The Italian programmes

The Italian Service's programming was constantly improved over the years of the conflict. When the service was established in 1938 there was only one daily fifteen-minute programme, which aired every evening at 7.45 p.m. At the end of 1939, there were four programmes broadcast. In May 1940, one month before Italy's entry into the war, the number of programmes increased to five. By the end of November 1943, there were thirteen daily programmes amounting to almost four and a half hours of broadcasts. These included the programmes from the Voice of America, which started being broadcast in Europe in 1942 through the BBC.[27]

Further evidence of the constant development of the Italian Service is provided by the increasing number of its staff. When Italy entered the war, there were only ten employees in charge of the Italian programmes; after only two years there were thirty-eight staff members working for the Italian branch.[28]

Like the other European Services, the Italian Service separated *News* and *Commentaries*. As we will see later when comparing the BBC and fascist radio propaganda, this choice was often described by Radio London as evidence of its reliability. The distinction, the BBC claimed, would allow the listeners to form their own opinions on the conflict.

> L'obbiettività è la dote più importante di un servizio di notizie. Buona o cattiva, favorevole o sfavorevole, una notizia va innanzitutto riferita; ed è una delle più rigorose norme della sala di redazione quella di non confondere e frammischiare il commento alla notizia vera e propria. Provvederanno poi i commentatori a interpretarla, a illustrarla, a metterla nella sua propria luce; essa deve innanzitutto venir riferita nella sua cruda realtà; il commento è libero, ma i fatti sono sacrosanti.[29]

> Objectivity is the most important feature of a news service. Whether it is good or bad, favourable or unfavourable, news needs to be reported above all; and this is one of the strictest rules in the drafting room: comments and actual news should not be mixed. Commentators will later be in charge of interpreting it, explaining it, and shedding proper light on it; above all, news needs to be reported in its harsh reality; comments are free, but facts are sacrosant.

The last sentence, 'Comment is free, but facts are sacrosant', had been pronounced for the first time by the *Manchester Guardian* journalist C.P. Scott. Despite this evident difference between British and fascist radio, the selection of news to include in the bulletins implied a choice, which cannot be considered neutral.

Among the most successful *Talks* were the programmes by Colonel Stevens and Candidus.[30] Another successful programme was called *London Diary* (*Asterischi Londinesi*), launched in 1942. *London Diary* informed Italian listeners about daily happenings in Britain. The scope of the programme was to demonstrate that, despite the bombings and the difficulties of war, civilians' lives carried on as usual.[31] This purpose was in line with some of the most common mottos of British domestic propaganda. Expressions like 'We can take it!' or 'Keep calm and carry on' were very familiar to ordinary British citizens in the 1940s. *London Diary* also provided the Italian listeners with an overview of what the British press published about Italy, usually reading out extracts from the most popular newspapers in Britain.

On 17 May 1943, the programme *Progress of Fascist Propaganda* was launched. The aim of this programme was to show how incoherent fascist propaganda was by pointing out the gap between what the regime had promised at the beginning of the war and the latest events in the conflict. The technique adopted to provide evidence of this discrepancy was simple and effective: extracts from fascist press or radio programmes from previous years of the war were quoted and compared to more recent declarations made by the regime.

Another well-known programme was entitled *Italian Round Up* (*Sul fronte e dietro il fronte italiano*), by Paolo Treves. As the title suggests, the programme described the military situation on the Italian front. After the liberation of Rome in June 1944 this programme was substituted by another called *Italian War Correspondent*. As Treves said in the first programme of the series, now that the Italian campaign was favourable to the Allies and freedom of expression was being gradually restored it was time to focus on the work of British correspondents in Italy. Among these correspondents was Cecil Sprigge, the former editor of the Italian Service.

Apart from *News* and *Commentaries* or *Talks*, another type of popular programme at the BBC Italian Service were the *Sceneggiati*, which, as suggested by the Italian word, comprised theatrical scenes acted out by two or more characters. Usually each character represented a different point of view on a specific theme. Among these was *Axis Conversations* (*Conversazioni dell'Asse*), whose protagonists were two men, a German and an Italian, who exchanged views on the war; *La Politica in Pantofole*, in which a nephew working for the Italian MinCulPop and an anti-fascist uncle animatedly debated controversial war issues; and *Undertone* (*Sottovoce*), dialogues between three Italians with divergent political ideologies. These kinds of programmes were more popular before the Allies' campaign in

Italy, since Italian civilians were probably less inclined to humour during the occupation.[32]

One of the most successful programmes of the Italian Service was the *Monologue of the Little Man* (*Il monologo dell'omo qualunque*) by Elio Nissim. Guglielmo Giannini's *Fronte dell'Uomo Qualunque* may have been named after the BBC programme. The comedy writer and journalist Guglielmo Giannini founded the movement known as *qualunquismo* in 1944; the movement was turned into a political party in 1945. The hypothesis that Giannini was inspired by Radio London seems to be confirmed by the work of Gino Pallotta and Sandro Setta. According to these two authors, Giannini sent a request to the Allied authorities for permission to publish two journals. These were *L'Uomo della strada* (*Man in the Street*) and *L'Uomo qualunque*.[33] It should be noted that *Man in the Street* was the title of another BBC programme.

During the Anglo-American occupation of Italy, the features of the BBC programmes changed slightly. In 1944 new programmes were launched with the aim of providing Italian civilians with information on their relatives who were either soldiers or prisoners of war in Britain. These included the *Piccola posta della voce di Londra*, in which a female radio broadcaster answered the requests for information sent by many Italian listeners to the Italian Service, and the *Italian Soldiers Programme*. In this programme, messages from Italian prisoners or soldiers to their relatives were broadcast, with the aim of reassuring their families. Their family members and friends, these programmes suggested, were receiving a very good treatment.[34]

As the case of Colonel Stevens has shown, radio broadcasters were not always the authors of their programmes. In some cases, the radio transcripts specify where the authors and broadcasters are different. Nevertheless, in many other cases it is not possible to find out who wrote the programmes. In Colonel Stevens's radio transcripts, the name of the real author, Aldo Cassuto, is never mentioned. The programmes were usually written in English and translated into Italian. It seems that the same rule was applied to other European Services.

It would be interesting to compare the original texts of the programmes and their translations. This would allow us to discover more about the linguistic choices made to mirror the culture of the country in which the programmes were broadcast. However, the Italian Service archives only hold the transcripts in Italian. The exception is Colonel Stevens's programme, for which we can access both the English and the Italian versions. In addition to that, the rule of translation from English into Italian may have been applied only to bulletins. As the next chapters will show, many Italian exiles wrote their own programmes. This is not surprising, considering that many of them were well-known personalities from the political and cultural Italian scene. This is further confirmed by Uberto Limentani, who claims that *Talks* were always written in Italian first.[35]

The translation of programmes from other languages into English or vice versa was a challenging operation for the BBC's foreign services staff members, especially during the first years of their activities. A bad translation would be ineffective or could cause communication problems. In October 1941, at one of the weekly meetings of the BBC Italian Service, the translation issue was discussed at the request of Leon Shepley, who had noticed a number of mistakes in the bulletins. At the meeting, a Mr Jeafferson suggested that translators should engage more with the Italian language:

> Mr Shepley drew attention to a number of bad mistakes in translation of bulletins which had come to his notice. Mr. Jeaffreson to investigate complaints re translating mistakes. The meeting considered suggestions to stimulate translators' interest and efficiency in their own language: Mr Jeaffreson to continue to urge translators to listen to Rome broadcasts, read Italian papers and speak Italian among themselves. Attention was drawn to translators' objections to use of alleged 'Fascist' words and phrases.[36]

The meeting concluded that a memorandum of all language questions would be prepared and circulated. The theme was at the centre of debates at other meetings. The most important questions regarding the formal aspects, content and targets of programmes were discussed at the weekly meetings of the Italian Service. These meetings were usually attended by the regional manager, the Editor of the Italian Service, a delegate from the Ministry of Information as well as other BBC employees.[37] Apart from the weekly meetings, at which more general issues were discussed, there were also daily meetings. The aim of these meetings was to analyse the news of the day and decide in which commentary or bulletin it would be used.[38]

Another important aspect to take into account was programme length. As Lawrence pointed out in an internal memo circulated in September 1940, an overlong programme would be difficult to follow in a country where listening to the BBC was forbidden:

> I listened to the Italian half hour from 18.30 to 19.00 the other night and I was much struck by the excessive length of the half hour period for broadcasts which are both jammed and prohibited in the country of destination. On this occasion, as on most evenings, the broadcast consisted of a quarter of an hour news followed by a quarter of an hour talk. The talk contained some very good points but was unnecessarily diffuse and would have gained by being cut down to ten minutes or even five. I think the experience of European talks suggests pretty clearly that there are not many talks which fill a quarter of an hour effectively. In any event, half an hour of straight speech unbroken by music or dialogue is excessive under the probable listening conditions. I suggest, therefore, that the policy for this very important half an hour should be reconsidered.[39]

The solutions suggested by Jeafferson to make the most of the 18.30–19.00 programme were either to introduce music and dialogue, or to cut down the programme to fifteen minutes. The reason why this half-hour was so important was that this transmission was mentioned in correspondence from listeners more often than others.[40]

The value that musical elements could add to the Italian broadcasts was also at the centre of a report by George Foa. The use of music in the French Service, wrote Foa, was proving to be really successful because it broke the monotony of a long talk:

> In order to catch the listener's mind and to divert him from the one item to the next, preparing him and putting him [sic] into the mood of what is to follow, musical links, varying between 15 seconds and 1 minute should prove, if carefully selected, effective, artistic and also of great propaganda value ... I feel, however, that if every day between each different item we were to introduce songs or slogans the repetition of this system might tend to tire or annoy the listener and thus defeat its own ends.[41]

He suggested that the Italian Service should use a wide selection of themes of famous composers who dealt with England and Italy. Among those mentioned by Foa were Mendelssohn's *Salterello*, Tchaikovsky's *Capriccio Italiano* and Bach's *Italian Concerto*. Other artists mentioned were Elgar, Delius and Purcell.

The attention the Italian Service paid to musical aspects so as to engage with Italians was publicised by a short article that appeared in the *Daily Telegraph* on 9 January 1941. The article was entitled 'Saying it with Music: BBC to Italy' and referred to 'a novel method of influencing the Italians against Fascism through their love of music'. In particular, the BBC had launched a series of interviews with famous tenors or musicians. The first interview was with Dino Borgioli, a friend of Arturo Toscanini. Like his friend Toscanini, who lived in the United States, Borgioli had left Italy because of his anti-fascist political position. When the BBC interviewer asked him why he had chosen Britain, his ironic answer was: 'To enjoy the sunshine. The sunshine of freedom.'[42] Borgioli was also invited to sing at the microphone on special occasions or festivities. This was the case in Christmas 1942, when Borgioli sang for the Italian listeners 'Notte Benigna, Notte Tranquilla' (Silent Night, Holy Night), 'Panis Angelicus' and Schubert's 'Ave Maria'.[43]

Similarly, the BBC made extensive use of special sound effects to make the above-mentioned *Sceneggiati* more entertaining. More details on the employment of music and sound effects, as well as on formal aspects such as linguistic registers, will be provided with an analysis of the radio transcripts in Chapters 5, 6 and 7. The next section will focus on the PWE directives for Italian programmes.

The PWE's directives to the Italian Service

As we have seen in Chapter 1, all the programmes and bulletins were based on directives sent weekly from the PWE. Every week the PWE released at least two kinds of directives for the BBC: some general directives were sent to all the foreign branches and other, more specific, directives to each individual branch. Among the Foreign Office records at Kew, there are several directives for the Italian Service. However, these directives do not cover the entire period of the war.

For the period between November 1942 and the end of 1943, all the weekly directives for the Italian programmes are available; for the years 1944–45, the directives seem to have been lost. As Garnett suggests in the introduction to his *Secret History of PWE*, many documents were destroyed at the end of the conflict.[44] This probably explains the lack of archival documents.

The weekly directives for the Italian Service were structured as follows. An opening sentence specifying that each branch was also supposed to refer to the general directives was followed by a report on the Italian situation that week. After the report there was a list of themes to be debated in the following week's programmes.[45] Some directives included informants' reports on the morale of the Italian civilians, as in that of 21 January 1943:

REPORTS FROM INFORMANTS:
1. Romans' sense of humour:
   The Romans retain their sense of humour, as shown by the following joke current in the Italian capital: A woman was taken to police headquarters for grumbling about the lack of butter. By way of punishment, she was ordered to repeat several times: 'We have enough butter! Long live the Duce!' She got confused and ended by transposing the words 'Butter' and Duce'!
2. Fear of the predominating sentiment in Italian circles:
   An informant who was recently in Italy states that the sentiment predominating in Italian circles is apprehension: apprehension of the Germans, the United Nations, air raids, hunger and the continuation of the war.[46]

In line with the Foreign Office document quoted at the end of Chapter 1, this extract shows how important it was to know the feelings and fears of Italian civilians.

Another directive carried references to the Italian listeners who were risking their lives by tuning in to BBC programmes despite the fascist regime's censorship laws:

WE MUST NOT WEAKEN IN OUR ATTITUDE TOWARDS ITALY. Constantly bear that in mind. Also remember that, by listening many Italians are running a great risk. Reliable information shows that many do listen to the BBC and we want to induce others to do so. We must therefore endeavour to maintain and even intensify the interest of what we have to say and avoid losing our audience by abusive treatment.[47]

References to the Italian audience who broke the fascist censorship laws about listening to foreign radio stations were very common in the Italian Service directives and programmes.

While the lack of PWE documents for the years 1944–45 does not allow for a systematic comparison between the directives and the programmes, it can be said that the directives for 1943 focus mainly on politics and tactical issues. The PWE indicated what were the main themes to be addressed, the fronts to mention and the political issues to debate in the Italian programmes. Moreover, when particularly important events happened, the PWE attached separate and more detailed guidelines to the usual directives. However, the directives never referred to any specific Italian Service programme title or broadcaster.[48] It is therefore possible that the BBC was actually free to curate formal aspects of its programmes independently from the PWE.

While this section has only provided a general description of how a typical weekly directive to the Italian Service was structured, the following chapters will explain in more detail how the political content of the programmes mirrored British military interests. The next two chapters will explore the careers of the most influential Italian employees, their memories of the BBC experience and BBC and their relations with the Foreign Office.

As this chapter has shown, in order to set up the Italian Service it was key to find employees who were familiar with Italian culture and language in order to engage with as many audiences as possible. It is not a coincidence that the two editors of the Italian Service, Sprigge and Whittal, had backgrounds in journalism and foreign languages. They had also lived in Italy prior to being hired by the BBC. The same reasoning applies to Colonel Stevens, who was Italian by origin and also lived in Rome.

As the Service developed, many Italians joined the BBC. These were political refugees forced to leave their country due to their anti-fascist activism or Jewish origins.

Chapters 3 and 4 will focus respectively on the biographies of some of these Italians and their relationships with the British Foreign Office during their years in London. These chapters will show two different aspects of their exile: while their accounts of their work at the BBC are extremely positive, their correspondence with British government institutions demonstrates that they also experienced serious political issues with the Foreign Office.

Notes

1 BBC, *Ecco Radio Londra*, p. 1.
2 Piccialuti Caprioli, *Radio Londra 1940–45*, p. xiv.

3 Lucio Sponza, *La BBC 'in bianco' e 'in nero': La propaganda britannica per l'Italia nella seconda guerra mondiale*, Storiamestre (18 December 2013), http://storiamestre.it/2013/12/bbcbiancoenero, 4, accessed December 2013.
4 Sponza, *La BBC 'in bianco' e 'in nero'*, 6.
5 Garnett, *Secret History of PWE*, p. 166.
6 *Manchester Guardian* Archive (hereafter MGA), A/S/50 – A/S/94, box 70, John Rylands Library (hereafter JRL), Charles Prestwich Scott to Cecil Sprigge, 19 December 1922.
7 MGA, JRL, A/S/50 – A/S/94, box 70, Sprigge to Scott, 27 March 1923.
8 MGA, JRL, A/S/50 – A/S/94, box 20, Scott to Sprigge, 18 January 1925.
9 MGA, JRL, A/S/50 – A/S/94, box 20, Scott to Sprigge, 27 January 1929.
10 MGA, JRL, B/S/215 – B/S/307 Sprigge to Crozier, 17 October 1941.
11 MGA, JRL, B/S/307, Sylvia Sprigge to Crozier, 16 July 1940.
12 MGA, JRL, B/S/215 – B/S/307; BBC to Crozier, 6 August 1940.
13 MGA, JRL, B/S/215 – B/S/307, Crozier to Sprigge, 16 July 1940.
14 MGA, JRL, B/S/215 – B/S/307, BBC to Crozier, 25 July 1941; Sprigge to Crozier, 17 October 1941; Sprigge to Wadsworth from the *Manchester Guardian*, n.d.
15 BBC Written Archives Centre (hereafter BBC WAC), Li/453, Left Staff, Whittal Cecil Frederick 10.2.1941–31.7.1945, Staff Record Form, 19 March 1941.
16 BBC WAC, Li/453, J. B. Clark to Whittal, 20 July 1945.
17 BBC WAC, Li/453, Interview with Mr C.F. Whittal, 21 January 1941.
18 Interview with Mr C.F. Whittal, 21 January 1941 Li/453, BBC WAC.
19 Piccialuti Caprioli, *Radio Londra 1940–45*, p. XVI.
20 Sponza, *La BBC 'in bianco' e 'in nero'*, p. 3.
21 MI7 was initially a section of the British War Office and then of the Ministry of Information from 1940. It specialised in Propaganda and Censorship.
22 BBC WAC, S107/15, *Colonel Stevens, Letters of Appointments, 1938–46*, Programme Division to Stevens, 24 November 1939.
23 BBC WAC, S107/15, *Colonel Stevens, Letters of Appointments, 1938–46*, Stevens's official letter of appointment as Italian News commentator, 15 December 1939.
24 BBC WAC, S107/15, *Colonel Stevens, Letters of Appointments, 1938–46*, Internal Circulating Memo of the BBC, 16 December 1940; *European Establishment Officer*, Gordon Yates to Stevens, 27 November 1942.
25 Sponza, *La BBC 'in bianco' e 'in nero'*.
26 Uberto Limentani recalled some of their names in a conference speech given in Tuscany. Among these were Alberto Casali, Massimo Coen, Giovanna Foà, Anny Foà, Italo Calma, W. Plank, P. Brookes, Platsheck, Cabib, Antona-Traversi, Grauberg, Mario Sarfatti, Vivante, Piero Mortara, Gino Valentine, Giulio Finzi, Mario Forti, Giulio Perugia, Carlo Ricono, Spani, Philipson and T. Gardini. Uberto Limentani, 'Radio Londra durante la guerra', in *Inghilterra e Italia nel '900: atti del convegno di Bagni di Lucca* (Florence: La Nuova Italia, 1973), p. 205.
27 BBC, *Ecco Radio Londra 1945*, pp. 25–27.
28 Sponza, *La BBC 'in bianco' e 'in nero'*, p. 3.
29 BBC, *Ecco Radio Londra*, p. 48; author's translation.

30 Chapters 5 to 7 of this work will focus specifically on themes and formal aspects of the programmes as well as on the different sections of society targeted by the Italian Service in each phase of the war. However, some preliminary information on main titles and themes of the broadcasts will be provided in this section.
31 Piccialuti Caprioli, *Radio Londra 1940–45*, p. xxvii.
32 Piccialuti Caprioli, *Radio Londra 1940–45*.
33 Sandro Setta, *L'Uomo qualunque: 1944–48* (Rome: Laterza, 1975); Gino Pallotta, *Il Qualunquismo e l'avventura di Guglielmo Giannini* (Milan: Bompiani, 1972).
34 BBC WAC, IS, series II, *Scripts*, G.R. Foa and D. Piani, *Italian Soldiers Programme*, n.1, 3 December 1944.
35 Limentani, *Radio Londra durante la guerra*, pp. 201–209.
36 BBC WAC, E1/1003, *Italian Weekly Service meeting*, 23 October 1941.
37 The BBC WAC does not hold a comprehensive series of meeting reports. It should also be noted that these reports do not include the names of the Italian anti-fascist exiles working for the BBC in their list of the attendees. It is therefore probable that they were not invited to the meetings.
38 BBC, *Ecco Radio Londra*, p. 45.
39 BBC WAC, E2/371, Foreign Gen. Italian Service 1940–1947, *BBC Internal Circulating Memo*, 5 September 1940.
40 BBC WAC, E2/371, Foreign Gen. Italian Service 1940–1947, *Times of Italian Evening Bulletin*, 3 April 1940.
41 George Foa, Suggestion for a co-ordinating scheme of the Italian programme to be run on the lines of an half an hour daily magazine, Foreign Gen. Italian Service 1940–1947, E2/371, BBC WAC.
42 BBC WAC, E2/371, Foreign Gen. Italian Service 1940–1947, 'Saying it with Music: BBC to Italy', *Daily Telegraph* (9 January 1941).
43 Lo Biundo, *London Calling Italy*, p. 67.
44 Garnett, *Secret History of PWE*.
45 See Lo Biundo, *London Calling Italy*, p. 71.
46 NA, FO371/37249, PWE, Weekly Directive for BBC Italian Service, week beginning Thursday 21 January 1943.
47 NA, FO371/37249, PWE, Special Directive for BBC Italian Service, 14 January 1943.
48 Lo Biundo, *London Calling Italy*, p. 72.

3

Exiles: biographies, memories and experiences of the Italian anti-fascist broadcasters

After providing information on the birth and development of the BBC Italian Service, this chapter concentrates on the Italian broadcasters working for the corporation. By exploring their biographies and the years preceding their emigration to Britain, the chapter aims to understand their political and cultural milieu. This in turn allows us to comprehend why they ended up working for British propaganda and to what extent their backgrounds and experiences as immigrants are mirrored in the content of the programmes.

The analysis of a selection of memoirs published by these broadcasters during or after the war will also reveal their intended mission at the BBC. Their aim, as suggested by the majority of these memoirs, was not to engage with their fellow academics, intellectuals or members of the Resistance. Rather, they wanted to support ordinary Italians whose lives were constantly at risk. This objective was in line not only with the broader BBC's aim of educating and entertaining the masses, but also with their personal life experiences in Britain. In Italy they were established academics, lawyers or politicians. Yet the forced emigration to another country and the outbreak of the war turned them into ordinary men. It is in their capacity as common people that they wanted to speak to the Italians who listened to the BBC.

The first section of the chapter will focus on anti-fascist political emigration from the early 1920s to the promulgation of the Italian racial laws, while each of the subsequent sections will refer to a specific Italian broadcaster. It is not among the aims of this chapter to analyse the biography of every single Italian working for the BBC, as the archival material consulted for this work does not provide exhaustive information about their role in Britain. It is not always possible, for example, to know when their collaboration with the British radio began or whether they played an important role at the BBC. The criteria for choosing the biographies for inclusion in this chapter are the importance of the broadcasters in the Italian political and cultural scene and the number of programmes under their names found at the BBC WAC.

Italian anti-fascist emigration

L'esilio come si intende generalmente e storicamente è la situazione di alcuni individui, molti o pochi, i quali, nello Stato in cui sono cittadini, per una serie di circostanze, si trovano in pericolo e nell'impossibilità di fare una vita normale, o addirittura di sopravvivere, per cui sono costretti, non volontariamente, non volentieri, non perché lo hanno scelto, non perché vogliono fare un viaggio turistico, ad andare oltre le frontiere, oltre i confini ad assicurare la propria sopravvivenza altrove ... In esilio si può stare in due modi: c'è un modo di andare in esilio semplicemente per salvarsi la pelle, insomma, per assicurare la propria sopravvivenza; c'è invece un modo di andare in esilio per continuare a lottare, perché nel proprio paese non è possibile, in quanto si finirebbe in galera, o addirittura fucilati.[1]

Exile, as we generally and historically know it, is the situation of few or many individuals who, due to a series of circumstances, are in danger in the State of which they are citizens. They are, therefore, forced, not voluntarily, not gladly, not because they chose it, not because they want to go on a holiday, to go beyond frontiers, beyond borders to ensure their own safety somewhere else ... There are two ways of being in exile: you can simply go into exile to save your own skin, in other words, to spare your own life; but you can also go into exile to continue to fight, since in your own country is not possible as you would be arrested or even executed.

These words, written by the Italian writer Joyce Lussu, can be applied to the experience of the Italian broadcasters at the BBC. Each Italian exile working for Radio London left Italy for a different reason and had a different cultural and political background. Some were involved in anti-fascist political activities prior to leaving their country; others left mainly because their Jewish origins prevented them from working in Italy; in some cases, the exiles were both anti-fascist activists and Jewish. Whether they left Italy simply to save their lives or to continue their political opposition from Britain, what associated all the Italian broadcasters at the BBC was their common enemy: the fascist regime. Another common element was the idea of having a mission to support the morale of Italian civilians whose lives had been destroyed by twenty years of Mussolini's dictatorship and the outbreak of the war. This common goal was pursued regardless of the specific political party or cultural group to which the exiles belonged. For this reason, the word 'anti-fascist' will be used in this book to refer to all the Italian refugees in Britain and the BBC's Italian broadcasters.

As we know, in October 1922 the March on Rome of about 16,000 *squadristi* brought Mussolini and the fascists to power. Mussolini's coup d'état was followed in 1925–26 by the proclamation of a series of laws known as *leggi fascistissime*. These laws banned all political parties, trade unions, newspapers and publications that opposed the fascist regime. They also obliged all Italian citizens working in public institutions to pledge loyalty to the fascist regime. Those who did not do so risked arrest, confinement or the death penalty. As a consequence, many Italian anti-fascist intellectuals and politicians who did not want to accept any compromise or risk their lives left their country.

According to historian Charles Delzell, the history of Italian emigration under the fascist regime can be divided into three main phases: a first wave covering the months from October 1922 to January 1925; a second wave from January 1925 to the proclamation of the 'exceptional decrees' in November 1926; and a third wave starting from the proclamation of the *leggi fascistissime*, also known as draconian decrees, in November 1926.[2]

The majority of the first wave of emigrants left Italy for economic reasons. They moved to wealthier countries such as Belgium, France and Switzerland in the hope of entering a better labour market. During this phase several anarchists and socialists also emigrated. Their aim was to continue abroad their activities against the state and 'of course, against fascism, which so passionately glorified the State'. In this period political personalities such as the former liberal premier Francesco Saverio Nitti and the leader of the PPI (Partito Popolare Italiano), Don Luigi Sturzo, left the Italian mainland.[3]

The second phase was characterised by the emigration of those opponents of fascism who 'feared that if they stayed home in silence the public must misconstrue their behaviour as tacit acceptance of their hated regime', or who wanted to protect their families. Among these people were the communist politician Giorgio Amendola, the journalist Piero Gobetti, the Catholic politician and journalist Giuseppe Donati, the politician and historian Gaetano Salvemini, the *Corriere della Sera* journalist Alberto Tarchiani and the law professor Silvio Trentin, to mention just a few examples. In this phase, passports were still valid and the emigration process was still relatively easy.[4]

The third wave saw the emigration of many important socialists, republicans and communists who assisted one another in escaping. While the socialists decided to leave as many young men as possible in Italy to organise the Resistance, older prestigious personalities were encouraged to escape. This was the case with politicians such as Ferruccio Parri, Claudio Treves, Filippo Turati, Giuseppe Saragat, Carlo Rosselli and Sandro Pertini.[5]

To establish whether the political activities of Italian exiles were as effective as the actions of those who remained in Italy is not an easy operation. This theme was at the centre of debates among well-known anti-fascist personalities such as the historians and politicians Benedetto Croce and Aldo Garosci. While Croce reached the conclusion that the actions of the exiles abroad were not as successful as the clandestine operations of those in Italy, Garosci claimed that it was pointless to consider domestic and foreign anti-fascism as two separate entities; rather, they were part of the same Resistance. Moreover, the two groups converged after July 1943 when many Italian refugees could finally return home.[6]

Italian anti-fascist groups and associations were more powerful in some countries than in others. One of the former was France, historically one of the preferred foreign destinations of Italian anti-fascists.[7] In many cases, the *fuorusciti*, as the anti-fascist exiles were disdainfully called by fascist sympathisers, did not have easy lives. They often experienced issues with fascist officials abroad and lived on very low salaries. Most worked as journalists or language teachers or held other similar part-time positions. In some cases, they also experienced problems with the governments of their host countries due to their political opposition to Mussolini. Moreover, communications with anti-fascists in Italy were often difficult.[8]

The problems encountered by these Italian exiles are not the only reason why it is difficult to judge the impact of their work in both their host countries and Italy. In the introduction to Antonio Varsori's *Gli Alleati e l'emigrazione democratica antifascista*, Ennio Di Nolfo explains why in the 1980s, this was still one of the most controversial themes in the historiography of Italian exiles:

> Difficile da esplorare, poiché la natura dell'azione politica antifascista, il fatto che essa fosse vincolata alla clandestinità o all'emigrazione, condiziona la natura delle fonti, che non potranno mai essere sistematiche, ma saranno sempre episodiche, legate allo scrupolo di qualche corrispondente e alla sensibilità di un protagonista; e che saranno sempre, nella migliore delle ipotesi, fonti 'nemiche', come quelle conservate negli archivi della polizia fascista, o fonti straniere, come quelle conservate negli archivi dei paesi che accolsero gli emigrati, e, talora, si valsero di essi per determinati obiettivi politici propri. E difficile da valutare storicamente, poiché su questo tema molto ha pesato, e pesa, la forza politica delle cose: il desiderio di trovare a tutti i costi nel filone dell'antifascismo gli elementi per ricostruire una continuità ideale di azione democratica e socialista; oppure, in senso inverso, il desiderio di ricreare una primogenitura, la volontà di affermare un primato o l'esclusività di un progetto, rivendicando paternità che non lasciano spazio a contributi diversi.[9]

> It is difficult to explore, since the nature of political anti-fascist activism, and the fact that it will always be bound up with secrecy and emigration, influences the nature of the sources. They will never be comprehensive, but will cover only a few episodes reported by some scrupulous correspondents or forward-looking people; they will always be, in the best-case scenario, 'enemy' sources

like those stored in the archives of the fascist police, or foreign sources, like those stored in those countries which welcomed the emigrants and, sometimes, used them for their own political ends. And it is difficult to assess from a historical perspective, since the topic is strongly influenced by politics: there is a desire to achieve – at all costs – some continuity of democratic and socialist ideals; or, conversely, there is the desire to take ownership, the wish to be the first and exclusive designers of a project, claiming paternity without leaving room for other contributions.

Di Nolfo's considerations on the nature of archival sources on the exiles can also be applied to this research on Radio London. In many cases, the documents held at the National Archives in Kew or the personal papers of the Italian broadcasters do not allow us to reconstruct comprehensively either the key phases of their exile or all the networks that they built in Britain with other anti-fascists. For these reasons, the next section of this chapter does not aim at extensively analysing their role in Britain. For the purpose of this work three main aspects will be examined: the cultural and political background of these exiles; their memories of their BBC experience; and their relations with British government institutions (Chapter 4). These three elements will allow us to discover more about their role at the BBC and to better understand the content of their programmes.

Paolo and Piero Treves

Paolo and Piero Treves were the sons of Claudio Treves (1869–1933), a well-known member of the Italian Socialist Party who was close to the political entourage of Filippo Turati and Carlo Rosselli. Claudio Treves escaped from Italy in October 1926 and moved to Paris. In *What Mussolini Did to Us*, published in 1940, Paolo Treves remembered the last night he saw his father at home. On 31 October 1926, there was an attempt on Mussolini's life during a ceremony to celebrate the anniversary of the fascist March on Rome. On that same evening Carlo Rosselli knocked on the door of Claudio Treves's house:

> My father was silent, wrapped up in his thoughts; perhaps, who knows, he already foresaw the consequences. Meanwhile there was no time to lose. We mustn't let ourselves be caught. We were more frightened than reassured by the soldiers picketed at the bottom of the stairs. Experience had taught us what 'protection' meant. What would happen tomorrow and tonight? It was not yet two months since the office had been destroyed, the doors were still without glass. At all once Rosselli's voice rang out in the silence: 'Let's go to my house. Tomorrow we'll see. Meanwhile it isn't safe for you to stay here, *onorevole* ...' ... After all, why not? It only meant spending one night away from home ... That was how father left us, with a pair of pyjamas in

his pocket, and an umbrella. We all thought he was coming back the next day, and instead he was never to come back, never more to see those rooms, the room where I was born, his study, his books and all his belongings. If someone had told us that night as we quietly went to bed, we would certainly not have believed it.[10]

This extract is a good description of the uncertainty and precariousness of the lives of anti-fascists living in Italy under the fascist regime. The same uncertainty would characterise the lives of Paolo and Piero who, a few years later, emigrated. Claudio Treves died in exile on the night of 11 June 1931, beside his son Paolo, who was in Paris for a visit. His death left a mark on Paolo and Piero who, as another extract from Paolo Treves's book suggests, continued their intellectual and political activities in their father's name:

After so many years of Fascism we could not go on fighting only with illegal arms: but our frenzy to 'do something' was to be given new and different objects to exploit. Fascism could not properly oppose us on critical and erudite grounds because it lacked competent apologists; the young, moreover, were notoriously ignorant; consequently, that 'something' could be partially achieved slowly but surely, by each man working in his own sphere and according to his opportunities and erudition ... Piero and I moreover had a different, more intimate purpose: to do something more for father. It was our duty in some way to restore to Italy that name which for years and years had been in its pages every day, and which now was banned. That name could return only with *our* name: that is why the books I published in Italy are dear to me, and why several of them are dedicated to father – it was in order that people should more readily connect the memory of him with the name of the new and unknown writer who was making his way in the world of authors.[11]

During and after the conflict Piero and Paolo Treves did return their father's name to Italy. Apart from working as BBC broadcasters during the war, they both contributed to Italy's political and cultural life and embarked on careers in academia and politics, respectively.

Piero, the younger, had a background in classics and graduated from the University of Turin. His mentor, Gaetano De Sanctis, specialised in the study of ancient history. De Sanctis was very well known in Italy, and not only for his excellent academic output; he was also one of the Italian academics who refused to pledge loyalty to the fascist regime.[12] Claudio Treves's anti-fascist political activities made Piero's academic career difficult during the fascist years. He therefore started working as a private tutor and author of school books. At the end of his employment at the BBC Piero Treves worked as a correspondent for the Italian newspaper *Corriere della Sera*. He moved back to Italy ten years after the end of the war, returned to the academic world and obtained a post at the University of Milan. In 1962 he became Professor of Greek History and taught in Trieste, Florence and Venice.

Paolo studied under the supervision and mentorship of Benedetto Croce. He first graduated in law from the University of Turin and took another degree in politics from the University of Milan. Before moving to London Paolo was an active member of the clandestine Socialist Party and worked with Filippo Turati for the socialist newspaper *Giustizia*. In 1938, after being arrested twice, Paolo moved to London, where he remained until 1944. During the years of his British emigration, he also taught Italian in Liverpool and London. On his return to Italy, Paolo worked for a short period as director of the Italian *Giornale Radio*. He also edited the famous socialist newspaper *Avanti*. He was a member of several post-war Italian parliaments as a Socialist Party deputy.

According to Charles Delzell, Paolo Treves was contacted by British intelligence and employed at the BBC. In the introduction to another of his books, Paolo explained the aim of his work at the BBC. The book in question is a selection of his series of programmes entitled *Sul fronte e dietro il fronte italiano*.[13] The reason for the success of the programmes, wrote Treves, was the nature of the subject itself, because the war was having a tremendous impact on the lives of Italian civilians. Moreover, Italian listeners – wrote Treves – identified themselves with the point of view of an Italian in exile who was speaking from a free country.

> Per questo, credo, ci siamo voluti bene. Infatti, mai ho voluto fare 'propaganda', come si dice, non solo perché detesto la parola e la cosa, ma sopra tutto perché non vi era nessun bisogno di 'propaganda' e si trattava invece di far sentire agli italiani che non erano soli nella tempesta e nella sofferenza purificatrice. Questo soltanto ho tentato di fare, e debbo pur dire che sempre, ogni giorno e ogni ora, mentre analizzavo sulle varie fonti le notizie della giornata e piano piano sorgeva il panorama cognito e amato e deturpato dalla doppia tirannide dell'Italia in travaglio, sempre ho sentito tutto il peso della mia responsabilità. Ogni volta che sono andato al microfono ho sentito qual era il mio dovere, e se in buona fede posso aver commesso errori di fatto ho sempre voluto dire tutta la verità e soltanto la verità.[14]

> This is why, I think, we liked each other. As a matter of fact, I never wanted to make 'propaganda', as they call it, not only because I hate the word and concept but, above all, because there was no need for 'propaganda'. It was rather a matter of making sure the Italians did not feel alone in the purifying turmoil and suffering. This is only thing I tried to do, and I must also say that I always – because every day and at all times, while I was analysing the day's news from various sources, I would gradually come to recognise the well-known and beloved landscape, disfigured by the dual tyranny of a suffering Italy – felt all the burden of my responsibility. Every time I was at the microphone I knew what my duty was. And if I made unintentional mistakes, it was in good faith as I only ever wanted to tell the truth. Only and always the truth.

Later in the same introduction, Treves declared that he was always free to express his political beliefs at Radio London, even in those cases where they differed from those of the British government. This freedom of expression made him feel part of an international civil war – a sentiment shared at the BBC, as the profiles of the other broadcasters at the Italian Service will show.

Uberto Limentani

Another well-known Italian broadcaster at the BBC Italian Service was the literary critic Uberto Limentani, who taught Italian literature at the University of Cambridge from 1945 on. He was the cousin of Piero and Paolo Treves and also had Jewish origins. As an academic, Limentani researched a wide range of topics and published on Salvator Rosa, Ugo Foscolo and Michelangelo Buonarroti il Giovane.

As we will see in the next chapter, a few days after the Italian declaration of war on France and Great Britain, Limentani, as well as the Treves brothers and many other Italians living in Britain, was arrested as citizens of an enemy country. According to Sponza, Limentani was arrested on 13 June 1940. He was initially taken to a camp in Surrey and then transferred to a disused cotton mill in Lancashire called the Warth Mills camp.[15] During his period of internment, as we will see in Chapter 4, he boarded the *Arandora Star*, the famous British ship hit by a torpedo while transporting around 2,000 internees to Canada.

In 1973 Limentani was invited to a conference in Tuscany on the relations between Britain and Italy in the twentieth century.[16] On that occasion Limentani remembered the years of his employment at the Italian Service. The first time his voice was broadcast from the Italian Service's microphones – on 21 November 1939 – he was only 25 years old and had lived in London for four months. The freedom of speaking to Italians over a microphone, claimed Limentani, was a great privilege for an inexperienced young man.

> Superato dopo i primi giorni il timor panico che incuteva il microfono, specialmente in chi, come me, non possedeva l'arte di controllare la dizione, di darle un ritmo nella lettura ad alta voce, e tendeva a mangiare la seconda metà delle frasi, potei guardarmi attorno e compiacermi di essere stato accolto in un'ambiente così congeniale; i miei nuovi amici (perché amici divennero subito e quasi rimasero) erano tutti uomini imbevuti quasi di missione, convinti di combattere una crociata, che non risparmiavano le energie.[17]

> After the first days of panic and fear of the microphone, especially for someone like me who had no experience of diction or rhythm when reading aloud, and tended to mumble the second half of his sentences, I was able to look around me and be pleased to have been welcomed in such a congenial environment; my new friends (since we immediately became long-lasting friends) were all

men with a mission, people who felt they were fighting a crusade and who spared no energy.

When Limentani joined the BBC, his first director, John Reith, had just left. The corporation was expanding rapidly to meet the needs of the war and counter enemy propaganda. At the time the BBC was perceived as a very mysterious and prestigious institution and its employees considered themselves to be privileged members of an elite. There were many rumours and myths about the BBC: people said that before the outbreak of the war, BBC broadcasters used to wear a dinner jacket to speak at the microphone; that every announcer was offered a glass of whisky prior to reading the news; that any female employee who 'dared' to get married would lose her job. With the outbreak of war, these habits would disappear.[18] Also in Limentani's case, there are references to the objectivity and independence of the corporation:

> Col ricordo fresco ancora della statolatria accentratrice del fascismo, non potevo far a meno di meravigliarmi della notevole indipendenza di cui godeva la BBC, e, in seno alla BBC, il Servizio Europeo. Il governo aveva letteralmente delegato all'ente radiofonico britannico il compito delle trasmissioni ai paesi stranieri, gli aveva lasciato, saggiamente, una libertà di movimenti e iniziativa che giovò assai alla freschezza e alla vitalità dei programmi.[19]

> Since I had a vivid memory of how acutely fascism controlled the state, I could not help being astounded about the great independence of the BBC and, within the BBC, the European Service. The government literally delegated the task of producing broadcasts to foreign countries to British national radio, giving the BBC freedom of action and initiative, which contributed to the openness and liveliness of the programmes.

Limentani's memories included references to the hectic and dangerous conditions in which BBC staff members undertook their daily tasks during the conflict. The bombings in the autumn and winter of 1940, for example, challenged the BBC, but despite the difficulties these caused, the most common motto was 'business as usual'.

> La sera del 15 ottobre mi trovavo, per pochi minuti di respiro fra due trasmissioni, nella concert Hall di Broadcasting House, quando con un boato pauroso una bomba ad azione ritardata scoppiò al quarto piano dell'edificio; non solo ci fu panico (ricordo la risata che, pochi secondi dopo l'esplosione, accolse il funzionario salito sul palcoscenico ad annunciare tranquillamente: 'This was a bomb'), ma ad onta dei danni e delle vittime, le trasmissioni continuarono come se niente fosse accaduto. Non così l'8 dicembre, allorché un'altra bomba costrinse il Servizio Europeo a sloggiare e a rifugiarsi dapprima in certi anditi e stretti corridoi degli Studi di Maida Vale, e poi dopo tre mesi a Bush House, che diventò la sua sede permanente.[20]

On the evening of 15 October I was having a few minutes' break between two broadcasts, when a delayed-action bomb blew up on the fourth floor of the building, making a frightening rumble; not only did people panic (I remember, a few seconds later, the broadcaster laughing and jumping on the stage to calmly announce: 'This was a bomb') but, despite the damage and the victims, broadcasts continued as if nothing had happened. That was not the case on 8 December, when another bomb forced the European Service to move to the pretty narrow corridors of the Maida Vale studios and, after three months, to Bush House, which would become its permanent headquarters.

Another common element between Paolo Treves's and Limentani's memories of the BBC is the firm belief that it was the Italian audience who made their work at BBC important. Limentani was aware of how difficult it was to judge whether Radio London was actually contributing to the Allies' victory. There was, however, no doubt that the BBC had many followers in Italy. These followers, as we will see in the final chapter of this work, sent many letters to their favourite broadcasters at BBC, including Limentani.[21]

> Che una gran parte della popolazione italiana si rivolgesse per sei anni alla BBC per avere notizie attendibili è un fatto concreto, e quindi incontrovertibile. Si può pertanto affermare che Radio Londra ebbe indubbiamente un profondo influsso sulla vita del popolo italiano durante la guerra o, più precisamente, fu uno dei fattori, e forse dei più efficaci, che forgiarono l'opinione pubblica a quei tempi; il segreto del loro successo, ripeto, era semplice: attenersi ai fatti; ammettere le sconfitte così come si annunciavano le vittorie; dire la verità; cose, queste, di cui gli Italiani erano assetati.[22]

> The fact that a great part of the Italian population tuned into the BBC for six years to access reliable information is real and unquestionable. Therefore, we can say that Radio Londra had, without doubt, a huge impact on the lives of Italians during the war or, we should say, was one of the factors, and maybe one of the most effective, that shaped public opinion at the time; the secret of its success was, again, simple: sticking to the facts; admitting defeats as well as announcing victories; telling the truth; all things the Italian were thirsting for.

Umberto Calosso

According to Piccialuti Caprioli, Umberto Calosso was one of the most intransigent broadcasters of the Italian Service.[23] It was he who coined the word *repubblichino* to refer to the members of the Italian *Repubblica di Salò*.[24] The word was broadly used by the other Italian broadcasters at the BBC and became an official entry in Italian dictionaries. In particular, as we will see in the next chapter, Calosso was critical of the BBC's position on the unconditional surrender of Italy.[25] Born in Belveglio, Piedmont, he graduated in literature from the University of Turin (1920), having written a thesis on Vittorio Alfieri, published by Laterza in 1924 under the title *L'Anarchia di Vittorio Alfieri*. Among his mentors were Piero Gobetti and the founder of the Italian Communist Party, Antonio Gramsci.[26]

On the day of the fascist March on Rome (28 October 1922) Calosso was arrested for armed resistance against some fascist gangs in Turin. The following year, in 1923, Gramsci's journal *Ordine Nuovo* was suppressed by the fascist authorities. All members of the editorial board, including Calosso, were arrested and subjected to a trial for sedition. On that occasion, thanks to the intervention of Benedetto Croce who acted as witness, Calosso was released.[27]

Between the two world wars Calosso worked as an Italian and Latin teacher in secondary schools near Turin. This work was interrupted by his emigration to Malta in 1931 to take Giuseppe Donati's post at St Edward's College in Malta.[28] In 1936 Calosso and his wife Clelia Lajolo went to Barcelona for their summer holidays, little expecting to become part of the Spanish Civil War.[29] Together with Carlo and Nello Rosselli, Calosso organised the first legion of Italian workers who fought against Franco.

It is possible to identify the key phases and dates of his anti-fascist emigration from a memorandum written by Calosso in 1944. He lived as an exile from 1931; his first destination was Malta, where he worked at St Edward's College. After Malta he moved to Tunis and Egypt, where he edited an Italian anti-fascist journal and worked for Radio Cairo. In 1940 he obtained a certificate of naturalisation and was granted British nationality.[30] In 1942 he moved to London and ran the BBC programmes called *Free Italy Talks*; he was also a member of the Fabian Society. According to some correspondence between Calosso and the British authorities based in Egypt, his collaboration with Radio Cairo was interrupted because of his pro-communist talks. Calosso was fired by the man responsible for the propaganda activities, Colonel Thornhill, in July 1941 after receiving letters of complaint from Federico Symons and Raffaello Battino from the Comitato Nazionale Italiano in Cairo. In the letter Calosso was accused of making decisions without consulting the other committee members. This behaviour, according to the letter, had nothing to do with politics, but was due to personal reasons, which Symons and Battino do not explain.[31] A few days later Calosso received a letter in which Colonel Thornhill informed him that his work for the British government was at end:

> Dear Sir,
> As it has been found that you are unsuited for propaganda work of the kind required by me and that you are not able to work in harmony with those who have been working with me for some time past, I am obliged herewith to give you notice of termination of your engagement, as provided in Clause 5 of your agreement signed by you in Lisbon on the 30th March 1941, and

> subsequently confirmed by contract signed by you in Cairo on the 4th May 1941 ... You will cease to work for His Britannic Majesty's Government as from to-day's date.[32]

Uberto Calosso tried, unsuccessfully, to defend himself from what he judged to be an unfair and mistaken version of the facts. In his letter to Colonel Thornhill, he pointed out that he was unfairly accused of being a communist and conducting anti-monarchy propaganda.

> Io sono da lungo tempo accusato segretamente presso di Lei e di altri, specialmente dal ten. Nacamuli, di aver portato nel giornale e nel giovane Battino un'influenza 'rossa'. Questa la vera ragione d'una atmosfera ostile e deleteria che mi circonda presso quanti non mi leggono e non mi ascoltano. I fatti, come le spiegai a voce, non sono solo diversi, ma contrari. Nel giornale io portai come novità, oltre a un tono morale che spesso faceva difetto, una polemica continua contro il materialismo storico marxista, polemica anche io solo di noi condussi, e condussi ostinatamente, essendo questo il centro della mia fede politica; e inoltre sottolineai continuamente il concetto di 'stirpe', ritenuto da me propagandisticamente utile parlando delle Camicie Nere di vent'anni, e rispettai nettamente l'impegno preso di non attaccare il Re e i Principi, cosa del resto opportune politicamente.[33]

> For a long time I have been secretly accused by you and others, especially by Lt Nacamuli, to have a 'red' influence on both the newspaper and young Battino. This is the real reason for the hostile and harmful atmosphere when I deal with people who do not read or listen to me. The reality, as I explained in person, is not only different, but is rather the opposite. My contributions to the newspaper contained, as well as a moral tone that was often lacking elsewhere, the novelty of constant criticism of Marxist historical materialism – and I was the only one who stubbornly expressed it, since this is at the centre of my political faith; moreover, I constantly focused on the concept of 'ancestry', since I found it useful from the perspective of propaganda to talk about the twenty-year-old blackshirts. I also complied with my commitment to not attacking kings and princes, which was, after all, a sensible political choice.

This was the first in a series of issues with British governmental institutions in Cairo. The Egyptian phase of his exile was followed by his exile in London. However, the move to Britain only came after an unsuccessful attempt to migrate to the United States. The British authorities refused to provide Calosso with a visa for the United States so he and his wife Clelia reached London after nine months of waiting in Lisbon. This was their second failed attempt to reach the United States, which caused great disappointment, as Calosso stated in a letter to the British ambassador in Cairo:

> In July 1940, at the very point to sail to America from Lisbon, I received a telegram signed by Y. E. asking me to Cairo to direct an antifascist newspaper. Owing to the impossibilities of the British authorities of Cairo to find a passport

in that critical moment, a second telegram declared my coming 'indefinitely delayed'. In the meanwhile, by British responsibility (as explained in a memorandum to the Embassy) I had lost my passage, my transit visa to the United States, my visa to Canada, an easy possibility to have granted a United States immigrant visa, and the job my friends Count Sforza, Lionello Venturi and Gaetano Salvemini had found for me in America...The British authority who asked me to Cairo in March 1941 (Colonel Thornhill) dismissed me on 31st July promising that arrangements were made to send me and my wife to the United States, provided visas could be obtained. My case has not passed entirely to the Embassy [*sic*].[34]

Despite the problems encountered at the British Embassy in Cairo and his intention of reaching Venturi and Salvemini in the United States, it was in London that Calosso continued his anti-fascist propaganda and co-founded the Free Italy movement, as we will see in the next chapter.

Umberto Calosso's papers reveal more about the reasons why he could not obtain permits for the United States. However, in a BBC programme entitled *Convoglio Britannico*, Calosso referred to a British ship on which he spent six months:

Sono arrivato recentemente da Suez a Londra, per il capo di Buona Speranza dopo un viaggio di alcuni mesi in un grande convoglio britannico. Non posso, naturalmente, dare particolari di questo viaggio e della sua organizzazione navale; ma l'ordine e l'efficienza di questa gran macchina di guerra che è un convoglio, mi impressionò, ed è appunto di questo che voglio parlarvi ... Solo italiano a bordo, fedele alla mia essenza italiana che è fatta di profondo umanismo e di rivolta morale contro l'anti-Italia fascista e nazista e avendo con me mia moglie italiana al cento per cento e sorella di Medaglia d'oro, non ci accorgemmo mai di essere stranieri durante una navigazione di mesi.[35]

I recently arrived in London from Suez, via the Cape of Good Hope, after a journey of several months in a large British convoy. I cannot, of course, provide details about this journey and its naval organisation; but I was impressed by the efficiency of this huge war machine, which is a convoy, and this is exactly what I want to tell you about ... I was the only Italian person on board, true to my Italian character, which is made up of deep humanism and moral rebellion against the anti-Italy fascists and Nazis. My hundred per cent Italian wife and Gold Medal-winning sister [the Gold Medal was awarded for help with the war effort] was with me and we never felt foreigners during a voyage of many months.

Later in the same programme, Calosso described his lifestyle on board the ship. What the programme did not explain is why Calosso and his wife Clelia lived on the British ship for six months. This was because, as Calosso stated at the beginning of the programme, the information was confidential and could not be revealed during the conflict. From his descriptions of the lifestyle on the ship, we can deduce that he and his wife were very comfortable. It is therefore possible that the issues experienced by Calosso in Cairo did not end his relations with the British government.[36] More information on his relations with the British authorities in London will be provided in the next chapter.

Elio Nissim

Elio Nissim was a lawyer from Tuscany. He lived in Florence from his birth in 1899 until the promulgation of the racial laws in 1938.[37] His employment at the Italian Service dated back to autumn 1940. In February 1946 he resigned from the BBC, but later on he would work for the corporation again, until 1960.[38] Like many other colleagues, at the outbreak of war he was interned on the Isle of Man as an enemy alien. On his return to London he was asked by Cecil Sprigge whether he wanted to run some programmes for the Italian judges and lawyers at the Italian Service. Nissim replied that politics was not his strength but that, certainly, he could address his colleagues by appealing to the historical bond of friendship between Britain and Italy, referring to Byron, Shelley and the exiles of the Italian Risorgimento.[39] Sprigge accepted and Nissim started working as talks assistant under the direction of Geoffrey Dennis. Dennis already knew Nissim, having met him during the latter's internment on the Isle of Man. As the letter that Dennis sent him at the end of his first job at the BBC shows, Elio was highly esteemed at the BBC: 'As we worked together for so long, I know perhaps better than anybody what a good colleague and good worker and good friend of this country you are.'[40]

After Nissim's first attempt to address his colleagues in Italy, however, he concluded that the most important thing was to familiarise Italians with the British. In particular, Italian people needed to know more about the British people, who were ready to make sacrifices to contribute to the war effort.[41]

Nissim was born and raised in a family of Sephardi Jews. Among the people named Nissim, as he learned from the *Encyclopedia Judaica*, there were many philosophers and astrologists. He liked to imagine himself the descendant of one of these brilliant minds:

> Potevo forse chiedere di meglio? Discendere da una lunga linea di dotti, di rabbini, di scrittori solleticava la mia vanità intellettuale, confermava le opinioni tradizionali di famiglia, che noi non eravamo volgari ebrei Ashkenazi, ricchi ma ignoranti, ma piuttosto Sefarditi, poveri ma colti.[42]

> What else could I ask? Descending from a line of scholars, rabbis and writers boosted my intellectual vanity, confirmed the opinions that traditionally circulated in my family, that we were not vulgar Ashkenazi Jews, rich but ignorant, but rather Sephardic Jews, poor but cultured.

The choice of London as his new home may not have been a coincidence. Florence was historically one of the preferred destinations of British and American tourists who visited the city on vacation or bought holiday houses there.[43] Moreover, Nissim had already lived in London; in 1923, when he was still a law student, his father had sent him there to introduce him to the British juridical system. Once in London, he visited a British lawyer who suggested he should familiarise himself with the new culture and enjoy the city before visiting the Courts of Justice. As Nissim jokingly wrote in his book *Il pappagallo del nonno: ricordi anglo-fiorentini*, he would never return to that lawyer's office and would learn nothing about British law until 1938, when he started working as a lawyer in London. Yet during his first British experience he learned 'various little useful things'.[44] These 'little things' mainly had to do with British society and life. He learned, for example, that British men never turned around to look at beautiful girls in the street but that, in spite of this, British girls did appreciate the glances of Italian men. He also learned that stereotypes about other cultures spread very easily and sometimes became truer than reality, as his experience with British fashion showed:

> Non avevo imparato proprio nulla sui tribunali inglesi, ma avevo scoperto varie cosette utili: che i gentiluomini inglesi non portano i vestiti di tweed nei giorni lavorativi, ma si vestono in modo sobrio, poco appariscente, e spesso trasandato. Mi ero perfino comprato un abito scuro, una cravatta scura, un cappello nero e un ombrello. Una volta in treno, però, pensai che i miei amici italiani sarebbero restati molto delusi al mio aspetto, e per apparire veramente inglese ai loro occhi, decisi di levarmi gli abiti che avevo comprato a Londra e di mettermi quelli che avevo comprato, partendo, in Italia.
>
> Il che mi ricorda la storia del Marchese Ginori, rinomato a Firenze per la sua perfetta eleganza stile inglese, che decise di andare a Londra e portò con sè il fedele cameriere. Come tutti i nobili italiani, si fermò al Ritz. Era stanco, e voleva riposare; disse al cameriere di uscire a fare una passeggiata per Mayfair e fargli rapporto. 'Dimmi le tue impressioni, Giovanni', disse al ritorno del cameriere. 'Le mie impressioni, signor Marchese, sono che lei è l'unico signore in tutta Londra vestito all'inglese'. Giovanni perse il posto. Il Marchese perse la fede nell'Inghilterra.[45]

> I had learnt nothing at all about the English court system, but I had discovered various little useful things: that English gentlemen do not wear tweed suits on workdays, but dress in a sober, inconspicuous and often scruffy manner. I had even bought a black suit, a black tie, a black hat and an umbrella. However, once on the train, I realised my friends would be very disappointed by my outfit and, in order to look really British to them, I decided to take the clothes I had bought in London off and to wear those I had bought in Italy before I left. Which reminded me of the story of Marquis Ginori, known in Florence for his perfect British-style elegance, who decided to go to London

and brought his trusted butler with him. Like every Italian aristocrat, he stayed at the Ritz. He was tired and wanted to rest; he asked the butler to take a walk around Mayfair and report back to him. 'Tell me your impressions, Giovanni', he asked when the butler returned. 'I think, Mr Marquis, that you are the only person in London dressed like a British person.' Giovanni lost his job. The Marquis lost his faith in England.

One of the reasons for these misleading ideas about Britain, argued Nissim, was the lifestyle adopted by the British in Tuscany. They had found a sort of compromise between their insular habits and the Italian way of life. 'They no longer drank tea, only strong Italian coffee. However, they still loved crumpets.'[46]

Nissim's life as an Italian immigrant in Britain influenced his programmes, which included many references to the differences between Britain and Italy and mirrored the experiences of Italian exiles in a foreign country.[47] As we will see when analysing the programmes, this was especially true for Nissim's most famous programme, the *Monologue of the Little Man*. His protagonist, an ordinary Italian man, was unfamiliar with the British political system and history, but wished to know more about the life of the British man in the street.

> Quando mi venne chiesto di parlare alla BBC nella sezione italiana di Bush House (la British Broadcasting House era stata colpita da una bomba), non avevo la più lontana idea dell' 'Omo Qualunque' fiorentino. Il microfono era per me qualcosa di inconcepibile. In quei giorni cadevano le prime bombe su Londra. Eppure (salvo rare eccezioni) non mi sentivo estraneo: i colleghi inglesi, gli amici inglesi, gli amici italiani conosciuti nel breve periodo che avevo passato nel campo di internamento nell'isola di Man erano, in un certo senso, parte di una vita stranamente nuova nel paese che mi aveva accolto da esule, che mi aveva aiutato nel mio lavoro e che era tutto unito nello sforzo comune della difesa della propria libertà.[48]

> When I was asked to work for the BBC Italian service in Bush House (British Broadcasting House had been hit by a bomb), I did not have the faintest idea in my mind about the Florentine 'Omo Qualunque'. The microphone was something inconceivable for me. In those days the first bombs were falling on London. And yet, apart from some rare exceptions, I did not feel a stranger: the English colleagues, the English friends and the Italian friends I had met during my internment on the Isle of Man were, somehow, part of an unexpected new life in the country that had welcomed me as an exile, had helped me find a job and that was united in the common effort of defending its own freedom.

When writing the texts for the programmes, Nissim recalled in his memoirs, it was natural for him to be himself – a man from Florence who happened to live in London suffering the Nazi-fascist raids: 'Our antifascism – I must confess – was not heroic, was not brave. We were all 'irresolute'; this is what they called us. We were, after all, ordinary men. And I was one of them when I talked at the BBC.'[49]

When speaking into the microphone, he soon realised, he tended to emphasise his Florentine accent and use regional vocabulary. Nevertheless, it was another BBC member of staff, Leon Shepley, who came up with the idea of calling the protagonist of his talks *Uomo Qualunque*. Nissim agreed and replaced the word *uomo* with its Florentine version *omo*.[50] Nissim identified so much with his BBC character that towards the end of his life he still compared himself to the *omo qualunque*. In another chapter of *Il pappagallo del nonno* he remembered the day – he was in his nineties – when he found in his wardrobe an old suit he used to wear before the war:

> Allora pensai perché non usarlo, perché non tornare, almeno nelle apparenze, a quello che ero una volta? Non più l'omo qualunque che lavorava per la BBC durante la guerra, ma l'ex-gentiluomo importante che sapeva benissimo come sostenere, anche alle apparenze del vestire, il suo ruolo.[51]

> Therefore, I thought: why not wear it? Why not be, once again, at least on the surface, the person I used to be? No longer the ordinary man who worked at the BBC during the war, but the former important gentleman who knew how to play his social role perfectly and how to dress to do it.

On that day Nissim realised that it was impossible to return to the past and change the present. This awareness resulted in the donation of the suit to charity. However, the episode was an occasion to learn something about himself: he was, claimed Nissim, a simple *omo qualunque* and there was nothing he could do to return to the Florentine lawyer he had been before the war. It was evident that his work at the BBC, the war and his emigration had had a huge impact on Elio Nissim's life.

Candidus

According to Piccialuti Caprioli, Joseph John Marus, better known by his pseudonym, Candidus, was almost as popular as Colonel Stevens.[52] Marus was a Londoner of Italian origins, born in 1903. As recalled by Elio Nissim, after being arrested and later put under the surveillance of the fascist regime, Candidus moved to Britain in 1937. Once in London, he started working for a chemical industry as an expert designer. When he started working for the BBC, he decided not to leave his former job as he wanted to keep his independence from the company. According to Nissim, Candidus was a fine, honest and straightforward commentator.[53]

Ruggero Orlando also refers to him as a man of a great charisma and compared him with the famous Italian writer Gabriele D'Annunzio. This charisma was clearly reflected in the passionate tone of his voice at the microphone.[54]

During the conflict a pamphlet was circulated with false information on his identity.[55] According to this pamphlet, Candidus was a member of the *Fascio* in London and worked in the British capital as correspondent for the Italian *Giornale d'Italia*. Candidus, the pamphlet stated, started collaborating with the BBC only on the outbreak of the Second World War with the aim of avoiding a forced repatriation. Like other BBC Italian broadcasters, at the end of the conflict he published a selection of his programmes. As he declared in the introduction, the decision to publish his programmes was made in answer to requests received by many friends and acquaintances, but also to give an insight into what Radio London actually was. While at the microphone, Marus's words seem to suggest, he was neither a hero nor a propagandist:

> Perché le lodi tributatemi sono eccessive, le censure arbitrarie, eccessive quelle perché io non ho fatto che compiere il mio dovere obbedendo ai dettami della mia coscienza di uomo libero, arbitrarie queste, perchè sono convinto di non avere mai ingannato gli italiani con false promesse.[56]

> Because the praises heaped upon me are excessive, the censorship unjustified, excessive since I only did my duty and obeyed my conscience as a free man, which is unjustified, as I know I never deceived the Italians with false promises.

Later in the same introduction, Marus defended himself from the false rumours about his identity circulating in fascist environments. The real reason he decided to hide his identity, claimed the radio broadcaster, was to protect his anti-fascist friends in Italy:

> V'è una questione preliminare da mettere in chiaro: la mia identità. Se durante la guerra tenni occulto il mio nome ... non fu già per amore del mistero o per timore che svelando la mia identità potessi subire danni alla mia persona (ero a Londra) negli averi (non esistono), o nell'onore (pulito), bensì per la paura di compromettere amici italiani con i quali ero in stato in intimo e stretto contatto durante il mio precedente soggiorno in Italia, e che da moltissimi anni conducevano un'assidua e pericolosa opera antifascista.[57]

> There is a preliminary issue I want to clarify: my identity. If during the war I hid my name ... it was not for the sake of mystery or because I feared that, by revealing my identity, I (I was in London), my goods (I own nothing) or my honour (clean) could be subject to any harm. I was rather afraid of putting in danger some Italian friends I had been in close contact with during my last trip to Italy, as they had been conducting constant and dangerous anti-fascist activities for years.

Among these friends in Italy was Massenzio Masia, a partisan from Emilia Romagna and a member of the Italian Partito d'Azione, killed by some RSI neo-fascists on 23 September 1944. Marus shared with his colleagues of the Italian Service the same idea about the main aim of his work at the BBC:

> Io credevo, allora, o forse mi illudevo, di essere per così dire uno strumento che interpretava i pensieri, i dubbi, i timori, le opinioni, e le speranze degli italiani, facendomi quasi uno di loro. – come per discendenza, per educazione e per animo, potevo invero considerarmi -, dando voce ai sentimenti che sapevo nascosti e repressi, della maggioranza del popolo italiano costretto a tacerli o per prudenza, o per paura di certe persecuzioni, o, in alcuni casi, per non dovere entrare in aperto conflitto con la propria dichiarata professione di 'fede fascista' cui contrastava l'intima coscienza repugnante alla ormai provata falsità di quella fede. Parlando da inglese agli italiani ho servito, più ancora che l'Inghilterra e la giusta causa per cui combatteva, la causa della dignità umana, della libertà e della comunità europea, al di là di ogni nazionalismo e frontiera statale.[58]

> Back then I thought, or perhaps hoped, I was acting as a kind of interpreter of the thoughts, doubts, fears, opinions and hopes of Italians. I was becoming almost one of them – my lineage, education and attitude made me think so – and giving a voice to the hidden and repressed feelings of the majority of Italians, who were forced to hide them either out of caution, for fear of being persecuted or, in some cases, to not question the official 'fascist faith', in contrast with their inner consciousness that was now rejecting the proven deceitfulness of that faith. As an English person talking to Italians, I served more than England and the cause it was fighting for, the cause of human dignity, freedom and the European community, going beyond every nationalism and state border.

References to the European community and the abolition of national frontiers was, as we will see in Chapter 6, very common in the BBC programmes broadcast in 1944–45.

Arnaldo Momigliano

Arnaldo Momigliano was an academic of Jewish origins who specialised in ancient history. Born in Caraglio, Piedmont, in 1908, he lived in Italy until 1938, when he moved to London. In 1925 Momigliano enrolled in the Faculty of Letters of the University of Turin and received a philosophical education. Among his cultural influences were Plato, Aristotle, Descartes and Kant.[59]

Momigliano, as Carlo Dionisotti stated in a volume dedicated to him, was part of that generation of intellectuals who, after the First World War, saw in Benedetto Croce a mentor and cultural guide in various fields such as philosophy, history, politics and literature. The Europe in which they lived, however, had changed considerably. As a consequence, this generation was in search of a guide who could respond to such changes.

> Era il distacco dai maestri, così dal vecchio e dal più che mai valido Croce, come dal giovane Gobetti, morto esule nel 1926 e che nessuno di noi aveva conosciuto vivo. Perché quei maestri, e le rispettive generazioni erano corresponsabili della disfatta subita dalla vecchia Italia nel 1924, dopo il delitto Matteotti.[60]

> It was the detachment from the great masters, from the older and ever more valuable Benedetto Croce as well as from the young Gobetti, whom none of us had met, since he died as an exile in 1926. Because those masters and their generations were responsible for the defeat of the old Italy in 1924, after the murder of Matteotti.

During his university years Momigliano met many fellow students whose names would become known on the Italian cultural and political scene. Among these were the writer and film director Mario Soldati; the writer Cesare Pavese; Paolo, Piero and Renato Treves; Aldo Garosci; the philosopher Norberto Bobbio; and the art historian Giulio Carlo Argan.[61]

In 1929 Momigliano graduated and moved to Rome to collaborate with the historian Gaetano De Sanctis. Between 1930 and 1931 he had his first experiences as a teacher of ancient history. In 1933, after De Sanctis's refusal to pledge loyalty to fascism, he took up a post as Professor of Ancient Greek History, a position he held until 1936, when he won a public competition for the post of Professor of Roman History at the University of Turin.[62]

In 1937, the year before the declaration of the racial laws against Jews, Momigliano experienced some issues with the Comunità Israelitica di Roma (the Jewish Community in Rome). As he wrote in a letter to the community, there were two main reasons why he wanted to leave it: he did not identify himself with its Zionist positions and disapproved of the fact that the community had adhered to the national politics.[63]

In spite of this attack and unlike his mentor, De Sanctis, Momigliano worked in a public university under the rules imposed by the fascist regime until 1938, when the racial laws left him no choice. Prior to leaving the country Momigliano tried, without success, to persuade the fascist Minister of National Education, Giuseppe Bottai, to make an exception for him and allow him to retain his post in Turin.[64] In an article published in the Italian newspaper *La Repubblica* on 16 March 2001, historian Luciano Canfora exposed Momigliano's attitude towards the fascist regime, questioning whether the real Momigliano was the university professor who tried to find a compromise with the regime or the anti-fascist who offered his help to the British.[65]

At the end of the war, Momigliano tried to return to his previous position in Turin. However, the position was no longer vacant and the Piedmontese historian returned to Britain where he worked in Bristol and London.[66] After trying to emigrate to the United States, the historian moved to Oxford, where he had the opportunity of meeting other exiles from Germany who had an expertise in classics, including Fraenkel, Jacoby, Maas and Pfeiffer.[67]

Unlike the Italian exiles mentioned so far, Momigliano was not a permanent member of staff at the BBC, but an occasional collaborator. His first contact with the BBC dated back to February 1941, when Momigliano asked whether the Italian Service was interested in receiving some talks by him.

> Dear Signor Momigliano, I understand that you would be willing to write an occasional talk on current events for broadcasting. We should be very glad if you would and would, of course, pay you a fee. As a start I would suggest you doing something to counter the Axis claim to represent the interests of the proletariat as against the capitalist class. This was one of the themes of Hitler's recent speech and it has also been taken up by Ansaldo. We should therefore, like to answer it fairly quickly. The length of the talk should be some 1000 to 1200 words. I should be obliged if you would treat any work you do for us as confidential and not discuss it with anybody.[68]

Momigliano's programmes mirrored his background as a historian and included many references to ancient history, the Italian Risorgimento and the history of Italian intellectuals such as Piero Gobetti and Benedetto Croce. Another characteristic of his programmes was his attention to issues like the concept of race in Nazi Germany.[69]

While Momigliano's contribution was highly appreciated by the BBC, his approach was slightly different from that adopted by the corporation. Moreover, while Momigliano's prose was regarded by the editor Geoffrey Dennis as excellent, it did not suit the style of a radio broadcast:

> As for the form of Talks, yours are about the right length – the simplest way to reckon is between 50 and 70 lines of ordinary type. It is not for me to criticise the style or Italian of your admirably written Talks, but two points to bear in mind, in writing them, 'how will it sound on the air', and to prefer rather shorter and crisper sentences than one might in one's ordinary literary style.[70]

In 1942 Momigliano made a proposal to the Italian Service for a series of programmes for Italian university professors and students. Geoffrey Dennis answered that the Italian Service was certainly interested. However, these programmes would have a limited amount of time since programmes for academics and intellectuals were not among the BBC's priorities.[71]

The BBC's schedule, as the analysis of the programmes will show, did include programmes for intellectuals and references to literary works. To mention just one example, in 1944 Piero Treves curated a series of broadcasts on the book *Fontamara* by the anti-fascist writer Ignazio Silone. However, such programmes constituted only a tiny proportion of Italian Service programming.

After April 1945, Momigliano contributed to a series of BBC programmes on British customs and lifestyle. His collaboration with the BBC concluded at the end of 1945.[72]

Ruggero Orlando

Ruggero Orlando was a mathematician who sometimes used the pseudonym 'Gino Calzolari' for his programmes at the BBC. After spending his youth as a member of fascist organisations, Orlando distanced himself from the fascist regime and therefore fell victim to persecution and arrests. In 1938 he moved to Britain, where he lived until 1944. In London, Orlando worked as a correspondent for the fascist radio EIAR until the outbreak of the war and his consequent internment. After his release, he started an occasional collaboration with the BBC Italian Service.[73] He was asked to work for British radio propaganda by the British authorities, who interrogated Italian prisoners of war for propaganda and intelligence purposes.[74]

As Orlando wrote in a memoir entitled *Qui Ruggero Orlando: Mezzo secolo di giornalismo*, prior to working for the BBC he was part of a clandestine British radio station called Radio Italia. A key personality involved in this project was Ivor Thomas, from the Labour Party.

> Scoppiata la guerra, subito l'internamento, liberato, mi ritrovai, come ho accennato, con compagni e connazionali a dirigere 'Radio Italia' che il governo britannico finanziava come arma di guerra e che tuttavia non era 'ufficiale' come i servizi europei della British Broadcasting Corporation (BBC) e quindi erano gestiti in libertà; venivano trasmessi a onde corte, e ci è risultato che avessero molto ascolto in Italia, soprattutto fra coloro che si sentivano attivamente antifascisti.[75]

> At the outbreak of war, after my internment and liberation I ended up, as mentioned, running 'Radio Italia' with comrades and fellow countrymen. It was funded by the British government as a weapon of war but was not 'official' like the European Services of the British Broadcasting Corporation (BBC) and was, therefore, independent; the programmes were broadcast on short wave and we found out that they were listened to a lot in Italy, especially by those who felt actively anti-fascist.

In 1941 Orlando published under the pseudonym of Pentad a book on fascism entitled *The Remaking of Italy*.[76] The book was co-authored by four other people involved in the Radio Italia project: Ivor Thomas, Lorenzo Minio, Pier Paolo Fano and A.F. Magri, who also worked for the BBC. More information about Magri will be provided in the next chapter. A note on the authors stated that the book was published anonymously for security reasons:

The writers of this book, as indicated by their pseudonym 'Pentad', are five in number. They are actively engaged in the task of liberating Italy from the Fascist and German yoke, and for this reason their names may not be divulged. But it may be stated that four of them are native Italians who, between them, represent the most aspects of Italian life; one is Lombard, one a Venetian, one a Sicilian and the fourth is an Emilian. With them is associated an English officer, who has recalled the help given by England in Italy's First Risorgimento.[77]

The book was dedicated to the 'glorious memory' of Fortunato Picchi, who was called 'a martyr of the new Risorgimento'. As we will see in Chapter 6, references to the anti-fascist war as a second Risorgimento were very common among the Italian exiles in Britain.

After his employment at the BBC, Orlando continued to work in the media industry. He was the first correspondent for the Italian national television station Radio Audizioni Italiane (RAI, now Radio Televisione Italiana) from New York and was arguably one of the most famous Italian journalists of the 1960s. In the 1970s Orlando left his post as a correspondent in the United States to start a political career in the Partito Socialista Italiano (PSI). In 1972 he was elected as MP for the Socialist Party. In 1976 he started working for RAI as a correspondent for the news programme TG2 and, from the 1970s onwards, collaborated with the weekly magazines *Europeo* and *Oggi*.[78] Among his publications inspired by his exile in England were *L'Inghilterra è un Castello in Aria*, on British politics, and the above-mentioned *Qui Ruggero Orlando*, which include references to his work at the BBC during the war.[79]

The analysis of the biographies of the Italian broadcasters has revealed that these exiles had diverse political and cultural backgrounds. Each left Italy for different reasons: the Treves brothers and Calosso emigrated because their political activism as members of the Italian Socialist Party put their lives at risk. Nissim and Limentani left mainly because their Jewish origins did not allow them to live in Italy any more. Moreover, as the cases of Ruggero Orlando and Arnaldo Momigliano have shown, there were also broadcasters who had either worked for the fascist regime or tried to obtain special treatment from the fascist authorities prior to leaving their country. This is clearly in contrast with the idea that all the Italian exiles working for Radio Londra were anti-fascist heroes. In spite of these premises, and whatever their past or milieu was, by the time they started working for the BBC, they all shared a mission: to defeat the fascist regime and support the morale of Italian civilians.

Another interesting aspect that emerges from their memoirs relates to the impact on their lives of forced emigration to another country. Although many of these broadcasters belonged to privileged social classes, the conflict and their experiences as political refugees had changed their perspective. As their memoirs seem to suggest, in Britain they were common people and it was in their capacity as ordinary citizens that they wanted to speak to their compatriots in Italy. This, as we will see in Chapters 5, 6 and 7, is clearly reflected in the programmes, in which there were frequent references to the negative impact that the war was having on the everyday lives of ordinary people.

As mentioned in the introduction, the duplicity of the BBC is a leitmotif of this work. This and the following chapter are, in this regard, complementary. While this chapter has shown that Italian exiles remembered their work at BBC as a very positive experience, Chapter 4 will focus on their controversial political relationship with the British Foreign Office. This difficult relationship, as will be explained, is in contrast with the myth of the BBC as the genuine supporter of the anti-fascist fight.

Notes

1 Joyce Lussu, 'Vita Vissuta', in Maria Sechi and Agnano Pisano (eds), *Fascismo ed Esilio II: la patria lontana: testimonianze dal vero e dall'immaginario* (Pisa: Giardini, 1990).
2 Charles Delzell, *Mussolini's Enemies: The Italian Anti-Fascist Resistance* (New York, 1974), pp. 46–53.
3 Delzell, *Mussolini's Enemies*, pp. 46–48.
4 Delzell, *Mussolini's Enemies*, pp. 49–50.
5 Delzell, *Mussolini's Enemies*, pp. 52–53.
6 Delzell, *Mussolini's Enemies*, pp. 43–45.
7 Antonio Varsori, *Gli Alleati e l'emigrazione democratica antifascista (1930–1943)* (Florence: Sansoni, 1982), p. 81.
8 Delzell, *Mussolini's Enemies*, p. 43.
9 Ennio Di Nolfo, introduction to Varsori, *Gli Alleati e l'emigrazione*, p. V.
10 Paolo Treves, *What Mussolini Did to Us* (London: Gollancz, 1940), pp. 70–72. The original book was published in English. An Italian edition was published in 1945.
11 Paolo Treves, *What Mussolini Did to Us*, pp. 333–334.
12 According to the royal decree n. 1227 dated 28 August 1931, university professors with a permanent contract as well as teachers in secondary schools were supposed to pledge loyalty to the king and the fascist regime. The other teachers and professors who refused to pledge loyalty to the fascist regime were: Ernesto Buonaiuti, Giuseppe Antonio Borgese, Aldo Capitini, Mario Carrara, Antonio De Viti De Marco, Gaetano De Sanctis, Floriano Del Secolo, Giorgio Errera, Giorgio Levi della Vida, Piero Marinetti, Fabio Luzzatto, Bartolo Nigrisoli, Enrico Presutti, Francesco Ruffini, Edoardo Ruffini Avondo, Lionello Venturi, Vito Volterra and Cesare Gobetti.

13 Paolo Treves, *Sul fronte e dietro il fronte italiano* (Rome, 1945).
14 Treves, *Sul fronte*, p. 5.
15 Sponza, *Divided Loyalties*, p. 109.
16 The conference took place in 1972 in Tuscany. The conference papers were published a year later in the already mentioned *Inghilterra e Italia nel '900*.
17 Limentani, *Radio Londra*, p. 203.
18 Limentani, *Radio Londra*, p. 201.
19 Limentani, *Radio Londra*, p. 203.
20 Limentani, *Radio Londra*, pp. 204–205.
21 The listeners' letters will be analysed in the final chapter. The majority of letters held at the BBC WAC in Caversham were sent to Colonel Stevens and there is almost no trace of correspondence sent to other broadcasters, but there are a few references to Elio Nissim's *Omo qualunque*. The popularity of this character is proven by the fact that Elio Nissim's papers, currently held by his son Danny Nissim, include letters to the *Omo qualunque*.
22 Limentani, *Radio Londra*, p. 209.
23 Piccialuti Caprioli, *Radio Londra 1940–45*.
24 Istituto Socialista di studi storici del Piemonte e Valle d'Aosta (ed.), *Umberto Calosso antifascista e socialista* (Venice, Marsilio, 1981), p. 8.
25 More information on the unconditional surrender of Italy and Calosso's position on this matter will be provided in Chapter 6.
26 Peresso, *Giuseppe Donati and Umberto Calosso – Two Italian Anti-Fascist refugees in Malta* (Malta: Gudja SKS, 2015), p. 89.
27 Peresso, *Giuseppe Donati*, p. 92.
28 Peresso, *Giuseppe Donati*, p. 97.
29 Peresso, *Giuseppe Donati*, pp. 125–139.
30 Peresso, *Giuseppe Donati*, pp. 144–145.
31 Fondo Umberto Calosso, Centro Studi Piero Gobetti (hereafter FUC, CSPG), Federico Symons and Raffaello Battino of the *Comitato Nazionale Italiano* to Colonel Thornhill, 24 July 1941.
32 FUC, CSPG, Colonel Thornill to Calosso, 31 July 1941.
33 FUC, CSPG, Calosso to Colonel Thornill, 25 July 1941.
34 FUC, CSPG, Calosso to the British Ambassador in Cairo, 18 October 1941. Another letter from Clelia Lajolo to the Ambassador's wife on the same matter, dated 19 October 1941, was attached to the same letter.
35 CSPG, FUC, *Interventi di Calosso da Radio Londra, Convoglio Britannico*, 5 and 8 August 1942.
36 Lo Biundo, *London Calling Italy*, p. 39.
37 Elio Nissim, *Il pappagallo del nonno, ricordi anglo-fiorentini* (Udine: Campanotto, 2001), p. 7.
38 DNPA, ENP, Gordon Yates of the BBC to Elio Nissim, 28 February 1946.
39 Nissim, *Il pappagallo del nonno*, p. 181.
40 DNPA, ENP, Geoffrey Dennis of the BBC to Elio Nissim, 18 April 1946.
41 Nissim, *Il pappagallo del nonno*, p. 181.
42 Nissim, *Il pappagallo del nonno*, p. 11.

43 A contribution about Florence and the British was published by Giuliana Artom Treves in the above mentioned *Inghilterra e Italia nel '900*.
44 *Il pappagallo del nonno*, p. 126.
45 Nissim, *Il pappagallo del nonno*, p. 125.
46 Nissim, *Il pappagallo del nonno*, p. 126; author's translation.
47 The same reasoning applies to other broadcasters and programmes. During his exile in Britain Paolo Treves wrote an essay entitled *England, The Mysterious Island*, trans. D. Forbes (London: Victor Gollancz, 1948). In the book Treves discusses his ideas on British culture and lifestyle.
48 Nissim, *Il pappagallo*, p. 181.
49 Nissim, *Il pappagallo*, p. 182. Author's translation.
50 Nissim, *Il pappagallo*, p. 183.
51 Nissim, *Il pappagallo*, p. 215.
52 Piccialuti Caprioli, *Radio Londra 1940–45*.
53 DNPA, ENP, *Scripts of Elio Nissim, Ricordi di Bush House, Articolo quarto*.
54 Piccialuti Caprioli, *Radio Londra 1939–45*, pp. V–XVI.
55 *Chi è Candidus*, p. 1944
56 John Marus, *Parla Candidus. Discorsi dal 13 Aprile 1941 al 3 dicembre 1944* (Milan, 1945), p. 5.
57 Marus, *Parla Candidus*, p. 5.
58 Marus, *Parla Candidus*, p. 6. Author's translation.
59 Carlo Dionisotti, *Ricordo di Arnaldo Momigliano* (Bologna: Il Mulino, 1989), p. 9.
60 Dionisotti, *Ricordo di Arnaldo Momigliano*, p. 11.
61 Dionisotti, *Ricordo di Arnaldo Momigliano*, p. 12.
62 Dionisotti, *Ricordo di Arnaldo Momigliano*, p. 15.
63 Fondo Arnaldo Momigliano, Scuola Normale Superiore di Pisa (hereafter FAM, SNSP), N-a 9, Letter to the *Comunità Israelitica di Roma*, 1937.
64 Riccardo Di Donato (ed.), *Ritorno al Risorgimento. Conversazioni a Radio Londra 1941–1945* (Pisa, Archivio Momigliano, 2013), p. 21. This publication is the preliminary version of a monograph on Momigliano at Radio London currently in progress. The project is based on about thirty radio transcripts by Momigliano, which were found in 1999 in Momigliano's former house in London. The programmes can be consulted at the Scuola Normale Superiore di Pisa.
65 Di Donato, *Ritorno al Risorgimento*.
66 Dionisotti, *Ricordo*, p. 22.
67 Dionisotti, *Ricordo*, p. 20. Documents attesting to his attempts to emigrate to the United States can be found in FAM SNSP, Documenti, *D-c 1.
68 FAM, SNSP, *British Broadcasting Corporation, G. Matelli of the BBC to Momigliano, 1 February 1941.
69 Di Donato, *Ritorno al Risorgimento*, pp. 15–17.
70 FAM, SNSP, *British Broadcasting Corporation, Geoffrey Dennis to Momigliano, 18 May 1942.
71 FAM, SNSP, *British Broadcasting Corporation, Geoffrey Dennis to Momigliano, 31 December 1942.

72 Di Donato, *Ritorno al Risorgimento*, p. 18.
73 Piccialuti Caprioli, *Radio Londra 1939–45*, pp. V-XVI.
74 Berrettini, '"To Set Italy Ablaze!" Lo Special Operations Executive e i reclutamenti di agenti tra enemy aliens e prisoners of war italiani (Regno Unito, Stati Uniti e Canada)', *Altreitalie*, 40 (2010), 1–19.
75 Ruggero Orlando, *Qui Ruggero Orlando: mezzo secolo di giornalismo* (Milan: SugarCo, 1990), p. 50.
76 Pentad, *The Remaking of Italy* (Hardmondsworth, Penguin, 1941).
77 Pentad, *The Remaking of Italy*, pp. 51–52.
78 'Ruggero Orlando', Dizionario biografico Treccani, 79 (2013), www.treccani.it/enciclopedia/ruggero-orlando_(Dizionario-Biografico)/, accessed 1 February 2022.
79 Ruggero Orlando, *L'Inghilterra è un castello in aria* (Milan, 1956).

4

The Italian broadcasters and the British Foreign Office

After exploring the biographies of the Italian broadcasters and their memories of employment at the Italian Service, this chapter will investigate their relations with British governmental institutions. It will focus on three aspects: their internment in British camps in June 1940, when Italy entered the war; the Free Italy movement, founded by Italian anti-fascists in Britain; and the problems encountered by some of them in 1943 when, after the Allied landings in Sicily, they wanted to return to Italy, where they felt they were needed for the liberation cause.

While Chapter 3 has shown that many exiles had a very positive experience at the BBC, this chapter will demonstrate that the same refugees who regarded Bush House as a second home encountered serious political issues in Britain. By analysing some correspondence between Italian refugees, the Foreign Office and the international department of the British Labour Party, this chapter will reflect on how the relations between these Italians and Britain's 'enemy-friend' government were not always easy.[1]

When Italy entered the war in June 1940, some of the Italian exiles, including Limentani and the Treves brothers, were already working for the BBC. Their contribution to the British war effort and their anti-fascist political faith did not spare them from the internment camps. Moreover, during their internment they experienced problems with fascist prisoners, malnutrition and poor hygienic conditions. The British government did not address these issues and it was only the intervention of the British Labour Party that led to a parliamentary debate and enquiry on the internment of anti-fascist and anti-Nazi refugees.

Another interesting fact that emerges from the Labour Party documents is that Carlo Petrone, the founder of the Free Italy Movement, which curated an independent programme at the BBC, was an ambiguous personality. According to reliable informants he was a former member of the Organizzazione per la Vigilanza e la Repressione dell'Antifascismo (OVRA), the fascist secret services. Moreover, other Italian anti-fascists were suspicious of him. Despite this, he contributed regularly to the *Free Italy Talks*.

The requests for repatriation, sent to the British Foreign Office by Calosso, the Treves brothers and Petrone after the Allied landings in Sicily, provide further evidence of the dual position of the British authorities. All these requests were at first rejected and the men did not return to Italy until over a year after the beginning of the Italian campaign. Clearly, the anti-fascist cause itself was not among the priorities of the British government. Winning the war was far more important. While these data are not surprising at all in a war context, they are evidently in contrast with the myth of the BBC as the guarantor of anti-fascism and Resistance.

Enemy aliens

The Italian declaration of war on France and Great Britain was considered a betrayal by the British government and population. Moreover, the fierce fascist propaganda against the British and the conflict of interest between Italy and Britain in the Mediterranean theatre contributed to the spread of anti-Italian feeling, regardless of the political beliefs of individual Italian immigrants.[2] This situation caused several debates about what to do with those Italian citizens living in Britain. Some months before the declaration of war, the British Foreign Office had discussed possible solutions to this issue in case of Italian participation in the war on the side of Germany.[3]

A meeting of the Home Office's Aliens Advisory Committee was scheduled to discuss the issue. During this discussion it was decided that it was necessary to repatriate as many Italian women and children as possible. Men were divided into groups: 1,500 Italians who were notoriously fascist, and all the others. The fascists should either be sent back to Italy or to Canada, the Canadian government having agreed to receive all of them. Fascists aged between 16 and 30 were to be interned in British camps; all other Italian men between the ages of 16 and 70 with less than twenty years' residence in Britain would be repatriated, with the exception of anti-fascists and Italians who were married to British women.[4] However, putting this plan into practice was more complicated than the British government had initially thought because there were not enough ships available for the repatriation. There were some Italian vessels in British waters that could be used for the operation, but the British government had no intention of releasing these to risk losing them.[5]

Despite the doubts about how to proceed, Italy had become an official enemy of Britain and some security measures had to be taken. In the days after Mussolini's declaration of war the police knocked on the doors of many Italians who were taken to British police stations and sent to internment camps. In the meantime, anti-Italian riots were hitting the streets of Little Italy in Soho and many Italian shops were vandalised.[6] Among those whose houses were visited by the British police were committed anti-fascist Italians.

Two years before, in October 1938, William Gillies had received an official request by the Home Office's Aliens department. He was asked to provide a list of Italian political refugees who needed protection in case of danger.[7] Gillies was the first secretary of the British Labour Party's international department. Born into a working-class family in Scotland in 1885, he was interested in politics and close to the Labour Party from a young age. Given his role as secretary of the international section of the party, he had the responsibility of dealing with the arrival of the first Italian refugees after Mussolini's March on Rome.[8] He therefore knew most of the politically active Italian anti-fascists in Britain and exerted pressure on the British government to obtain the liberation of the Italian anti-fascist internees in the summer of 1940.

Gillies kept the Foreign Office informed about changes to the list and sent copies of it to Military Intelligence 5 (MI5), in charge of security and espionage. An updated list, compiled by Gillies with the help of Decio Anzani, the secretary of the Italian League for the Rights of Man, was sent to the Home and Foreign Offices on 24 and 27 June 1940. The updated list included forty-five names, including those of the Treves brothers and Umberto Limentani.[9] It also included the name of Carlo Petrone, who collaborated occasionally with the BBC's Italian Service.

After receiving the document, some individuals at the Foreign Office blamed MI5 for the internment of the anti-fascists. Among these were Nigel Ronald and Harold Farquhar. According to them, the security services were responsible for the internment of the Italian refugees. Moreover, many Italian anti-fascists believed that MI5 was given a list of people to arrest by Mussolini's secret service, although only a few 'subversives' from the fascist lists had actually been interned.[10]

As soon as William Gillies discovered the internment of known Italian anti-fascists, the British Labour Party sent a letter to Nigel Ronald at the Foreign Office. The letter enclosed an informative statement by Gillies. The statement had been forwarded to the British prime minister on behalf of the National Executive Committee of the Labour Party, with the aim of pressing the prime minister for an enquiry on the unacceptable internment of political refugees.[11]

> It is within the knowledge of Mr. Gillies, and must also have been known both to the Home Office and the War Office, that at least three well-known anti-Fascists were included in the War Office lists for sending to Canada. One

of them has since been released by order of the Home Secretary. Another will be released when the Home Secretary's instructions for release have been carried out. A third was drowned.[12]

The three men were Decio Anzani, Uberto Limentani and Paolo Treves. Treves was released first, together with his brother Piero.[13] Paolo Treves, Anzani and Limentani were included in the War Office's list of internees for deportation to Canada on board the *Arandora Star*. The ship left Liverpool on 30 June 1940 and sank a few days later after being hit by a torpedo. Around 446 internees and prisoners of war being transported to Canada, including Decio Anzani, lost their lives.[14] Limentani was one of the lucky ones who survived the tragedy, whereas, as we will see shortly, Paolo Treves never boarded the ship, despite his name being on the War Office's list. When it became known that there were several anti-fascist refugees on board the *Arandora Star* and that Anzani had lost his life, the government was asked by some MPs to provide an explanation for the inadmissible mistake.[15] On 16 July, the Secretary of State for War, Anthony Eden, declared that only Italian fascists and category-A Germans and Austrians were on board the ship.

Eden's words were refuted by the MPs Eleanor Rathbone and George Strauss. The latter added that also among the German internees were some well-known anti-Nazis.[16] An inquiry was therefore set up, conducted by Lord Snell. As a result, in October 1940 a summary of the investigations was published. The document attested that a number of mistakes had been made when the list was compiled. Lord Snell's full report was never published.[17]

The internment of political refugees led to huge disappointment among the community of the Italian *fuorusciti* in Britain, but greater discontent was caused by the treatment refugees received in the internment camps. Uberto Limentani, Ruggero Orlando and Paolo Treves's reports on their internment revealed that the British authorities who administered their camps did not differentiate between anti-fascist and fascist prisoners. In the next section of this chapter accounts of their internment will be examined.

The internment camps

As we have seen in Chapter 3, Limentani was arrested on 13 June 1940. He was interned at two camps, one in Surrey and a second in Lancashire. After his release he sent a report on the *Arandora Star* incident. He also exposed the inhumane conditions of his period of internment.

> I was interned on the 13th of June, and sent to Lingfield (Race-course Aliens' Internment Camp) on the same day. I was housed with 9 other people in a horse-box; no distinction whatsoever was made either at that time or after

> between refugees or other people; after nine days better accommodations became available, but on the 11th day of my permanence I was transferred to Warth Mills Internment Camp-Bury-Lancs. In this camp, I found very deplorable accommodation and insufficient hygienic facilities for the 1800 people who were packed in a very restricted space (no possibility of having a proper wash, the dirt and grease of an abandoned factory spread all over the place, practically inexistent lavatories). The food, both in Bury and in Lingfield, was often insufficient, and the evening meal frequently consisted in some bread, a piece of cheese and a cup of tea. Five days after my arrival at Bury, the so called Lingfield Group was summoned by the Commandant, who announced that a certain number of them was going to leave on the following date ... As I thought there was a possibility that I should be parted from the group of Italian refugees with which I was staying, on the same evening I informed the Commandant Braybrook of the camp and some other officers about my position as a refugee and as an official of the BBC and I asked them not to split our group of refugees. I was told that, if I was a refugee, my position was certainly being considered. I was therefore very surprised, on the following morning, when I heard that my name was included in the list of those who were going to leave, and that I had to part from all other refugees.[18]

Limentani's attempts to persuade the British authorities that they were making a huge mistake and interning anti-fascist refugees proved unsuccessful. Limentani and his fellow anti-fascist internees were even more shocked when, once in Liverpool, they realised they would be shipped to Canada on board the *Arandora Star*. Later in the same document Limentani stated that, even after the sinking of the *Arandora Star*, he was not allowed to send telegrams to anybody.

> When my friends reported to the War Office about my whereabouts and asked for the immediate enforcement of the order of release, the official reply was that they were waiting for an official news about my whereabouts. I understand that during my internment at Donaldson's Internment Camp, many letters and wires were sent to me in connection with the proceedings for my release, one of them signed by Mr William Gillies, secretary of the international section of the Labour Party, and one signed by Mrs B. Pritchard, Hon Secretary of the relief Committee for Refugees from Italy. I never got any of them. Incidentally, I should like to mention that I never got a penny back from the money, which was taken from me on the first day of my internment.[19]

Evidently, in the eyes of the British authorities, Limentani's contribution to British official radio propaganda against the fascist regime, as well as his well-known anti-fascism, did not constitute a good enough reason to allow him better treatment.

Paolo Treves's account of his internment was very similar. As his wife, Lotte Dann Treves, wrote in her memoir *Ricominciare sempre da capo*, Paolo was interned on 11 June 1940. Both Paolo and Piero were initially interned at Kempton Park racecourse and then transferred to the Bury camp, the same camp where Limentani was held before he boarded the *Arandora Star*. Also in this case, the account refers to a list provided of people to be transferred to another camp. Paolo was supposed to be transferred to another camp the day after. The news disappointed him because he was unwilling to leave the group of anti-fascist refugees remaining at Bury. Paolo tried to persuade the camp's chief officer to remove his name from the list and, as evidence of his anti-fascism, showed him a copy of his *What Mussolini Did to Us*. Like his cousin and colleague at the BBC, Limentani, he received a negative answer. However, as Lotte recalled in his memoir, a lucky encounter changed his destiny.

> Paolo, disperato, uscì dall'ufficio, e gli si presentò un signore, dicendo: 'Credo di poterle essere utile; permetta che mi presenti, mi chiamo Paolo Treves'. Era un'ufficiale di marina, sposato con un'inglese, il quale appunto per questo aveva preferito rimanere a Londra quando l'Italia aveva dichiarato guerra. Diceva ancora, quell'altro Paolo Treves, che nel gruppo di coloro che dovevano partire c'erano tutti i suoi amici e lui era contento di andare con loro. Così i due tornarono dal comandante, il quale acconsentì a mandare via la mattina dopo l'ufficiale di marina, pure essendo sull'elenco il numero di matricola di Paolo.[20]
>
> Paolo, desperate, left the office and a man introduced himself, saying: 'I think I might be able to help you; let me introduce myself, my name is Paolo Treves.' He was a naval officer, married to a British woman, who had decided to stay in London when Italy declared war. The other Paolo Treves also said that all his friends were in the group of those who were supposed to leave, and he was happy to join them. So the two went back to the commander, who agreed to send the naval officer away the next day, despite the fact that Paolo's registration number was on the list.

This encounter spared Paolo's life, since his namesake and the other internees on the list were sent to the *Arandora Star*. But the episode, reported by Lotte Dann Treves, contradicts Paolo's versions of the facts. According to an article he published about a month after his release from internment, the time of arrest was the criterion that determined who was sent to the ship, and this was the reason he had not boarded. The article was published anonymously in the 9 August 1940 issue of the weekly magazine *The Tribune*.[21] It is therefore possible that Paolo Treves did not want to include details that could reveal both his identity and the way he managed to remain in the camp. The article started with his account of what happened on the morning when 'two gentlemen' knocked on his door. 'Suddenly flashes of old remembrances' of his past life in Italy came back to him. As we saw in Chapter 3, Paolo Treves had moved to Britain in 1938, after being arrested more than once in Italy. When the policemen asked Paolo to follow them, he tried, in vain, to explain who he was. The officers refused to listen to his explanations or to let him contact any of his influential acquaintances. Also in Paolo Treves's account there are references to the 'filthy and unhealthy' environment and to the poor hygiene of the camps where he was interned for over a month. His description of the Bury camp confirms what Limentani stated in his report.

There were 2,000 men in only two dirty rooms. All his personal belongings were taken and he was 'lucky enough' to get two blankets and a military bed – others had to sleep on a straw mattress on the floor. Once a day they were allowed, in shifts, to get some fresh air for 45 minutes and food rations were far from satisfactory.

Another analogy between Limentani's report and Treves's article relates to political refugee status – both wrote that protection from the fascist prisoners was not guaranteed in the camps. It was during his period of internment, wrote Treves, that he again heard the official fascist anthem, *Giovinezza*.

> In that camp we found out there were some 70 anti-Fascist refugees. We tried to keep together to avoid incidents and threats from the Fascists. Fascist songs, threats and anti-British talk were the normal amusement of an overwhelming majority of the internees. I tried to point this out and to explain our intolerable position to the officers in charge, but the only reply was: 'We don't care a damn about politics. Here everyone is the same.'[22]

Referring to another camp, Paolo Treves commented on the difficult situations he had been through, declaring that he felt as if he was back in Italy, the country from which he had escaped.

Another broadcaster at the BBC Italian Service, Ruggero Orlando, had similar thoughts on his status as an enemy alien. Unlike many other Italian broadcasters, Orlando was not a political refugee. He was neither a Jew nor an anti-fascist activist and had freely chosen to live in Britain. When Italy entered the war, Orlando could easily have returned to Italy, but he decided instead to remain in Britain, what he judged to be the right moral decision. Despite this, as he wrote in a letter to his fiancée, Miss Friedl Bamberger, that was intercepted by the Prisoners of War section of the postal censor, the British government was treating him as an enemy. Here is an extract from the intercepted letter, dated 5 September 1940:

> My position was not that of a refugee. I could go away with a nice salary, in touch with my mother; mopping up the things I could have boasted at home to be a war hero. I chose the more uncomfortable business, the only one possible from a moral point of view ... After a free choice, after an acknowledged right to go back, dropped for the sake of the conscience, I became an enemy to this country!![23]

Orlando had been advised by the British Home and Foreign Office 'to miss the train' when many Italians were being repatriated. His situation was therefore made worse by the fact that he had followed the advice of the British authorities in deciding to stay. Hence the Ministry of Information and the Political Intelligence Department pressed for his release from internment in order to employ him in official propaganda against Italy.[24] The postal censorship slip on Ruggero Orlando was therefore sent by the Home Office to the Isle of Man Committee in order to obtain his release.[25] Once released, as we have seen in Chapter 3, he started working for the Italian Service.

A different opinion on internment was expressed by Elio Nissim in *Il pappagallo del nonno*. Referring to the Isle of Man, Nissim wrote that he received very good treatment and that food was better than in London. Moreover, since it hosted foreign internees and prisoners, enemy planes were not allowed to drop bombs on the island. As Nissim jokingly wrote, he was almost shocked when the chief officer of the camp, Geoffrey Dennis, announced his release:

> Restai interdetto: al campo si mangiava bene e non c'erano bombe naziste, perché l'isola, secondo le convenzioni di guerra, era protetta appunto perché vi si trovavano i campi degli internati stranieri. A Londra invece le bombe – e che bombe! – infuriavano di giorno, ma soprattutto di notte, le provai per tutta la durata della guerra. Dopo un po' ci si fa l'abitudine, e comunque a me andò bene, scampai senza danni.[26]

> I was shocked: in the camp we used to eat well and there were no Nazi bombs since the island, according to the conventions of war, was a protected area precisely because the camps for foreign internees were situated there. Conversely, in London the bombs – and what bombs! – flared up during the day, but especially at night, I had to cope with them for the entire conflict. After a while you get used to it and, in any case, I was lucky, I was not harmed at all.

During his detention Nissim also had the chance of meeting Arnaldo Momigliano and Piero and Paolo Treves, since the Isle of Man was where almost all Italian internees were eventually taken. Nevertheless, it is not surprising to read such contrasting comments about his captivity, since internment conditions varied depending on the specific camp and the individual internee. As mentioned in Chapter 3, while Elio Nissim was an anti-fascist, he had not been actively involved in political action against Mussolini when he lived in Italy. It is therefore possible that he was considered a less potentially 'dangerous character'. Moreover, it is crucial to take into consideration the dates on which the accounts of internment were written. While Limentani, Orlando and Paolo Treves wrote their reports during their internment or shortly afterwards, Nissim's extract is taken from his memoir, written after the war and published in 2001, nearly ten years after his death. Time might have played a substantial role in softening the memories of those years. Moreover, in 1940, Treves, Limentani, Orlando and Nissim had not yet seen the fruits of their sacrifice: the Allied victory and the partisan Resistance over the Axis. This could also explain why the memoirs published by Limentani and Treves after the war, examined in Chapter 3, made no references to difficult relations with British government institutions. These relations, as will be explained in the next two sections of this chapter, continued to be uneasy after their release from internment and in 1943–44, after Italy's unconditional surrender.

The Free Italy Movement

By autumn 1940 many of the Italian anti-fascist internees had already been released. Yet the fact that they had regained their freedom did not solve the issue of their relations with the British government. The events of summer 1940 had shown that the Home and Foreign Offices had no idea who the Italian refugees in Britain were. Moreover, even after releasing the Italian anti-fascists from internment, the government still had no plans for them. Some of them, as this book shows, were employed in official propaganda against Mussolini. However, the British government remained distrustful of many of them. It was thanks to the actions of a group of anti-fascists in Britain that the British government realised that the presence of Italian refugees was a political issue that could no longer be ignored.[27]

This group included Carlo Petrone, Alessandro Magri and Decio Pettoello, who founded an association of Italian *émigrés*. Established in September 1940, the association was originally called the Comitato Nazionale Libera Italia and was renamed the Movimento Italia Libera (Free Italy Movement) in July 1941. The movement was not very successful because of internal friction between its members; by the beginning of 1943, only a few members were still part of the movement and these then merged with a newly founded group called Friends of Free Italy. Friends of Free Italy was the project of a group of British intellectuals and politicians who were politically and culturally interested in Italy, among them the Labour Party member Ivor Thomas. Together with some friends of the British Institute in Florence, Thomas tried to safeguard the historical good relations between Italy and Britain. However, following the failure of the Friends of Free Italy as a political association, the movement, renamed the British Italian Society, became a cultural institution and played no significant political role during the years of the Anglo-American occupation of Italy.[28]

For the purpose of this work, the movement founded by Petrone is important because some of its associates were permanent members of staff or occasional collaborators with the BBC Italian Service. These included Umberto Calosso, who was also the director of the *Free Italy* journal, the Treves brothers, Giovanni Giglio, Giuseppe Gatti and Livio Zino Zencovich. Moreover, the BBC hosted a series of programmes run by Calosso and other members of the association called *Free Italy Talks*.

Carlo Petrone was a member of the Partito Popolare Italiano (PPI), an Italian Catholic party founded in 1919 by Don Luigi Sturzo. When Petrone decided to set up the Free Italy Movement, MI5 and the Foreign Office were unsure what position to take because Petrone was considered an unreliable person. Nevertheless, the Ministry of Economic Warfare welcomed Petrone's idea. Such an association could be of great help to the clandestine propaganda activities of the Special Operations Executive, in charge of subversive activities in the German-occupied territories.[29]

Petrone and the Free Italy movement were the subject of a Foreign Office meeting held in December 1940. The benefits and drawbacks of future official collaborations with Free Italy were evaluated during the meeting. Among the benefits was the fact that the movement could inspire similar initiatives around Europe and attract other Italians willing to help the British government. The drawbacks had mainly to do with the reception of such an initiative because the British government doubted that the association would be successful among the Italians who lived in Italy. Petrone was not considered capable of exerting any influence on Italy, due to his lack of contacts there. Moreover, the presence of an anti-fascist movement would force the Italians to side with either the regime or anti-fascism. According to the British Foreign Office the Italian population was not ready to make such a choice. There was also the issue of the younger generations: while young Italians were not necessarily fascists, they might have considered the fascist model of modernity and efficiency more appealing than the old-fashioned Italian liberal state.[30]

The Labour Party also expressed doubts about Carlo Petrone as a suitable leader of an anti-fascist movement. As the case of the internment of Italian anti-fascists has shown, the party supported the cause of Italian refugees in Britain. However, Petrone's political past was in question since, when Gillies was asked by the Home Office to compile a list of Italians who should be protected in the event of danger, his anti-fascist acquaintances made no recommendation for his release.[31] Doubts on the authenticity of Petrone's anti-fascism have emerged from some correspondence between Gillies and other political personalities close to the international department of the Labour Party. While the Labour Party would certainly welcome a movement of anti-fascists, it was necessary to collect information on Free Italy's members before offering official support to Free Italy. As Angelo Crespi stated in a letter to Gillies, Petrone 'was unknown to all anti-fascists here [in Britain] before he started the *Free Italy Movement*'. 'I do not doubt his good faith,' said Crespi, 'but I think he is unbalanced, suffering from egomania and mania of persecution and he is unable to agree with anybody; and I fear that this is already at the root of the possible failure of that Movement.'[32]

In a letter to David Margesson from the War Office, Sylvia Pankhurst warned him that it would be very dangerous to share any confidential military information with the Free Italy committee. Those Italians who collaborated closely with the intelligence services should not disclose any sensitive information to the members of the movement. The reason for Pankhurst's apprehension was that Carlo Maria Franzero had told her that Petrone was an OVRA agent. The OVRA was Mussolini's secret police and Franzero was likely to be well informed since he had previously worked as a propagandist for the fascist regime. Moreover, continued the letter, Petrone had taught in Italian schools and had practised in the Italian courts until recently. He could not even be considered a refugee as he had left Italy with an ordinary passport and visa.[33] In another letter to Gillies, Pankhurst declared that a former fascist lawyer to the Italian embassy, Del Giudici, confirmed that Petrone was an OVRA agent. This information was also reliable as it had been passed on by Mrs Massey, a friend of Gaetano Salvemini, who acted as his agent in Britain. In the same letter there are references to the Treves brothers and other known anti-fascists in Britain:

> It was then brought to my notice that neither Professor Angelo Crespi who, though an Italian, is a British subject, nor the brothers Treves – sons of the well-known Italian Socialist leader – who are Italian refugees working for the BBC, nor any of the others recently released from internment, were willing to attend any gathering where Petrone was present; they all expressed the greater distrust for him.[34]

In particular, Paolo Treves had told her that even the leader of the PPI, Don Luigi Sturzo, did not want to have anything to do with Petrone.[35] Very similar concerns were expressed about a month before by Bertha Pritchard, the Honorary Secretary of the Relief Committee for Refugees from Italy, in a letter to Gillies.[36] Two other Italian broadcasters at the BBC, Limentani and Marus, had told Pritchard that Petrone was dishonest.[37] As for the Treves brothers, while they did become associates of the movement, disagreements with other members led to their decision to distance themselves from Free Italy in December 1942.[38] Umberto Calosso was among these others and the problems had mainly to do with the manifesto of the Italian Socialist Party in London.[39] Calosso would be expelled from the PSI in London less than a year later, in September 1943.[40] Another problem raised by Paolo Treves and other members of the association was the absence of coordination between Free Italy and other influential associations of anti-fascists such as the Mazzini Society set up by Salvemini in the United States.[41]

Despite the failure of Free Italy as a political movement in England and its internal friction, its members did contribute to the British war effort by curating some programmes for the BBC Italian Service and launching a weekly magazine called *Notiziario Italiano*, which was published between December 1941 and November 1943. The reason for this cessation may be attributed to the crisis of the movement, since it coincided with the last programmes broadcast by Calosso on behalf of Free Italy, in December 1943.[42] The first issue was a sort of manifesto, stating that one of the movement's aims was to broadcast radio programmes and to print informative material against Mussolini.

The *Free Italy Talks* were curated independently from the PWE and, as its members liked to point out, did not mirror the interests of Britain or any other state involved in the conflict. The audience for the programmes were mainly Italian factory workers who were encouraged to resist Mussolini's regime. References to the Italian Risorgimento were very common in the programmes curated by Free Italy. Moreover, as we will see later, unlike official British propaganda, some members of the movement promoted the idea of a separate Italian peace rather than unconditional surrender.

Despite the independence of the movement from the PWE, the *Free Italy Talks* were subsidised by the BBC. In April 1942 the director of the Italian Service, Whittal, raised the issue of payment for Free Italy members. The quality of the programmes, stated Whittal, was not that high and could not justify such an expense for the corporation.

> At the present the movement gives four talks a week, totalling about two minutes on the air. The payment they receive for these talks is, for the most part, handed over to the *Free Italy Movement*, and is used to support their various activities. The *Free Italy Movement*, in fact, is maintained in existence by the BBC, for if we were to take them off the air, or even substantially to reduce their time on the air, they would have to give up their offices, their Weekly Newsletter, etc.
>
> Quite often their talks are of poor quality, but I feel the greatest reluctance in taking them off the air because it would mean putting them in a position of great financial difficulty. I think it is quite wrong that the BBC should be put into the position of being the sole means of support of the Movement. H.M. Government has made it clear that it wants the Movement to go on, and I feel, therefore, that it should take over the financial support of Free Italy. If the Movement were to receive a Government subsidy and no payment from the BBC, we would be in a much stronger position.[43]

The issue was debated at a meeting of the Propaganda Policy Committee on 28 April 1942. It was decided that the BBC should not continue to financially support the movement at the rate of fifteen guineas a week, regardless of the quality of the programmes. Payment should instead be based on the merit of the individual programmes.[44] As soon as Colonel Stevens was informed of the decision, he expressed concern to Ivone Kirkpatrick and Bruce Lockhart. The support provided to the Free Italy movement, claimed Stevens, was more than a mere economic problem and the BBC should not take the responsibility of deciding whether or not Free Italy should fail. The Movement could be of political help in dealing with the United States. As for the *Free Italy Talks*, Stevens pointed out that, in order to respect the nature of a 'free' movement, its members should continue to work independently from the PWE. After all, continued Stevens, the movement could deal with those political subjects that, despite being worthy of attention, were totally unsuitable for BBC broadcasters. Above all, Stevens mentioned the delicate issue of the form of government that should prevail in case of the overthrow of the fascist regime.[45]

Stevens was very far-sighted since, as we will see in Chapter 6, one of the main concerns of the Italian broadcasters after the fall of the fascist regime in summer 1943 was the political future of their country. The debate on the Free Italy movement did not lead to its end, yet, as we have seen, it did not last for long.

Returning home

As this brief history of the Free Italy movement has shown, after the release from internment of several Italians, the British government realised that the presence of anti-fascist organisations in Britain could be beneficial to the war effort. Even an ambiguous character like Petrone ended up working occasionally for the BBC. As Petrone's case shows, not all exiles who defined themselves as anti-fascist had always been opponents of Mussolini. It is therefore not surprising that the British government and the Labour Party monitored such exiles. Nevertheless, those who were regarded as trustworthy anti-fascist personalities also continued to experience issues with the Foreign Office in 1943–44.

Towards the end of the war, when the Italian broadcasters were free citizens who had been working for the BBC for years, the Foreign Office still had an influence over their lives. At the end of 1943, after the defeat of Mussolini's dictatorship and the Allied landings in Italy, some Italian broadcasters, including Paolo Treves, Umberto Calosso and Carlo Petrone, wrote to the Foreign Office, expressing their desire to return to their country, where they felt they were needed to pursue the cause of liberation and political reconstruction. The British Foreign Office initially refused them permission to leave Britain. It took many months before they were able to reach Italy. What connects these letters is their disappointment and inability to understand why an answer from the Foreign Office took so long to arrive.

As Petrone stated in a letter to Dixon, Churchill and Eden had promised that 'the British government would then facilitate the repatriation of all Italians of prominence'.[46] Nevertheless, four months after his first letter to Dixon regarding his return to Italy, he was still waiting for an answer. While this delay can be attributed to the fact that the British authorities had not placed full trust in Petrone, the situation was no different for Calosso and the Treves brothers.

As pointed out by Calosso, 'after the Moscow conference, the Anglo-American authorities in Italy declared that they were looking for anti-fascists to help in the reconstruction of the country', but could not find a 'sufficient number'.[47] Calosso is here referring to the conference in Moscow of October–November 1943 between the foreign ministers of Britain, the United States, the Republic of China and the Soviet Union. Calosso argued that identifying anti-fascists to repatriate should not be that difficult since there were very few Italian political refugees in Britain who met the Allies' requirements. In addition, it was not clear why the few anti-fascist exiles who had lived for many years in Britain were not given permission to return home, while non-political refugees and ex-fascists had left for Italy.[48]

At the end of the letter Calosso mentioned Major Geoffrey Dennis. In his capacity as the editor of the Italian *Talks*, Dennis had read hundreds of Calosso's talks and could therefore confirm his political position. Calosso sent another request to Marshal Badoglio to ask for the reinstatement of his rank of reserve lieutenant in the 49th infantry, of which he had been deprived by the fascist regime after his participation in the Spanish Civil War.[49]

These feelings were shared by the Free Italy movement and the Committee of Italian Socialists in Britain. The Free Italy movement had sent two resolutions to Churchill and Eden after the fall of Mussolini's government (25 July 1943) and on the occasion of Italy's unconditional surrender (8 September 1943). Both resolutions referred to Garibaldi and the battle of Volturno. During the battle, the documents stated, Britain was the only country that helped the political refugees return to Italy. Unfortunately, exactly the opposite was happening to the anti-fascist immigrants in Britain. Many exiles had already been repatriated from Switzerland, France, Russia and the United States, whereas Britain seemed to be the only country from which it was very difficult to return home.[50]

In a letter to the Italian Advisory Committee of the Foreign Office the Committee of Italian Socialists called attention to the fact that hundreds of socialists had not yet been able to return home.

> Hundreds of Italian Socialist exiles, whose party until the Fascist coup d'état of October 1922 was the strongest single party in Italy, with 165 M.P.s in the last freely elected Chamber of Deputies and with majorities in over 4,000 Municipal Councils are still now being denied the right to return to Italy, their homeland. At the same time, members of the Fascist-Nationalist 'Partito Azzurro', namely the same party chiefly responsible for the coup d'état of October 1922, which never had more than 8 M.P.s in freely elected Parliaments and never was able to muster a Majority in one single municipal Council, are at this moment being allowed in Allied-occupied Italy to regroup and openly to engage in political activities the purpose of which is avowedly the one of bringing about a restoration of House of Savoy rule over Italy.[51]

Among the reasons why the bureaucratic procedure was so slow, claimed the Foreign Office, was Britain's agreement with the United States.[52] Prior to invading Italy, the United States and Great Britain had agreed that they would not allow the return of political refugees to their respective homes without consulting one another.[53] However, this did not seem to be a valid reason for the delay, since the US government had already decided to allow individuals of standing to return to Italy to participate in the political life of their country.[54]

One possible explanation for the British authorities' reticence can be found in Philip Noel-Baker's answer to a letter from Paolo Treves. Paolo Treves had requested permission to leave Britain at the end of 1943, but it took him several months to obtain the necessary permits. Noel-Baker was Under-Secretary to the Ministry of War Transport at the time. Treves and Noel-Baker, who were also friends, were constantly in touch during the negotiations between the former and the Foreign Office. In the letter, dated 20 December 1943, an extract from a Foreign Office's message was reported by Noel-Baker:

> We have consulted the British Broadcasting Corporation, who have strongly expressed that there is little to gain in facilitating the return of Paolo Treves to Italy at present. The same goes for his brother, mother and fiancée. On the contrary, we would lose two capable and almost irreplaceable members of the British Broadcasting Corporation's Italian team. The British Broadcasting Corporation are strongly of the opinion that the Treves brothers are certainly of better use to the war effort in England than they are likely to ever be in Italy.[55]

Paolo Treves's answer to this letter was extremely frank. He would not take no for an answer:

> I quite see the BBC and the Foreign Office point of view but I feel it is our duty to go back to our country as soon as possible and work there for its reconstruction. We are certainly not moved by reasons of personal interest. By going back my brother and I would lose very good jobs and embark once again on a very difficult adventure. But perhaps may be useful to our friends who are now in the Italian cabinet.[56]

The comments made by the Foreign Office about the Treves brothers are certainly flattering. Yet, despite their praiseworthy and useful work undertaken for British propaganda, the two exiles were not free to exercise their will to continue their anti-fascist activity in Italy. Although the brothers did eventually manage to help their friends in Italy, they only obtained authorisation to return home at the end of 1944, more than a year after Paolo Treves's first request to the Foreign Office. Clearly, the anti-fascist cause and the political reconstruction of Italy were not among Great Britain's priorities.

It is clear from Chapter 3 that the majority of the broadcasters at the BBC Italian Service were extremely proud to work for British national radio and serve their country from abroad. Some of the broadcasters, as we have seen, wrote that in the majority of cases they felt free to express their own opinions using the BBC's microphones and to provide accurate information rather than propaganda.

However, the documents and existing literature on the Italian exiles examined in this chapter show another side of the Italian refugees' experience in Britain. As the case of Carlo Petrone has shown, not all exiles were authentic anti-fascists. It is therefore not surprising that the British government and the Labour Party launched official as well as informal investigations to obtain information on the political background of the refugees.

Yet, what the community of Italian exiles regarded as unacceptable was that even refugees of undoubted anti-fascist political commitment faced arrest and harsh internment in the British camps. As Paolo Treves and Uberto Limentani wrote, they were not even granted protection from fascist prisoners interned alongside them in the camps. The same applies to the difficulties encountered by the Treves brothers, Calosso and Petrone, when trying to obtain permission to return to Italy.

The obvious incongruity between what the anti-fascist exiles declared about their experience at the BBC and what the documents of the Foreign Office disclose show British radio's problematic position as both moral support for the Italian population and the official voice of an enemy country. This contradiction, as the following chapters will show, is evident in the Italian Service's programmes.

Notes

1 The expression 'enemy-friend' has been used by David Ellwood, Claudio Pavone and many other historians of the biennial 1943–45 to refer to the dual nature of the relations between the Allies and anti-fascist Italians. Ellwood, *Italy 1943–45*; Pavone, *A Civil War*.
2 Varsori, *Gli Alleati e l'emigrazione*, p. 17.

3 Bernabei, *Esuli ed emigrati*, p. 9.
4 Sponza, *Divided Loyalties*, p. 98; Bernabei, *Esuli ed emigrati*, p. 11.
5 Sponza, *Divided Loyalties*, p. 99.
6 Bernabei, *Esuli ed emigrati*, p. 11.
7 Sponza, *Divided Loyalties*, pp. 100–101.
8 Bernabei, *Esuli ed emigrati*, p. 108.
9 Sponza, *Divided Loyalties*, p. 101.
10 Sponza, *Divided Loyalties*, p. 102.
11 National Archives (hereafter NA), Foreign Office (hereafter FO) 371/25210, William Gillies to Nigel B. Ronald, 30 July 1940.
12 NA, FO371/25210, Attachment to Gillies's letter of 30 July 1940.
13 According to Paolo Treves's wife, Lotte Dann, the release from internment of Paolo and Piero was approved almost immediately. However, it was difficult to identify the camp in which they had been interned. The camp was identified after the two brothers sent a telegram to their mother in London. When they were released, a month after their arrest, they realised they had been on the Isle of Man. Lotte Treves, 'Ricominciare sempre da capo', *Rivista di Storia dell'Università di Torino*, I (2012), 63, www.ojs.unito.it/index.php/RSUT/article/view/280, accessed 1 February 2022.
14 Sponza, *Divided Loyalties*, pp. 105–112; Bernabei, *Esuli ed emigrati*, pp. 178–190.
15 Sponza, *Divided Loyalties*, p. 110. Peter Gillman and Leni Gillman, *'Collar the Lot!': How Britain Interned and Expelled its Wartime Refugees* (London: Quartet, 1980), p. 221.
16 Gillman and Gillman, *'Collar the Lot!'*, p. 221.
17 Sponza, *Divided Loyalties*, p. 110.
18 NA, FO371/25210, Statement by Umberto Limentani on his internment and the incident of the *Arandora Star*, August 1940.
19 NA, FO371/25210, Statement by Umberto Limentani on his internment and the incident of the *Arandora Star*, August 1940.
20 Treves, *Ricominciare sempre da capo*, p. 63.
21 Fondo Paolo Treves, Fondazione Filippo Turati (hereafter FPT FFT), box 4, s. *Scritti*, 'I Was Anderson's Prisoner', *Tribune* (9 August 1940). I found the article among Paolo Treves's personal papers in a box containing a copy of his publications. This is the reason why he is considered most likely to be the author.
22 Treves, *I was Anderson's Prisoner*.
23 NA, FO371/25210, Extract of an intercepted letter from Ruggero Orlando to his fiancée, Postal Censorship, Prisoners of War Section, 17 September 1940.
24 NA, FO371/25210, Letter from Wilson Young (Foreign Office) to the Loraine Committee, 28 September 1940.
25 NA, FO371/25210, Letter from the Home Office to Wilson Young (Foreign Office), 6 December 1940.
26 Nissim, *Il pappagallo del nonno*, pp. 179–180.
27 Varsori, *Gli Alleati e l'emigrazione*, p. 81.
28 Pietro Sebastiani, Laburisti inglesi, p. 27.

29 Varsori, *Gli Alleati e l'emigrazione*, p. 83.
30 Varsori, *Gli Alleati e l'emigrazione*, pp. 85–86.
31 People's History Museum, International Department Labour Party, William Gillies Papers (hereafter PHM, IDLP, WGP), Gillies to Miss Massey, 19 November 1940.
32 PHM, IDLP, WGP, Angelo Crespi to Gillies, 21 March 1941.
33 PHM, IDLP, WGP, Sylvia Pankhurst to David Margesson (War Office), 29 April 1941.
34 PHM, IDLP, WGP, Pankhurst to Gillies, 13 March 1941.
35 PHM, IDLP, WGP, Pankhurst to Gillies, 13 March 1941.
36 PHM, IDLP, WGP, Bertha Pritchard (Hon. Secretary of the Relief Committee for Refugees from Italy) to Gillies, 26 February 1941.
37 PHM, IDLP, WGP, Pritchard to Miss Howie, 23 February 1941.
38 PHM, IDLP, WGP, Piero and Paolo Treves to Gillies, 20 March 1943.
39 PHM, IDLP, WGP, Piero Treves to Gillies, 11 December 1942.
40 PHM, IDLP, WGP, Giovanni Giglio to Gillies, 14 October 1943.
41 PHM, IDLP, WGP, Piccialuti Caprioli, 'Umberto Calosso da Radio Londra', in *Umberto Calosso Antifascista*, p. 98.
42 Piccialuti Caprioli, 'Umberto Calosso da Radio Londra', in *Umberto Calosso Antifascista*, p. 97.
43 BBC WAC, E2/371, Foreign Gen. Italian Service, BBC Internal Circulating Memo. Free Italy Movement, 27 April 1942.
44 BBC WAC, E2/371, Foreign Gen. Italian Service, David Stephens and Colonel Stevens, 29 April 1942.
45 BBC WAC, E2/371, Foreign Gen. Italian Service, Colonel Stevens to Ivone Kirkpatrick and Bruce Lockart, 30 April 1942.
46 NA, FO371/37258, Petrone to Dixon, 30 November 1943.
47 NA, FO371/37258, Calosso to the Foreign Office (name of addressee not specified), 16 December 1943.
48 NA, FO371/37258, Calosso to the Foreign Office (name of addressee not specified), 16 December 1943.
49 NA, FO371/37258, Calosso to Marshall Badoglio, 22 November 1943.
50 NA, FO371/37258, Calosso to Anthony Rumbold, *Memorandum: On the Return of the Political Exiles*, 4 November 1943.
51 NA, FO371/37258, Francesco Frola and Giovanni Giglio from the Provisional Committee of the Italian Socialist Party Operating Outside Italy to the Italian Advisory Committee of the Foreign Office, 3 December 1943.
52 Institute for Social History, Paolo Treves Papers (hereafter ISH, PTP) Philip Noel Baker to Paolo Treves, 20 December 1943.
53 NA, FO371/37258, Anthony Rumbold to the Foreign Office (full name of addressee not included), 20 December 1943.
54 NA, FO371/37258, Anthony Rumbold to the Foreign Office (full name of addressee not included), 20 December 1943.
55 ISH, PTP, Philip Noel-Baker to Paolo Treves, 21 April 1944.
56 ISH, PTP, Paolo Treves to Philip Noel-Baker, 26 April 1944.

5

The enemy: Ente Italiano per le Audizioni Radiofoniche (EIAR)

Analysis of the memoirs of Italian broadcasters (Chapter 3) and the examination of British government sources (Chapter 4) have already shown the BBC's contradictory position as the voice of a friend and as an enemy of Italy. While the Italian exiles working for British radio described their experience at the BBC as a time when they could freely express their anti-fascist opinions, the British Foreign Office did not allow them complete freedom. Despite their work at the BBC, many had been treated as criminals in internment camps. Moreover, when the Italian campaign began, some of them did not obtain permission to return home to continue their anti-fascist fight in Italy.

After offering an insight into the evolution of the fascist EIAR and the features of its programmes, this chapter will analyse another aspect of the ambiguous role played by Radio Londra. While British propaganda described Britain as a genuine and convinced supporter of the anti-fascist cause, what follows will show that British anti-fascist propaganda only really began when British interests in the Mediterranean were at risk. Moreover, despite the anti-Italian propaganda in Arabic broadcast by the BBC from 1937, it was only with the Italian declaration of war on Britain that contact between the BBC and the EIAR ceased. Before this time, the two radio stations were constantly in touch with each other, exchanging material for use in their programmes.

An analysis of the anti-Axis programmes in the last two sections of the chapter will also show how the BBC's Italian Service contributed to the distribution of false information about the Italian army's defeat at El Alamein at the end of 1942, as well as about the unconditional surrender of Italy. In order to win the war, it was key to persuade the Italians that they had been dragged into the war by an unreliable ally. It was also vital to convince them that an unconditional surrender of Italy to the Allied forces would have no negative consequence on Italy's political position in post-war Europe. These data are unsurprising in a war context; however, they are clearly in contrast with the BBC's reputation as the authentic voice of the Italian Resistance and anti-fascism. The reception of the programmes in Italy, as the sample of listeners' letters in Chapter 7 will show, contributed extensively to this reputation.

The birth and evolution of fascist radio

Fascist radio was set up in 1924, two years after the foundation of the BBC. However, there was a crucial difference between the BBC and the EIAR. While the British national broadcaster was established in a democratic state, the Italian radio station developed in parallel with the fascist regime. The previously mentioned Mussolini's March on Rome took place in 1922, only two years before the institution of Unione Radiofonica Italiana (URI). As Franco Monteleone emphasises: 'Unlike in other countries, in Italy the development of modern mass communication techniques is contemporary with the birth of the totalitarian State.'[1]

Moreover, despite the fact that the radio pioneer Guglielmo Marconi was Italian, Italy's technical development in the field of radio communications was slow in comparison with countries such as Britain and the United States. While Marconi's invention opened a debate in Italy on wireless communications, there were no significant efforts to put his ideas into practice, and interest in radio was limited to the military. As a consequence, Marconi began promoting his invention abroad. Monticone locates the reasons for the slow development of early Italian radio communications in the general backwardness of Italian industry, since only some particular sectors and geographic regions had benefited from the industrial revolution.[2]

Legislation relating to radio telegraphy and radio telephony mirrored this backwardness. The first law regulating these developments dated back to 30 June 1910 (law n. 395) and decreed that the Italian government would establish new radio-telegraph and radio-telephone systems.[3] However, the 1910 law was the only regulation approved by ordinary parliamentary procedure until 14 April 1975, when a second law on radio and television programmes was implemented. In the 65-year gap between the two laws, radio and television had been regulated by decree-laws. According to the law of 1975 (n. 103), radio and television should be treated as essential public services. Therefore, it was decided that the government would no longer be allowed to pass new laws regarding radio and television matters without parliamentary approval.[4]

Neither the Italian nor British government realised immediately that radio could be a powerful tool of propaganda as well as entertainment for civilians. As we have seen in Chapter 1, it was the initiative of private firms that led to the institution of the British Broadcasting Company, which became a public institution only five years later. Similarly, the early years of Italian radio were characterised by the competition between private Italian and foreign radio telegraph and telephone companies.[5]

> The main difference was that in Britain the manufacturers then allowed the government to take responsibility for the provision of programmes, and the BBC was transformed from a private company to a public corporation ... In Italy, on the other hand ... the state showed very little interest before the Thirties in developing radio, whether for propaganda or any other purpose.[6]

It is not within the scope of this chapter to analyse in detail the years of the competition between private firms in Italy. For the purpose of this work some general information on the key phases of the development of Italian radio and its production is sufficient. This will allow for a better understanding of the BBC programmes analysed in this and the following chapters. In order to counter the enemy propaganda and engage with Italian civilians it was crucial for the BBC to be familiar with the radio programmes and news bulletins aired by the EIAR. As we have seen in Chapter 1, knowledge of the enemy was so important that in 1939 the BBC Monitoring Service was set up. Its aim was to monitor the radio propaganda and press of foreign countries. The material collected by BBC monitors was examined and taken into consideration when preparing the schedules of the various foreign branches of the BBC. While this book does not analyse the records of the BBC Monitoring Service, as we will see later in this chapter, the programmes themselves show how the texts of the Italian programmes often referred to what had been said or written by fascist propagandists.

When Mussolini came to power, Italian music programmes and news bulletins were still in an experimental phase. Moreover, no single radio station was broadcasting regularly.[7] As stated by Philip Cannistraro, 1922 was a crucial year for the development of Italian radio. In that year the under-secretary of state, Giacomo Acerbo, received a secret memorandum in which some private companies expressed their interest in an investment in radio. On 27 August 1924, URI was established as a result of the merger of two firms interested in radio: Società Italiana per le Radioaudizioni Circolari (SIRAC), based in Milan, and Radiofono, based in Rome.[8] URI created a private radio station in Rome with Marconi's help. After this first experiment in Rome, Radio Milano and Radio Napoli were set up. The birth of these new radio stations led to Mussolini's decision to institute a Royal Committee chaired by Augusto Turati, the Secretary of the Partito

Nazionale Fascista (PNF). This committee, created in 1926, decided that Radio Roma should become a bigger radio station and that new stations should be set up in Genoa, Florence, Palermo, Turin and Trieste.[9] Moreover, the committee decided that these radio stations and their production should be monitored by a governmental committee.

The Royal Decree Law n. 2526 of 15 December 1927 turned URI into the EIAR. The EIAR was composed of the former URI's shareholders as well as some new ones such as radio manufacturers and traders. A new committee was created, the main task of which was to ensure that the programmes aired by the EIAR were in line with the political agenda of the fascist regime. The first EIAR administrative council included four delegates of the fascist government; among these Mussolini's younger brother, Arnaldo. Moreover, a new committee called the Comitato superiore di vigilanza (Higher Committee of Surveillance) was created. This committee played an active role in designing the EIAR's programming and included representatives of the regime's industrial confederations and cultural institutions of the fascist regime. A few months after its establishment, it was decided that the fascist government would choose the committee's members and take decisions on the number of people involved. According to article n. 8 of the Royal Decree Law, EIAR radio stations would be used to broadcast concerts, theatre performances, conferences, sporting events, important ceremonies, talks and lectures, and religious sermons.[10]

The EIAR's programmes

The transformation of URI marked the transition from a *radio d'elite*, which focused mainly on cultural programmes, to a *radio di regime*.[11] Yet the transformation of fascist radio into a more popular medium was gradual and slow.

Among the most well-known cultural programmes were those curated by the futurist intellectual and poet Filippo Tommaso Marinetti. Marinetti welcomed radio as an apt instrument for the dissemination of Futuristic ideas.[12] Another core programme was *Giornale Radio*. Born as a simple news bulletin, *Giornale Radio* soon developed into a programme that mixed news with commentary from the broadcasters. Moreover, radio commentaries on cultural, political and sports-related events became another feature of the EIAR.[13]

Once the fascist authorities understood that the regime's political propaganda would benefit from the new medium, more programmes were created. These included broadcasts for children and competitions to encourage listeners to tune into the EIAR regularly. In 1930 Costanzo Ciano proposed the creation of special programmes for farmers to provide technical advice and weather forecasts. In 1933 Ente Radio Rurale was created, its aim being to distribute public radio transmitters to rural schools and villages. These public radio transmitters, called *uditori collettivi* by the regime, were installed in places where peasants gathered in their spare time. Another attempt at increasing the number of listeners was the creation of the *radio balilla*, a cheap radio that Italians could buy in instalments.

The study of broadcasting techniques was also promoted in universities. In 1933 the Centro Sperimentale di Radiofonia (Experimental Centre for Radio) was created. In addition, the Gioventù Universitaria Fascista (GUF, or Fascist University Youth, the fascist organisation of university students) played a key role in encouraging the study of radio. Students from Milan, Rome and Naples also created their own radio stations.[14]

Among the most important EIAR broadcasts between the 1930s and the 1940s was a programme called *Commenti ai fatti del giorno*. Broadcast for the first time in 1936, it was often attacked by the BBC, as we will see shortly. In 1939 a programme for workers, called Radio Sociale, was launched and broadcast at lunchtimes and in the evenings, when no one was at work. Some public radio transmitters were also installed in factories. The collaboration of factory owners was vital in this regard. Yet, the outbreak of the Second World War interrupted the process of distributions of radio transmitters in workplaces.[15]

After the promulgation of the race laws, new anti-Jewish programmes were launched. These included titles such as *Protocolli degli Anziani di Sion*, *Il giudaismo contro la cultura occidentale*, *L'Internazionale ebraica* and *Il giudaismo voleva questa guerra*. A very popular type of programme was the radio drama, a radio theatrical piece that resembled the German Hörspiel, popular in Germany since the 1920s.

With the outbreak of the war, fascist programmes were subjected to stronger political control. Among the wartime programmes was *Signor X* (Mr X), launched in 1942 and often mentioned by the BBC. This consisted of sarcastic conversations read by an anonymous announcer. The texts were often written by Mussolini. The announcers' voices, as Mussolini himself suggested, should resemble that of the Duce.[16] According to Anna Lucia Natale, fascist broadcasters never became stars, because the only legitimate celebrity in fascist Italy was Mussolini.[17]

Despite fascist attempts made before the war to turn radio into a popular medium, the economic backwardness of Italy, as well as the high cost of radio sets, were still limitations.[18] Another limitation of the EIAR was its inability to empathise with its listeners and address them as individuals rather than as a mass. This was especially true for the years of the conflict, during which fascist radio programming changed considerably. Neither civil servants working at MinCulPop) nor the officials of the EIAR seemed ready for the war. A month before the Italian declaration of war a special section of the Ispettorato per la radiodiffusione, called Ente Radio Guerra, was created. Its main tasks consisted of collecting and distributing military news. The Ispettorato was, moreover, divided into three sections: the home section, the foreign section and a third section in charge of intercepting enemy propaganda.[19] Ente Radio Guerra received directives from MinCulPop.

The institutional readjustment of the bodies in charge of radio propaganda was not, however, followed by an appropriate reorganisation of the EIAR's programming. The content of fascist broadcasts did change, but the new programmes' features did not seem to meet the needs of the Italian population. The number of entertainment and cultural programmes was considerably reduced and replaced by military programmes. There was no more space for innovation and imagination; the news bulletins became boring and impersonal.[20] The incapability of understanding how important it was to target individuals and talk directly to the listeners contributed to the failure of fascist journalism and information.[21]

The EIAR's impersonal style may be one of the reasons that made BBC radio broadcasts appeal to many Italians. As Luigi Petrella notes, the EIAR 'often showed an appalling incapacity to grasp people's real feelings'. For example, in March 1942 many Italians listened to foreign radio stations because the EIAR did not broadcast light music. [22] More generally, the failure of fascist propaganda, Petrella claims, can be attributed to both 'the catastrophic impact of the European crisis on civilians' lives and to institutional and political flaws'.[23] The BBC, however, was able to handle this crisis by continuing to entertain and reassure Italians. As we will see in the next two chapters, Radio London made use of music, different linguistic registers, styles and themes to entertain and meet the interests of a wide range of Italians.

Another aspect that led to the failure of fascist radio propaganda towards the end of the war was the way in which the arguments were presented, since the broadcasters' declarations were never supported by any factual evidence. This strategy was successful while the conflict went in favour of the Axis coalition. However, things changed when the Italian population started to experience bombings, hunger and power cuts.[24]

The BBC and the EIAR before the outbreak of the war: correspondence and music exchanges

As Franco Monteleone notes, until Italian foreign policy began to go against the interests of the western democracies, the fascist regime was not opposed by other countries. It was only in the 1930s, when a conflict of interest between Italy, France and Great Britain arose, that the British had a strong reaction to fascist propaganda.

This, Monteleone argues, was particularly true at two specific moments of fascist political warfare: the Ethiopian war in 1935, and the declaration of war on France and Great Britain in June 1940.[25] As Manuela Williams has written, the early 1930s opened a new phase of aggressive policy in the Middle East:

> The rise of the threat of an expansionist Germany opened the way for Mussolini to play an initial role of balance between major power blocs. At the same time, the growing popular consent generated by both Arab nationalism and Zionism attracted the attention of the Fascist regime.[26]

The Foreign Office's records for those months, continues Williams, referred to 'rumours of possible Italian claims to Syria, Lebanon and Palestine'. The Italian presence in North Africa could certainly put British and French colonial interests at risk. It was not a coincidence that after the Italian military campaign in Ethiopia, Mussolini's regime was constantly attacked by the foreign press and radio in that area, leading to the birth of European anti-fascist radio propaganda.[27]

An example of this is the battle against Radio Bari conducted by the BBC Arabic Service in North Africa and the Middle East. Radio Bari was set up on 24 May 1934 and broadcast in Arabic until the day of Italy's unconditional surrender to the Allied forces (8 September 1943). After this date the station was used by the Anglo-American occupying forces in Italy. Radio Bari was the first European radio station to broadcast in a non-European language and was an instrument of anti-Semitic and imperialist propaganda.[28] Its main aim was to persuade the populations of the Middle East and North Africa that the Italian presence in the area was preferable to the British and French dominations. The contradiction of conveying anti-colonial messages on behalf of a colonising country led to a failure of Italian propaganda in the area. Yet, in the summer of 1935 the British Foreign Office was seriously concerned about Radio Bari. It was in response to the fascist programmes that the BBC Arabic Service was set up in October 1937. However, since the British government was trying to influence the political line of the programmes, the BBC clarified that its independence from the government should be maintained.[29]

In spite of the conflict of interests in the Mediterranean theatre, communications between the BBC Italian Service and the EIAR only stopped after June 1940. Prior to the Italian involvement in the war, the two radio stations were often in touch to exchange favours, and material to use in the programmes. Radio broadcasts were a relatively new phenomenon and it was extremely useful to know what the other stations in Europe broadcast or what technical improvements were applied. This section of the chapter will examine some correspondence between the BBC and the EIAR before the outbreak of the Second World War. This correspondence includes letters referring to exchanges of music between the two radio stations. As we have seen in Chapter 1, music was a very important propaganda tool, since Italians were known as music lovers. Hence the BBC needed to make the most of this interest, and broadcast music by either famous Italian composers or English composers who had some connection with Italy. Similarly, fascist radio was interested in knowing what kind of music was popular in Britain. This was especially true for the pre-war period, since the outbreak of the war did not leave much space for entertainment in EIAR's programming.[30]

On 26 February 1937, at the request of EIAR's officials who had asked for some advice on music for broadcasting in Italy, the BBC sent them a list of popular dance music and dance-show records. The list included musical comedies and dance songs:

MUSICAL COMEDIES
Careless Rapture
Swing Along
Over she goes
Balalaika

DANCE MUSIC
A fine romance
You turned the tables on me
This'll make you whistle
When a lady meets a gentleman down south
I've got you under my skin
Good evening, pretty lady
Bye, bye baby
The way you look tonight
Serenade in the night
I'm in a dancing mood
Organ grinders' swing
Shoe shine boy
It's a sin to tell a lie
When the poppies bloom again
In the chapel in moonlight
There's a small hotel
Pennies from heaven
When did you leave heaven
Who loves you
I'm in a dancing mood[31]

Similar requests were sent to the BBC the following year. On 7 September 1938 the EIAR asked for summaries of radio comedies and musical radio comedies by modern authors popular among the British listeners.[32] A few days later, on 16 September, a list was sent to the EIAR. The document included the following comedy titles: *At your Service, Madame!*, the story of some male escorts and their clients; *The Silver Spoon*, about a man who escapes from his wife to go to a nightclub where he discovers that his daughter is having an affair with one of the singers; *You're the Girl*, the love story of a man who follows his girl to South America and gets involved in a revolution; *Mr Barley's Abroad*, the story of a businessman who leaves his job to join a concert party as a pianist-composer; and *The Three-Cornered Hat*.

The summary of this last radio comedy, written by a BBC member of staff, is particularly interesting. In this summary the Italians were labelled with the racial slur 'wops'. The word 'wop' refers to southern Europeans and derives from the Neapolitan word *guappo*. It came into use at the end of the nineteenth century as a label for Italian immigrants in the United States and is no longer acceptable because of its racist connotations.[33] As we will see in Chapter 7, the word was also used in England during the Second World War to refer to Italian prisoners of war.[34] The word was removed in the version of the document sent to the EIAR:

> This is more operetta than musical comedy. It has a delightful score, and the story is based on the same folk tale which is responsible for the famous ballet. It is of course Spanish through and through, but the Wops might like to put it on a Franco Gala night.[35]

At the end of 1938 the EIAR was still interested in British music, as shown by a request for some catalogues of records produced in Britain.[36] The BBC, in its turn, wanted to know more about the Italian music scene. In January 1940 Italian radio returned the favour by sending the catalogues of records produced between December 1939 and January 1940 by a company called Cetra Parlophon.[37]

Sometimes the BBC and EIAR exchanged other kinds of material or artists. This was the case with the BBC's request for EIAR programme plans and an invitation to Britain for the orchestra conductor Tito Petralia, who directed a concert at the BBC.[38]

In February and March 1940, the BBC expressed its interest in two activities run by Italian radio: the radio competition and radio referendum.[39] As mentioned before, competitions were a pretext to encourage the Italian audience to regularly listen to EIAR:

> Dear Signor Gorini,
> We were very interested to see in *Radiocorriere*, details of a questionnaire in connection with which prizes were being offered. We should very much appreciate

it, if you were so kind as to let us have any report you may prepare on the results of this questionnaire, since, as you know, we ourselves do a considerable amount of listener research work of this kind and we are always interested to hear of any new developments of this kind.[40]

As for the radio referendum, it aimed at investigating what Italians liked or disliked about radio programmes and the BBC asked the EIAR to send to London any outcomes and statistical figures obtained from the referendum.[41]

On other occasions some BBC and EIAR members of staff asked to visit the studios of the Italian and British radio, respectively. This was the case with the visit of a British conductor, Mr Henry Braithwaite, who was in Milan to attend some performances at the Italian theatre, *La Scala*. Given his interest in opera, Braithwaite wished to take a tour of the EIAR music department. The BBC interceded on his behalf by requesting a tour for him.[42]

But the aim of these visits was often to obtain information on technical and practical aspects of other radio stations. This was the case of the visits of Gorino, from the studio department in Rome, Ermanno Agostinetti, Manager of EIAR's Turin studio, and Banfi. In particular, Banfi wanted to discuss a recent improvement at Alexandra Palace with the director of BBC television.[43]

With the outbreak of the Second World War in September 1939 relations between the BBC and the EIAR continued, though some issues started to arise.[44] One of these related to the use of Italian material for the BBC Forces programme:

> Dear Mr Ogilvie,
> according to reports I am receiving from my staff, I understand that, in the projected arrangements for relays, which we are successfully exchanging in spite of technical difficulties arising from present conditions, a number of light music concerts from Italy were to be included in the recently started BBC's programmes for the Forces.
>   While I can fully appreciate the importance of this new feature, as we also endeavour, in Italy to assist the services with entertainment and educational broadcasting, I would point out that the EIAR strictly restrains to national sources the production of any programme to that effect; and therefore, in case my information is correct, I thought it advisable to submit friendly such matter to your consideration.
>   Framing all programme items from abroad, I mean from Italy or from Great Britain alternatively, in the general Home Service, without of interfering with features of a more special purpose and character, as those for the Forces unquestionably are, would prove, in my opinion, more profitable to the development and the improving of our programme exchanges. That, I am certain, both of us will agree to be the most suitable result which we might aim to.[45]

The BBC answered the letter by confirming that relays from Italy would only be broadcast in the Home Service and not in the programme to the

Forces, and took the opportunity of saying how much the BBC and the British listeners had enjoyed the programmes from Italy in the previous months.[46]

Exchanges of information and music between the two radio stations ceased with the Italian declaration of war, but contact between the BBC and EIAR would be re-established with the end of the conflict and the beginning of the Cold War.[47]

As this section has shown, neither Mussolini's coup d'état nor the Ethiopian war interrupted the exchanges between the EIAR and the BBC. While the BBC Arabic Service was attacking Radio Bari, the BBC home service was regularly in touch with EIAR employees based in Rome and Milan. These employees, as explained in the first section of this chapter, worked under the direction of committees chosen by the fascist regime. Nevertheless, for the BBC this did not constitute a valid enough reason to distance itself from the EIAR home service. This ambivalent position could no longer be maintained after June 1940, once Italy was officially at war against Britain.

By analysing a selection of programmes in which the EIAR is described as the propaganda tool of a totalitarian regime, the next section will focus on the shift in British attitudes towards fascist radio.

Democracies vs totalitarian states in Colonel Stevens's commentaries

As will be explained in more detail in the last chapter of the book, despite the censorship laws that forbade tuning in to foreign radio stations, Radio Londra had many listeners in Italy. Since the first months of the war against Italy, the Corporation seemed to be very aware of this. In an extract from one of the European Service's weekly bulletins, dated 13 February 1941, it was stated that the fascist regime had officially recognised the existence of Colonel Stevens. His commentaries had been described by Radio Rome as *idioti e avventati* (idiotic and reckless). Moreover, Stevens was mentioned in a fascist programme broadcast on 7 January 1941.[48]

As we have seen in Chapter 1, one of the features of the BBC programmes was the separation of news and commentaries, a choice presented by the British radio station as the evidence of its objectivity. The topic was often at the centre of the Italian Service's programmes and was used to illustrate the difference between the BBC and the EIAR. The BBC often referred to fascist radio broadcasts or publications to expose the lies told by the fascist broadcasters and the lack of freedom of expression in Italy.

In a programme broadcast in January 1943, Stevens focused on the differences between democracies and totalitarian regimes. The programme began with references to a recently published article in the fascist journal

Gerarchia, written by the fascist philosopher Francesco Orestano. In the article, entitled 'La vita religiosa nella nuova Europa', the philosopher addressed the issue of the future of Europe in the event of Germany's victory.[49] Germany, the article suggested, was not a Christian country. Therefore, Orestano wondered whether what he identified as the European Christian identity would be put at risk by a German victory. In Orestano's opinion Germany would not embrace the Christian religion, which was the only force that could unify all European countries. Stevens used Orestano's article as a pretext to show that fascist policy on freedom of expression was contradictory and unfair. While an article questioning Germany's leading role in the post-war period had been published in an official fascist journal, any common citizen expressing similar ideas in a public space or over the telephone risked arrest or a substantial fine.

> Qua sta la contraddizione che condanna il regime totalitario. Si deve servire, per scopi politici spesso oscuri, degli uomini di pensiero; i quali se non vogliono perdere l'autorità acquistata con grande fatica debbono esporre obiettivamente e secondo verità, le deduzioni cui dovevano necessariamente giungere. Ma quando l'uomo medio è attratto dalla verità rivelata attraverso il lavorio della mente colta, allora sorge il pericolo che l'inganno ordito dal regime ai danni delle masse venga rivelato ad un numero troppo grande di persone. Ne segue la repressione illogica, stupida e ingiusta che, comprimendo le reazioni più violente le giustifica e le provoca.[50]

> This is the contradiction to which the totalitarian regime is condemned. It needs men of thought for its shady political purposes; who, if they do not want to lose the authority they have gained through such great effort, are expected to present the conclusions they have logically reached, objectively and truthfully. But when the average man is interested in the truth revealed by the intellectual activities of a cultured mind, there is the risk that the deceit of the regime towards the detriment of the masses is revealed to too large a number of people. Thus follows an illogical, silly and unfair repression that, by suppressing the most violent reactions, actually causes and justifies them.

Similar considerations dominated a programme dated 22 March 1943. In this case Stevens commented on a speech made by Winston Churchill in which the British prime minister had stated that governments deprived their citizens of their freedom only when they could not rely on a solid tradition. Stevens expanded on Churchill's speech, adding that Britain had chosen the tradition some centuries before. While the Glorious Revolution of 1688 was not mentioned explicitly in the programme, Stevens's reference to the solid, non-written British constitution was evident.

References to important British and Italian historical moments were very common in the Italian programmes. Brave and virtuous historical characters or corrupt politicians from past eras were often mentioned. This was the case on 26 March 1943. The broadcaster was again Stevens, who opened the programme by referring to the popular saying that Napoleon would not have been able to govern if he had allowed freedom of the press. A similar reasoning, the programme seemed to suggest, applied to Italy; Mussolini remained in power only because Italian civilians were not free to act according to their will:

> Vietare i comizi non serve; quando i discorsi sediziosi serpeggiano per le code malinconiche che si allungano davanti ai negozi, nelle lunghe attese per le magre razioni. Nè d'altra parte, è possibile collocare una spia ad ogni tavolo dei locali pubblici. E c'è, soprattutto, la radio la cui voce converge sull'Italia da tutti i punti cardinali da microfoni che sono fuori dalla portata delle grinfie di Mussolini, e che parlano la lingua del popolo. Il regime predica che non è patriottico ascoltare le radio straniere; e nessuno ascolta la predica. Il regime emana leggi che puniscono gli ascoltatori con la multa e la prigione; e le leggi non vengono rispettate. Triplica le sanzioni; e la gente continua ad ascoltare. Limita la fabbricazione di nuovi apparecchi, proibisce la vendita di apparecchi usati ad onde corte, nega agli utenti l'impiego di antenne esterne. E gli ascoltatori delle radio straniere si moltiplicano, eludendo con ogni accorgimento, la vigilanza dei carabinieri, del capo fabbricato, dei vicini astiosi, dei portinai, e delle donne di servizio.[51]

> There is no point in forbidding public speeches when seditious talk spreads among the mournful people queuing in front of the shops during the long wait for meagre rations. After all, it is not possible to place a spy at every table in public places. And there is, above all, radio, whose voice reaches Italy from all the points of the compass and microphones that are out of Mussolini's clutches and speak the language of ordinary people. The regime preaches that is not patriotic to listen to foreign radio stations; and no one listens to the preacher. The regime issues a law that punishes listeners with fines and imprisonment; and the laws are not respected. It triples the sanctions; and people keep on listening. It restricts the manufacture of new radio transmitters, bans the sales of second-hand short-wave radios, forbids the use of external aerials. And the listeners to foreign radio stations multiply, by avoiding – in every way possible – control by the Carabinieri, the concierges, spiteful neighbours, caretakers, and maids.

As suggested by the text of the broadcast, the 1940s were very different from the Napoleonic era. From newspapers to textbooks and other forms of publication, fascist and Nazi regimes had taken control of the entire cultural production of their countries. Yet, technology had introduced something that was out of their control: radio. At the end of the programme, Stevens announced that in the coming days the BBC would increase the number of its programmes to keep on informing and encouraging the Italian population.

A month later, on 28 April 1943, Stevens once again exposed fascist propaganda. This time his target was the aforementioned fascist programme *Commenti ai fatti del giorno*. Late spring 1943 was a difficult moment for the Italian war. As we will see later in this chapter, after the Anglo-American victories in North Africa, Italy feared an Allied landing in Sicily from the North African coast. Yet, claimed Stevens, fascist programmes did not address the issue at all:

> Buona sera. I *Commenti ai fatti del giorno* sono morti, ingloriosamente, alla chetichella, come avviene di tutte le istituzioni fasciste quando la loro utilità e la loro impopolarità cominciano a creare delle seccature per il Regime...E' logico che i commenti hanno una ragione di essere solamente quando c'è qualcosa da commentare. E se il governo, per ragioni sue proprie, comincia a proibire di parlare di questo e parlare di quest'altro, specialmente delle cose che più interessano al pubblico, meglio era giungere alla soppressione, lasciando così il compito di parlare regolarmente degli eventi politici che riguardano l'Italia ai commentatori di Londra, Mosca e Nuova York.[52]

> Good evening. The *Commenti ai fatti del giorno* died with no glory, on the sly, as happens to every fascist institution when its purpose and unpopularity start causing trouble to the regime. It is obvious that comments have reason to exist only if there is something to comment on. And if the government starts forbidding, for its own reasons, talks about one topic or another, especially about the issues of the greatest interest to the public, it is better to abolish them, leaving the task to give regular talks about the latest Italian political events to the commentators of London, Moscow and New York.

This extract is a good summary of one of the most debated topics on the BBC and the EIAR. Radio Londra often accused the EIAR of hiding the truth about the war fronts and broadcasting misleading information on the conflict. On the other hand, Radio London's choice of reporting on both victories and defeats was described by the EIAR as an opportunistic propaganda strategy. In May 1943 the BBC created a new programme entitled *Progress of Fascist Propaganda*, the aim of which was to unveil the incongruity between what was happening to the Italian troops in North Africa and what was being said by the EIAR broadcasters. In the programmes in this series, recent declarations by fascist politicians and propagandists were compared with the regime's statements on the same date in previous years. The scope was to demonstrate that the promises made by Mussolini in 1940, when Italy entered the war, had not been kept.

> COMPERE: Il 17 maggio 1940, tre anni fa, radio Roma annunciava:
> ANNOUNCER: Il Senato ha discusso il bilancio. Il senatore Tondirelli dichiarò, fra l'altro, che gli sforzi del regime erano diretti a ottenere l'autarchia voluta dal Duce e che si era mostrata un sicuro fattore di Potenza ed una garanzia di vittoria ...

COMPERE: Il 17 maggio 1941, due anni fa, Radio Roma annunciava:
ANNOUNCER: La Gran Bretagna combatte su otto fronti, senza disporre di materiale bellico, di navi o di aeroplani in quantità sufficienti. La situazione della marina mercantile britannica è davvero pietosa ...
COMPERE: Il 17 maggio 1942, un anno fa, radio Roma commentava:
ANNOUNCER: L'affondamento avvenuto ad opera di una nostra torpediniera di scorta ad un convoglio, dimostra ancora una volta che per le unità inglesi, anche le più insidiose, la navigazione nel Mediterraneo è assai difficile. E' appena il caso di dire che la Gran Bretagna ha finito di vantare la sua padronanza nel nostro mare.
COMPERE: Oggi, 17 marzo del 1943, che cosa dice la propaganda fascista?[53]

COMPERE: On 17 May 1940, three years ago, Radio Rome announced:
ANNOUNCER: The Senate discussed the annual financial report. Senator Tondirelli declared, moreover, that the regime's efforts to obtain the autarky the Duce wanted and which had proved to be a certain tool of power and a guarantee of victory ...
COMPERE: On 17 May 1941, two years ago, Radio Rome announced:
ANNOUNCER: Great Britain is fighting on eight fronts, with insufficient war equipment, ships or aeroplanes. The British Navy is in a really pitiful situation ...
COMPERE: On 17 May 1942, one year ago, Radio Rome announced:
ANNOUNCER: The sinking of a convoy by one of our emergency torpedo boats proves, once again, that for English units, even the most dangerous ones, navigating the Mediterranean is really difficult. It is time to admit that Great Britain no longer dominates our sea.
COMPERE: What does fascist propaganda say today, on 17 May 1943?

The final rhetorical question in which the BBC broadcaster asks what fascist propaganda had said in 1943 is present in the other programmes in the series. According to the documents held at the BBC Written Archives Centre, the programme was broadcast only in May and June 1943.

After analysing the ways in which the BBC attacked the fascist regime and its repressive political system, the next section will focus on key arguments used by the Italian Service to conduct its anti-Axis propaganda.

The representation of the Nazi-fascist enemy: Germany, an unreliable ally

As has been mentioned earlier, in the 1930s there was a conflict of interests between Italy, France and Great Britain in the Mediterranean theatre. The outbreak of the Second World War exacerbated this conflict. A key moment in the development of the war in North Africa was the end of 1942; in November that year the Axis coalition was defeated at El Alamein by troops under General Montgomery.

The Allied victories in North Africa inaugurated a season of Anglo-American military victories in Tunis, Algiers and Morocco. The outcome of these successes was the occupation of Vichy France's colonies. The code name for the Anglo-American operation in French African territories, led by General Eisenhower, was Operation Torch.[54] The conquest of North Africa was only the beginning of the Allied expansion in the Mediterranean. The next step was the Allied landings in Sicily, known as Operation Husky.[55] Operation Husky was planned in January 1943 at the Casablanca conference. The Allies would land in Sicily on 10 July 1943. According to some astronomical calculations, there would be four hours of darkness between midnight and 4.30 a.m. on the night of 9–10 July. Hence there were more chances of going unnoticed while approaching the southern Sicilian coast.[56]

The decision to land in Sicily had some consequences for Allied propaganda. The Allies' occupation of Italy needed to be supported by the Italian Service. It was crucial to obtain the collaboration of Italian civilians or, at least, the non-obstruction of Anglo-American military operations. This goal was attained in various ways, particularly by depicting Germany as an unreliable ally for Italy and showing that Mussolini was taking no security measures to protect Italian civilians.[57] As Winston Churchill declared in a speech to the Italians, Mussolini was the only man to blame for dragging Italy into a war against the British Empire. The speech was quoted in a BBC broadcast and was in line with Italian Service propaganda:

> CHURCHILL: Italiani, vi voglio dire la verità. E' tutta colpa di un uomo. Un uomo, un uomo solo ha schierato il popolo italiano in lotta mortale contro l'Impero britannico, ha tolto all'Italia le amicizie e la simpatia degli Stati Uniti d'America ... Ecco a che punto un uomo, un uomo solo vi ha ridotto e qui lascio la storia incompiuta, fino a che non venga il giorno- ed il giorno verrà- in cui la Nazione italiana ancora una volta riprenda a foggiare da se stessa i propri destini.[58]

> CHURCHILL: Italians, I want to tell you the truth. It is all because of one man. One man, one man alone has deployed the Italian population into a mortal fight against the British Empire, has taken away from Italy the friendship and favour of the United States of America ... Here's what one man, only one man did to you and I will only end my story on the day – and this day will come – on which the Italian nation will start forging its own destiny once more.

Since the initial victories in North Africa, the BBC had pointed out that these developments were a turning point in the conflict and started mentioning the possible retreat of General Erwin Rommel's troops. When this retreat became reality the BBC exposed Germany's treason towards Italy and argued that Italy could no longer rely on its ally, as a programme titled *Il Grande Tradimento* suggested:

ANNOUNCER: Italiani che mi ascoltate, date ai Vostri amici questa notizia: i Tedeschi vi hanno tradito ad El Alamein.
COMMENTATOR: Italiani che mi ascoltate: segnate a caratteri indelebili nella vostra memoria questo nome: El Alamein. Ricordatelo bene, questo nome, perché negli anni a venire dovrete vendicarlo. Esso segna una disfatta militare tremenda per i tedeschi, ma per voi italiani segna il più grande tradimento che un popolo abbia subito per mano dei propri alleati. Siete stati pugnalati alle spalle, siete stati trattati da straccioni, siete stati insultati nel modo più sanguinoso che la storia di questa guerra ricordi. Siete stati abbandonati. Da chi? Lo sapete bene.
1st VOICE (calm and clear cut): DAI TEDESCHI.[59]

ANNOUNCER: Italians who are listening to me, break this news to your friends: the Germans betrayed you at El Alamein.
COMMENTATOR: Italians who are listening to me, engrave your memory with this name: El Alamein. Remember this name well since in the future you will have to avenge it. It marks a terrible military defeat for the Germans but for you, Italians, it is the biggest betrayal of a population by its own allies. You have been stabbed in the back, you have been treated like tramps, you have been insulted in the bloodiest way this war remembers. You have been abandoned. By whom? You know it.
1st VOICE (calm and clear cut): BY THE GERMANS.

Dialogues between two or more broadcasters were very common at the BBC, since they could entertain listeners while conveying propaganda messages. In this case the employment of more broadcasters and the rhetorical question '*Da chi?*' (By whom?) turned the programme into a theatrical drama. The upper case used for the answer '*DAI TEDESCHI*' (BY THE GERMANS) conveys that the line was meant to be shouted by the broadcaster. Later in the same programme the broadcaster George Foa provided a detailed description of how the treason occurred: the Germans stole Italian aeroplanes, tanks and motor vehicles and escaped, leaving the Italian troops in danger.

In this and other Italian Service programmes, Italian civilians were not blamed for the twenty years of the fascist regime or Italy's declaration of war on Britain. The same applied to the Italian troops, who were never depicted as responsible for the Italian defeat at El Alamein. Rather, both the Italian population and troops were described as the victims of an unfaithful ally and an irresponsible regime. This is not surprising, since a tired and disillusioned army was more likely to desert or refuse to fight against the Anglo-American occupying forces.

According to Filippo Focardi, who has extensively analysed the creation of the myth of the 'bad German' and the 'good Italian' in the post-war period, Anglo-American propaganda misinformed the Italians about El Alamein. The real responsibility for the defeat of the Italian troops lay with the Italian Supreme Command, which had not formulated a plan for retreat. Moreover, Hitler and Mussolini had prevented a first attempt at retreat, when it would have still been possible to escape the British attack.[60] Despite this, as Focardi's study suggests, the Anglo-American propaganda was very effective in persuading the Italians that their soldiers were victims of ruthless German soldiers and generals. This was not the only falsehood that issued from BBC microphones. As Aga Rossi has shown in *A Nation Collapses*, the Anglo-American forces misinformed Italians about the military equipment they held in order to persuade the Italian government that an unconditional surrender to the Allies was the only possible solution.[61] This false information regarding Allied military superiority of the Allies was often repeated by the BBC in 1943.[62]

In December 1942 Germany's presumed opportunism was still being attacked in one of the programmes in the series *Axis Conversation*. The protagonists of *Axis Conversation* were usually a German character and an Italian character who debated controversial issues. The Italian used by Gerlach, the German, included grammar and spelling mistakes. This was an expedient to create a radio character. Gerlach claimed that, despite the damage and the casualties caused by the bombings of Genoa and Turin, the German losses were qualitatively more important, given the superiority of the Germany's factories and cities.

> GERLACH: Quantità di danno a Genova o Torino può essere stato grave. Ma qualità in confronto a Essen è molto meno grave, non è vero?
> MANCINI (scalda): Lei è pazzo. Vada a contarli a quelli di Genova o Torino questa storia! Ma è ridicolo!
> GERLACH (coldly): Eppure dottore, se lei guarda la guerra dal punto di vista dell'alto Comando Tedesco, questa è evidentemente la verità.
> MANCINI: Me ne frego io dell'Alto …
> GERLACH: L'alto comando tedesco deve considerare la qualità del danno. Non può diminuire difese di Essen o Bremen o Koln o altre importantissime città tedesche solo perché Milano o Torino o Napoli non sono state difese bene da Mussolini.[63]

> GERLACH: The amount of damage in Genoa and Turin might have been great. But, in terms of quality, it's nothing compared to Essen, is it?
> MANCINI (angrily): You're mental. Tell it to the people in Genoa or Turin! It's ridiculous!
> GERLACH (coldly): Actually, Doctor, if you look at the war from the High German Commander's point of view, this is clearly the truth.
> MANCINI: I don't care about the High …
> GERLACH: The High German Commander must consider the quality of the damage. It can't remove the protection from Essen, Bremen, Cologne or other very important German cities only because Mussolini didn't provide enough protection for Milan, Turin or Naples.

As the last lines show, Mussolini was accused of not defending Italian cities. This theme was also at the heart of other programmes. Another idea that was challenged by the BBC in those days was the concept of *Lebensraum* (living space), used by Hitler to justify the German expansion into East-Central Europe:

> Ed è vero, poi che gli Italiani si battono per uno spazio vitale? Io credo -e molti sono della mia opinione- che lo spazio vitale degli italiani sia in primissimo luogo l'Italia. Ed il guaio di questa guerra è che la stragrande maggioranza degli italiani è convinta che oggi si combatte non già per l'Italia, ma per la Germania. Infatti più proletari italiani vanno a morire al fronte o a lavorare nel Reich e più dirigenti tedeschi vengono a prendere posizioni di comando in Italia dove essi trovano quello che negli altri Paesi occupati chiamano senza tanti ambagi 'spazio vitale'.[64]

> Is is true that the Italians are fighting for a vital space? I think – and many agree with me – that the vital space of the Italians is, above all, Italy. And this is the problem of this war, that the great majority of the Italians think that today they're not fighting for Italy, but for Germany. As a matter of fact, more and more Italian proletarians are sent to the front to die or to work in the Reich, while more and more executives come to take leadership positions in Italy, where they find what they explicitly call 'vital space' in the other occupied countries.

As Stevens pointed out, the Italians deserved their living space too. Yet the latest developments of the conflicts showed that many Italians were instead working and dying for Germany's space.

A few months later, in April 1943, the defeat at El Alamein was still the subject of many programmes, for example in a broadcast in the series *Sottovoce* (Undertone). The protagonists of *Sottovoce* were a convinced anti-fascist, a fascist and a third person who was disillusioned with Mussolini's regime. In the spring of 1943 it was clear that the situation on the North African front could not be reversed, and the conflict was still going in the Allies' favour. As the anti-fascist character, Paolo, pointed out, this was the only possible consequence of the initial defeats of November 1942. Fascist propaganda, Paolo suggested, should not have hidden the truth from Italians. By doing so the regime had deceived many Italians who were now faced with disappointment and fear:

> PAOLO: Insomma, caro Rossi, concludiamo: ha finito anche lei di sperare nell'Africa
> ROSSI: Per forza ...
> PAOLO: Ha visto. Proprio come le avevamo sempre detto. La sconfitta ad Alamein è stata decisiva. Tutti quei discorsi che si facevano a quell'epoca erano poi tutte chiacchiere. Si ricorda? Ci contavano su che la guerra nel deserto era fatta di altalene ... prima avanzavano gli inglesi ... poi le forze dell'Asse

> ... poi di nuovo gli inglesi e così via di seguito. Tutte balle. Evidentemente la cosa era già messa per il peggio ad El Alamein.
> ROSSI: Va bene, ma anche così, Pravesi: perché avrebbero dovuto venire a dircelo?
> PAOLO: Perché almeno avrebbero detto la verità. E allora anche i tipi come lei si sarebbero resi conto che la guerra in Africa non era più che una gigantesca azione di retroguardia. Allora anche i tipi come lei avrebbero aspettato il crollo del settore meridionale in Tunisia per accorgersi che i combattimenti in Africa si svolgevano già sugli avamposti del territorio italiano. I tipi come lei, infine, avrebbero forse avuto tempo di accorgersi che la guerra italiana- e cioè, più precisamente, la guerra voluta dal Duce- era già persa, finita, seppellita, e che i combattimenti in Africa erano solo una funzione del più ampio piano di strategia difensiva della Germania. Invece lei, Rossi, è andato avanti per un pezzo ad illudersi ancora che in Africa si combattesse ancora- che so io? Per la Tripolitania e la Cirenaica ...[65]

> PAOLO: Anyway, dear Rossi, let's get straight to the point: even someone like you doesn't trust to Africa any more ...
> ROSSI: Of course ...
> PAOLO: See? Exactly like we've always told you. The El Alamein defeat was crucial. All the discussions we had at the time were, after all, chit-chats. Remember? They used to tell us that the war in the desert had ups and downs ... before the English advanced ... then the Axis forces ... then the English again, and so on. All lies. The situation was obviously worse in El Alamein.
> ROSSI: OK, but even in this case, Pravesi, why should they have told us?
> PAOLO: Because at least they would have told us the truth. And even people like you would have realised that the war in Africa was only a giant rearguard action. Even people like you would have waited for the defeat on the Southern front in Tunisia and realised that the African battles were already taking place in the outposts of Italian territory. Finally, people like you would have had time to realise that the Italian war – more precisely, the war the Duce wanted – was already lost, over, buried, and that the battles in North Africa were only part of Germany's broader defence strategy. But you, Rossi, kept on deluding yourself into thinking that in Africa we were fighting for, I don't know, Tripolitania or Cyrenaica.

If Germany was a traitor, the other side of the coin was the irresponsible fascist administration and the lack of effective security measures for the protection of Italian civilians. This topic was debated in a May episode of *La politica in pantofole*, whose characters were an anti-fascist uncle and a nephew working for the fascist MinCulPop:

> UNCLE: Fortificazioni ... fortificazioni ... non si sente parlare d'altro. Non mi verrai a dire che stiamo fortificando anche il Brennero per caso?
> MARIO: Noi no, ma pare che lo stiano fortificando i tedeschi.
> UNCLE: E' un po' strano, non ti pare?

> MARIO: Non è strano, è un gran brutto segno: significa che si stanno preparando per il caso che debbano difendere la fortezza di Europa, <u>al di là</u> della frontiera italiana.
> UNCLE: Avevo ragione allora, ma tutte le volte che ti dicevo che al momento critico la Germania non avrebbe esitato a liberarsi dell'Italia come di un brutto debito, mi hai sempre chiamato pessimista e germanofobo.[66]

> UNCLE: Fortifications ... fortifications ... It's all anybody ever talks about. You don't want to tell me that we are even fortifying the Brennero border, do you?
> MARIO: Not us, but it seems that the Germans are doing it.
> UNCLE: It's a little bit strange, don't you think?
> MARIO: No, it's not strange, it's a really bad sign: it means that they're getting ready in case they'll have to defend fortress Europe over Italian borders.
> UNCLE: I was right, then, but every time I told you that should there be problems Germany wouldn't hesitate to get rid of Italy as if it was a bad debt, you called me a pessimist and a hater of the Germans.

The uncle is here exposing Germany's decision to defend 'Fortress Europe' and strengthen the Eastern front, rather than Southern Italy. As claimed in another programme, broadcast in January 1943, Italians were silently suffering an injustice:

> Il silenzio è un monumento elevato alla concordia dal popolo che soleva offendersi, prima di nascere in nazione, se la sua patria veniva chiamata la terra dei morti...E di stare zitti, come si conviene al condannato costretto a scavarsi la fossa con le proprie mani'.[67]

> Silence is a monument erected to celebrate harmony by people that used to feel offended if, prior to becoming a nation, their country was called the land of the dead. And the Italians need to shut up, exactly like a person who has been sentenced to death and is forced to dig his own grave.

Terra dei morti was the expression used by the French poet Alphonse Delamartine in his *Le Dernier Chant du pèlerinage d'Harold* to refer to nineteenth-century Italy. The decadent political situation of the time was compared to the glory of Italy's ancient past, the only thing the country could be proud of.

In another programme, Mario and his uncle debated the food question. The uncle asked his nephew whether he could provide him with two tickets for a Christmas meal at the *Deutsches Haus*. When the nephew asked his uncle why he wanted to spend Christmas at the *Deutsches Haus* and not somewhere else, the answer was that it was the only place where he could get a decent festive meal:

> MARIO: Vuoi dire alla Deutsches Haus qui a Roma?
> ZIO: Si, proprio quella: la Deutsches Haus.

MARIO: Ma si può sapere perché proprio alla Deutsches Haus?
ZIO: Andiamo Mario non far finta di non sapere perché proprio lì. Tutti sanno che anche nei giorni comuni la Deutsches Haus dà da mangiare delle portate che non si possono ottenere in nessun ristorante di Roma; uova, porzioni di carne spettacolose, burro e qualsiasi altra cosa. Ti puoi quindi immaginare cosa sarà il loro pranzo di Natale!!!![68]

MARIO: Do you mean at the Deutsches Haus here in Rome?
UNCLE: Yes, exactly: the Deutsches Haus.
MARIO: But can you tell me why the Deutsches Haus and not anywhere else?
UNCLE: Come on, Mario, don't pretend not to know why. Everybody knows that, even on an ordinary day, the Deutsches Haus offer courses that you can't find in any other restaurant in Rome; eggs, spectacular portions of meat, butter and any other thing. You can easily imagine what kind of Christmas lunch they will offer!!!

Another aspect of Italian subordination to Germany, suggested a programme aired on 2 March 1943, was Germany's cultural domination of Italy. Again in this case the protagonists were Mario and his uncle. As an employee of the MinCulPop, Mario was supposed to attend a German evening course and had to set a good example by attending every class.

MARIO: Scusami tanto zio, è solo questione di un minuto (parlando con voce differente) Allora, è chiaro signorina? Non dimenticate che questa sera mi sarà impossibile di prendere parte alla lezione di tedesco. Dite che mi dispiace molto, ma che ho un lavoro enorme da sbrigare (parlando allo zio). Ed ora caro zio eccomi tutto a tua disposizione!
UNCLE: Mario, non sapevo che frequentavi un corso di tedesco.
MARIO: Ti dirò che faccio a meno di andarci tutte le volte che posso. Ma sai com'è: il Comitato Interprovinciale dei Giornalisti ha organizzato queste lezioni di tedesco per i suoi membri ed è naturale che anch'io nella mia condizione ufficiale debba dare il buon esempio.
UNCLE: (pensoso) E così la penetrazione continua sempre più profonda e senza soste ...
MARIO: (nervoso) Cosa vuoi dire?
UNCLE: Oh nulla! Pensavo ad alta voce, sai a volte mi succede! Mi pare che (almeno per i miei gusti) ci ammanniscano un po' troppa KULTUR tedesca. (Annoiato) Ogni giorno qualcosa di nuovo: una mostra tedesca, una conferenza tedesca, lezioni di tedesco nelle scuole...e ora non è nemmeno più possibile essere un giornalista a meno che non si sappia leggere *Voelkische Beobachter* nell'edizione originale tedesca.[69]

MARIO: I'm so sorry, Uncle, it will only take a minute (speaking in a different voice) Is it clear, Miss? Don't forget that tonight I won't be able to go to my German class. Tell them I'm so sorry, but I have a huge task to deal with (Talking to his uncle). And now here I am, my dear Uncle, I'm all yours!
UNCLE: Mario, I didn't know you were attending a German course.

MARIO: Well, I try to skip it every time I can, but you know? The Interprovincial Committee of Journalists organised these German classes for its members and obviously, as a public servant, I have to set a good example.
UNCLE: (thoughtful). So the brainwashing continues, deeply and without cease ...
MARIO: (nervous) What do you mean?
UNCLE: Oh, nothing! I'm talking to myself, you know, it happens to me sometimes! I think (at least in my opinion) they teach us too much German KULTUR. (Bored) Every day something new: a German exhibition, a German conference, German classes in schools ... and now you can't even be a journalist any more unless you can read the original German edition of *Voelkische Beobachter.*

The fascist regime is very effectively ridiculed here, with Mario, an official of the regime, depicted as a child who does not want to go to school. Ridiculing the enemy was common in Italian Service programmes. This was especially true for the *Sceneggiati* and the *Monologue of the Little Man*. Some extracts from this programme will be analysed shortly.

The representation of the Nazi-fascist enemy: Badoglio and the RSI

As the programmes analysed thus far have shown, until the Allied landings in Sicily and the fall of Mussolini's regime on 25 July 1943, the Italian Service aimed mainly at discrediting Mussolini and Nazi Germany. This remained unchanged after July 1943. Two new enemies were, however, at the centre of the BBC's programming in Italian: Badoglio's government and the newly formed RSI.

Prior to the fall of Mussolini's regime, the Allies had tried to find a valid political personality who could act as their point of contact in Italy and as the new Italian head of government. The main challenge was to find someone who was both anti-fascist and pro-monarchy. The Italian king's support was crucial. Badoglio was at first considered a suitable candidate. However, his relationship with the Anglo-American forces worsened once he succeeded Mussolini and set up a new government in Brindisi.[70] As will be explained in Chapter 6, this was mostly concerned with the negotiations that led to Italy's unconditional surrender. Moreover, as soon as Badoglio became the head of the government, the Allies realised that he was not a real alternative to Mussolini.

On 26 July, the day after the fall of Mussolini's regime, Radio Londra said that the overthrow of the regime had not resulted in an immediate end of the Italian war on the part of Germany: 'Badoglio afferma di voler afferrarsi a questo trapezio, probabilmente fino a che qualcheduno non gli stenda sotto una rete di salvataggio contro il pericolo di una caduta mortale. Perciò si tiene in casa i tedeschi e continua la guerra' ('Badoglio wants to grab this trapeze, probably until someone puts a safety net under him to prevent the danger of a fatal fall. Therefore the Germans are kept at home and the war continues').[71] Moreover, as Stevens stated in another programme, the end of Mussolini's government was described as a simple administrative crisis, rather than as a radical change of the status quo.[72]

As a programme dated 17 August 1943 suggested, Badoglio's government, in line with Mussolini's regime, kept on repeating to the Italians that the British and the Americans were enemies of Italy:

> Che le nazioni unite abbiano fatto la guerra al fascismo nessuno lo può negare. Il fascismo fu soppresso nelle zone da noi occupate molto prima che Badoglio venisse al potere, ed assai più radicalmente che egli non si sia assunto di fare … Quanto all'affermazione che gli americani e gli inglesi odiano gli italiani, bisogna convenire che Mussolini ed i suoi accoliti queste cose le dicevano in modo molto più pittoresco. Il fascismo soppresso, rivive nelle sue tesi riesumate. La seconda tesi, poi (che l'Italia non vuol divenire campo di battaglia) sembra implicare che il governo Badoglio sarebbe disposto a non rispettare il patto d'acciaio, purché nessuna parte del territorio nazionale venisse usata per le operazioni belliche, e l'Italia tornasse ad essere neutrale come lo era prima del 10 giugno del 1940.[73]

> No one can deny that the United Nations fought fascism. Fascism was suppressed in the areas we occupied, long before Badoglio took power and way more radically than he managed to do … As for the assertion that the Americans and the English hate the Italians, it must be said that Mussolini and his friends used to say these things in a much more colourful way. The suppressed regime has returned to life in the form of his old theories. Moreover, the second theory (that Italy doesn't want to become a battlefield) seems to imply that the Badoglio government will be willing to respect the Pact of Steel only if the national territory is not involved in the military operations and Italy goes back to the neutrality it had before 10 June 1940.

The Pact of Steel ratified the military and political alliance between Italy and Germany, signed on 22 May 1939 by the Italian minister Galeazzo Ciano and the German minister Joachim von Ribbentrop. The implicit message was that the only way of avoiding military operations on the Italian mainland was to break the Pact of Steel because Germany would certainly take advantage of the Italian territories.

On 4 August 1943 Elio Nissim's *Omo Qualunque* (the 'little man') commented on the same topic. His considerations expressed the worries and fears of ordinary Italians. Despite the formation of a new government, Italian civilians could still die at any moment due to a bomb. Italy's destiny was still in Hitler's hands:

> Ma insomma –per zio– a che gioco si gioca? S'è liquidato il capo grosso, s'è sciolto il P.N.F., s'è sciolto un sacco di altra roba ... e l'Asse? Cosa si aspetta a scioglierlo? Perché, intendiamoci bene, qui passano i giorni e si ricomincia con la questione delle bombe. Ma ... ma ... una cosa alla volta, non bisogna avere furia, chi va piano va sano (e si rompe l'osso del collo). Balle! Storie![74]

> But I mean, for God's sake, what's their game? We finished the big boss off, the PNF was banned, a lot of other stuff was banned ... and the Axis? Why don't they ban it? What are they waiting for? Because, let me make this clear, days go by and the bombs come back. But ... but ... one thing at the time, we musn't rush things, whoever goes slowly goes far (and breaks his neck). Bullshit! Lies!

Scepticism towards the Badoglio government was a frequent feature of the BBC programmes during the so called forty-five days.[75] A similar scepticism was used to discredit the RSI as well as those fascists who claimed to be different from Mussolini and his corrupt administration. The RSI was created by Mussolini in the town of Salò at the request of Nazi Germany. This government would control the German-occupied territories in Northern Italy. Only the German-occupied territories and other members of the Axis coalition officially recognised it. Fascists who supported the RSI were called *repubblichini*. The word had been coined in 1793 by the poet Vittorio Alfieri to refer to the founders of the Republic after the French Revolution.[76] It was reused for the first time by Umberto Calosso in a BBC broadcast to label the members of the RSI and its supporters.[77]

After the unconditional surrender of Italy, many fascists who were now supporting the RSI claimed that there had been many faults in the previous regime but that the new Salò government would be different. Moreover, many ex-fascists offered their help to the Allies and declared that they had never supported the regime or that their political beliefs had changed.[78] This, as often repeated by the BBC since the beginning of 1944, was only an opportunistic strategy to save their skins and jump on the bandwagon.

> L'aria diventa sempre più cattiva per i fascisti, dovunque essi si trovino, e anche per quei facili furbacchioni che, tentando di farsi passare per convertiti e compunti democratici, offersero i loro servigi agli Alleati nell'Italia libera. Si apprende oggi che nuove misure sono state prese dalle autorità militari alleate per rimuovere dai pubblichi impieghi tutti i fascisti, e restituire le cariche a coloro che ne erano stati privati per motivi politici.
>
> Questa notizia sarà certo accolta con soddisfazione dai patrioti che combattono soprattutto per sradicare il fascismo, in ogni sua forma e manifestazione, e l'occupazione germanica è solo il culmine logico e naturale di vent'anni di regime. Ed è proprio divertente che i signori fascisti neo-repubblicani ci vengano adesso a dire che tante cose non andavano nel 'blocco granitico' e che a suo tempo (ma sì, a suo tempo, tanto non c'è premura) a suo tempo l'assemblea

costituente metterà tutto a posto. Perché le cose che non andavano nel defunto regime son proprio quelle che ne formano l'essenza stessa, la natura inconfondibile del fascismo, e che i patrioti hanno già condannato con la loro attiva e organizzata resistenza.[79]

The atmosphere is worse and worse every day for the fascists, wherever they are, and for those old foxes who, by trying to pass themselves off as converted and remorseful democrats, offered their help to the Allies in liberated Italy. Today we have heard that new measures were taken by the Allied authorities to remove all the fascists from the public sector and give their jobs to those who had lost them for political reasons.

This news was certainly welcomed by the patriots who are fighting, above all, to eradicate fascism in every form and feature. The German occupation is only the logical and natural culmination of twenty years of the regime. And it is really hilarious that these fascist neo-republican gentlemen now come and tell us that many things did not work in that 'granite rock' and that, when the time comes (yes, the time will come, there is no hurry!) the Constituent Assembly will make things right. Because what did not work in the defunct regime was the essence of it, the unmistakable nature of fascism that the patriots have already sentenced to death with their active and organised resistance.

The word *patrioti* is used in this programme to describe Italian partisans fighting against the German occupying forces and RSI soldiers. As will be explained in more detail in Chapter 7, the word was used to suggest that there were some similarities between the Resistance to the Germans and the Italian Risorgimento against the Austrian Empire of the Hapsburgs.

This programme was broadcast in January 1944. At the end of the year the *repubblichini* and their opportunistic political identity was still being ridiculed in a comic monologue by the 'little man'. Unlike the majority of the other broadcasts of the series, this programme was a dialogue, with the *omo qualunque* being constantly interrupted by annoying characters who burst into the studio. These characters were a *repubblichino* and a turncoat:

ANNOUNCER: E ora vi trasmettiamo 'Un monologo dell'omo qualunque'
OMO QUALUNQUE: Ecco, a me mi viene la rabbia quando penso a tutte le sgraffignature che stanno ancora facendo nell'Italia occupata dai tedeschi, quei farabutti delinquenti dei fascisti repubblichini ...

SPOT: DOOR OPENING SUDDENLY

REPUBBLICHINO: Chi mi chiama? Eccomi qua!
OMO QUALUNQUE: O questo pappagallo in camicia nera? 'Oh che 'un si sta più tranquilli neanche in sala di trasmissione. Fuori! E' uno sbaglio, via ... via ...
REPUBBLICHINO: Ma io sono il neo-repubblichino ...
OMO QUALUNQUE: 47, morto che parla.

REPUBBLICHINO: Sono io, con la fede inconcussa, la devozione indistinguibile, l'obbedienza inconfondibile dei giorni indimenticabili di quelle belle porcherie ... Noi fascisti dell'ante-marcia, dell'ante-ora, dell'ante-rivoluzione, e dell'ante-tutto, della rivoluzione ce ne facciamo un baffo ...
OMO QUALUNQUE: Basta, per carità! Signori tecnici, aiutatemi! Disturbi, interferenze! Fermatelo![80]

REPUBBLICHINO: And now we will broadcast 'Un monologo dell'omo qualunque'
OMO QUALUNQUE: I get mad when I think about the larcenies that those republican fascist scoundrels and criminals are committing in German-occupied Italy ...

SPOT: DOOR OPENING SUDDENLY

REPUBBLICHINO: Who is calling me? Here I am!
OMO QUALUNQUE: Who is this parrot in a black shirt? Can't they leave us alone at least in the broadcasting room? Out! You don't belong here, out ... out ...
REPUBBLICHINO: But I am the neo-republican ...
OMO QUALUNQUE: 47, it's a dead person speaking.
REPUBBLICHINO: It's me, with my everlasting faith, the same devotion, the unmistakable obedience of those unforgettable days of dirty tricks ...
We, the fascists from before the march, before the present, before the revolution, before everything, couldn't care less about the revolution ...
OMO QUALUNQUE: Stop, for God's sake! Technicians, help me! Jamming, interferences! Stop him!

One line of this extract ('47, it's a dead person speaking') is particularly interesting, as it refers to an important aspect of Italian popular culture, a game called *tombola*. The game was often played on the occasion of big family gatherings and it is still an important Italian Christmas tradition, especially in the Southern regions. In the game the number 47 is associated with death. In this case the 47 is connected to the *repubblichino*, who is the expression of a past regime, exhumed under a new guise. The *repubblichino* is followed by the turncoat:

SIGNORE: Scusi, si può? E' permesso?
OMO QUALUNQUE: Oh, quest'altro? Oh che 'un mi lascian più fare neanche il monologo qualunque, per zio?
SIGNORE: Ah, lei sarebbe l'uomo qualunque ...
OMO QUALUNQUE: Qualunquissimo, almeno fino a prova in contrario – e lei?
SIGNORE: Quanto a me, ci tengo subito a dichiarare che io non sono uno di quelli ...
OMO QUALUNQUE: Oh, meno male.

SIGNORE: ... , uno di quelli che dicono: ho fatto questo, ho fatto quello e ho fatto quell'altro ...
OMO QUALUNQUE: Insomma, ho bell'e capito: lei 'un ha fatto nulla.
SIGNORE: E ci tengo a dire che io non sono uno di quelli che vogliono onorificenze, riconoscimenti, decorazioni, gloria, ricchezze, compensi, beni materiali, eccetera eccetera eccetera ... perché io non sono di quelli ...
OMO QUALUNQUE: E ridai!
SIGNORE: Ma certo ci tengo anche ad affermare che se non mi danno un posticino ben pagato ...
OMO QUALUNQUE: Ho capito: è un cavaliere.
SIGNORE: ... Un bell'ufficio riscaldato ...
OMO QUALUNQUE: Ho sbagliato: è un commendatore!
SIGNORE: ... e una bella poltrona girevole ...
OMO QUALUNQUE: Ci sono! E' un uomo politico dell'era fascista. E allora ci vuole una poltrona di molto ma di molto girevole.
SIGNORE: Io non sono uno di quelli ...
OMO QUALUNQUE: Per carità![81]

GENTLEMAN: Excuse me, may I? Can I come in?
OMO QUALUNQUE: Hey, who's this other one? What the hell, they won't even leave me to do my monologue any more!
GENTLEMAN: Would you be the *omo qualunque*?
OMO QUALUNQUE: Yes, very *qualunque*, at least until you can prove the opposite. And you?
GENTLEMAN: As for me, I want to clarify that I am not one of those ...
OMO QUALUNQUE: Oh, thank God!
GENTLEMAN: ... one of those who say 'I did this and that and this other stuff ...'
OMO QUALUNQUE: I got you, you didn't do anything.
GENTLEMAN: And I also want to say that I'm not one of those people who want awards, recognitions, decorations, glory, wealth, rewards, material goods, et cetera, et cetera, et cetera, because I'm not one of those ...
OMO QUALUNQUE: And again!
GENTLEMAN: Of course, and I also want to say that, if they don't give me a well-paid job ...
OMO QUALUNQUE: I got it: you're a knight.
GENTLEMAN: ... A nice warm office ...
OMO QUALUNQUE: I was wrong: you're a commander!
GENTLEMAN: ... and a good swivel chair ...
OMO QUALUNQUE: I got it! You're a politician from the fascist era so you need a really, but really good swivel chair.
GENTLEMAN: I'm not one of those ...
OMO QUALUNQUE: For pity's sake!

As the extract shows, the turncoat is trying to secure a well-paid job in the post-war Italian government. Hence the *omo qualunque* suggests that a chair on wheels is the perfect piece of furniture for his new office, as he will then be able to comfortably change party and political position.

In the dialogue between the *omo qualunque* and the *repubblichino* the word revolution is mentioned. This seems to be a reference to Mussolini's early years as a socialist and editor of the socialist newspaper *L'Avanti*. The theme is also at the centre of a programme in the series *Italian Round-up*:

> Ma certo, proprio di socialismo, del loro socialismo si intende, perché dopo aver sbraitato in tutti i toni che ormai gli Alleati hanno venduto a prezzi rotti l'Europa e specialmente l'Italia al bolscevismo, dopo aver invocato dagli italiani una chiara scelta per l'ordine contro il disordine, soggiungono che il loro neo-fascismo è socialismo della più bell'acqua e che il tempo del capitalismo e della borghesia è finito per sempre.[82]

> Socialism, of course, but their own socialism, as you can imagine. Because, after shouting in every corner that the Allies had already sold the broken pieces of Europe, especially Italy, to bolshevism, and after asking the Italians to choose between order and disorder, they claim that their neo-fascism is nothing but fine socialism and the time of capitalism and bourgeoisie is over forever.

Mussolini and the *repubblichini* called themselves socialists. However, as the BBC pointed out, after twenty years of fascism, they should not expect to be taken seriously.[83]

While the fascists were trying to deny their past or redefine their identity, Italy was still at war. In this case also the *Omo Qualunque* did not miss his opportunity of expressing his opinion as an ordinary man. As in other programmes of the series, the pragmatism of Nissim's little man stood out. There was one common interest that associated all the Italians regardless of their social, cultural or political backgrounds, the end of the war:

> So, as I was saying, at a time like this, when so much can happen from a day to the next, I have said before and I say again: think for yourselves and do not let yourself be muddled by anybody. But now, Badoglio or not Badoglio, all of us in Italy, workers, gentlemen (and there must be precious few of those left), partisans, guerrilla fighters, democrats, right, left and all the rest, we must all agree and get it over faster. All the Allies have recognised that we Italians must govern ourselves as we want: on one hand Badoglio must make room for others and stop being so bossy; and on the other those who were pulling faces at him must stop that and must stop being so stiff.
>
> That is all very well in ordinary times, but now one must be practical above all and think that there is nothing finer than peace without the Germans. Just think of being able to gaze up at the sky without being afraid of getting a bomb on your head. Think of throwing open the windows with all the lights on (someone will have to pay the bill after). And that is the least of it, because what really matters is that no more young men of any country will

be losing their lives. And what matters most to us is that our people will no longer suffer.[84]

The *omo qualunque*, as well as Italian civilians, would still have to face over a year of conflict and bombings instead. The theme of the bombings, as well as the last eighteen months of the conflict, will be further investigated in Chapter 7, where we will analyse BBC programmes about partisan resistance and the actual Anglo-American occupation-liberation of Italy.

One of the aims of this chapter has been to provide some contextual information on the main adversary of the Italian Service, the fascist EIAR, and the ways in which this was challenged by the BBC. The BBC and the EIAR shared a similar institutional history: they were both created on the initiative of private companies and became public institutions after a few years. They also shared an educational function, with both radio stations wanting to turn broadcasts into an instrument for educating the masses.

However, there was a key difference between the BBC and the EIAR. The BBC was the national radio of a democratic country, while the EIAR was born in a totalitarian state. This difference is mirrored by the laws promulgated by the two countries concerning radio and can be considered as one of the reasons for the failure of fascist propaganda. As we have seen, by the beginning of the Second World War the EIAR was strongly controlled by the fascist regime. Moreover, with the outbreak of the conflict the station lost its ability to engage with Italians as individuals rather than as a mass.

Another aim of this chapter has been to demonstrate that many contradictions characterised the BBC's battle against the EIAR. During the war the BBC depicted itself as an ally of the anti-fascist cause. Nevertheless, its anti-fascist propaganda in Arabic only began at the end of the 1930s, when Britain's interests in North Africa and the Middle East were at risk. In addition, the BBC Home Service was constantly in touch with the EIAR even after the Ethiopian war.

These data confirm that the BBC's attitude towards the fascist EIAR was ambivalent. The BBC claimed to be an independent and fair voice. Nevertheless, it clearly manipulated the truth on at least two key moments of the conflict: the battle of El Alamein and the unconditional surrender of Italy. While manipulating the truth in the context of a conflict is a common practice, this is evidently in contrast with the BBC's reputation for objectivity.

As the last two chapters will show, the reception of the programmes in Italy played an important role in building the image of the BBC as a champion of democracy. Moreover, the absence of freedom of expression, the co-operation between the Allies and the partisan brigades, and the precarious living conditions in Italy led to the creation of many legends and myths about Radio Londra.

Notes

1. Franco Monteleone, *La radio italiana nel periodo fascista: studio e documenti 1922–1945* (Venice: Marsilio, 1976), p. 9. Author's translation.
2. Monticone, *Il fascismo al microfono: radio e politica in Italia 1942–45* (Rome: Studium, 1978), p. 1.
3. Monticone, *Il fascismo al microfono*, p. 3.
4. Monteleone, *La radio italiana*, p. 11.
5. There were three main groups competing for Italian radio telegraphy and telephony. These were the Societé Générale de Télégraphie Sans Fil, the German Telefunken and the Società Italiana Servizi Radiotelegrafici e Radiotelefonici (SISERT), connected to Britain (Monticone, *Il fascismo al microfono*, p. 4).
6. David Forgacs, *Italian Culture in the Industrial Era 1880–1980: Cultural Industries, Politics and the Public* (Manchester: Manchester University Press, 1990), p. 64.
7. Cannistraro, *La fabbrica del consenso*, p. 225.
8. Monticone, *Il fascismo al microfono*, p. 9.
9. Cannistraro, *La fabbrica del consenso*, p. 228.
10. Monteleone, *La radio italiana*, pp. 37, 39, 67.
11. Monticone, *Il fascismo al microfono*.
12. Monticone, *Il fascismo al microfono*, p. 45.
13. Cannistraro, *La fabbrica del consenso*, p. 232.
14. Cannistraro, *La fabbrica del consenso*, pp. 234–236; 245.
15. Cannistraro, *La fabbrica del consenso*.
16. Cannistraro, *La fabbrica del consenso*, p. 264.
17. Anna Lucia Natale, *Gli anni della radio (1924–1954): contributo ad una scienza sociale dei media in Italia* (Naples, Liguori, 1990).
18. More information on the cost of radio transmitters as well as numbers of radio owners will be provided in the last chapter of this book.
19. Monteleone, *La radio italiana*, p. 201.
20. Monteleone, *La radio italiana*, pp. 203–206.
21. Monteleone, *La radio italiana*, p. 207.
22. Petrella, *Staging the Fascist War*, p. 171.
23. Petrella, *Staging the Fascist War*, p. 213.
24. Monteleone, *La radio italiana*, p. 208.
25. Monteleone, *La radio italiana*, p. 163.
26. Williams, *Subversion in the Mediterranean*, p. 35.
27. Monticone, *Il fascismo al microfono*, p. 147.
28. Marzano, *Onde fasciste*, pp. 13–14.
29. Marzano, *Onde fasciste*, p. 280.
30. On the employment of music for propaganda purposes at the EIAR see Gioachino Lanotte, *'Segnale radio': musica e propaganda radiofonica nell'Italia nazifascista, 1943–1945* (Perugia: Morlacchi, 2014); *Il 'quarto fronte': musica e propaganda radiofonica nell'Italia liberata, 1943–1945* (Perugia, Morlacchi, 2012).
31. BBC WAC, E1/984/1, EIAR 1930–45, BBC to EIAR, 26 February 1937.

32 BBC WAC, E1/984/1, EIAR 1930–45, EIAR to BBC, 7 Sept 1938.
33 Isabella Insolvibile, *Wops: i prigionieri italiani in Gran Bretagna (1941–1946)* (Naples, Edizioni Scientifiche Italiane, 2012), 27.
34 Insolvibile, *Wops*, 27.
35 BBC WAC, E1/984/1, EIAR 1930–45, List of musical comedies for Italy, 16 September 1938.
36 BBC WAC, E1/984/1, EIAR 1930–45, EIAR to BBC, 28 November 1938.
37 BBC WAC, E1/984/1, EIAR 1930–45, EIAR to BBC, 21 January 1940.
38 BBC WAC, E1/984/1, EIAR 1930–45, BBC to Dr. Crochetti of EIAR, 7 February 1938; EIAR to BBC, 19 May 1939, *Invio fascicoletto con programmi italiani ad onda corta per il mese di giugno*; EIAR to BBC, *Scambio internazionale di artisti*, 4 April 1939.
39 More information about this will be provided in Chapter 7.
40 BBC WAC, E1/984/1, EIAR 1930–45, BBC to Gorini from EIAR, 9 February 1940.
41 BBC WAC, E1/984/1, EIAR 1930–45, EIAR to BBC, 9 March 1940, Info on referendum radiofonico and request of BBC material; BBC to EIAR, Answer to the referendum letter, 21 March 1940.
42 BBC WAC, E1/984/1, EIAR 1930–45, BBC to EIAR, 15 December 1938.
43 BBC WAC, E1/984/1, EIAR 1930–45, EIAR to BBC, 22 September 1937; Chiodelli from EIAR to BBC, 20 July 1938; EIAR to Noel from BBC, 1 February 1939.
44 'Dear Sirs, We wrote to you at the beginning of the month telling you how sorry we were that we should have to discontinue international relays owing to the outbreak of war. We now find that, contrary to expectation, lines between our two countries will be available for broadcasting purposes, so that we should very much like, if you agree, to continue to exchange programmes with you.' BBC WAC, E1/984/1, EIAR 1930–45, BBC to EIAR, 23 September 1939.
45 BBC WAC, E1/984/1, EIAR 1930–45, Chiodelli of EIAR to F. W. Ogilvie of BBC, 4 March 1940. According to Sean Street's definition, a radio relay is 'the dissemination of radio programmes down telephone wires opposed to wirelessly from transmitters ... The idea of sending material down a telephone wire for public –as opposed to private- consumption, had been present from the 1980s. With the development of radio on a mass audience scale in the late 1920s and early 1930s, the idea of wired relays, under license to the Post Office as controllers of the lines, became a key issue in British radio' (Sean Street, *Historical Dictionary of British Radio* (Lanham, MD: Scarecrow Press, 2006)).
46 BBC WAC, E1/984/1, EIAR 1930–45, BBC to EIAR, 15 March 1940.
47 BBC WAC, E1/984/1, EIAR 1930–45, RAI to BBC, *Questioni musicali*, n.d., most likely 1946.
48 BBC WAC, E2/371, Foreign Gen, 1940–47, Extract from the European Service Weekly Bulletin of the BBC, 13 February 1941.
49 Francesco Orestano, 'La vita religiosa nella nuova Europa', *Gerarchia*, December 1942, 476–484.
50 BBC WAC, IS, Scripts, s. I, b. 8, H.R. Stevens, 14 January 1943, 6.40 p.m.; author's translation.

51 BBC WAC, IS, Scripts, s. I, b. 9, H.R. Stevens, 26 March 1943, 6.40 p.m.; author's translation.
52 BBC WAC, IS, Scripts, s. I, b. 9, H.R. Stevens, 28 April 1943, 6.40 p.m.; author's translation.
53 BBC WAC, IS, Scripts, s. II, b. 18, L. Shepley. G.R. Foa, *Progress of Fascist Propaganda n. 1*, 17 May 1943, 5.30 p.m.; author's translation.
54 See Harold Macmillan, *War Diaries: Politics and War in the Mediterranean, January 1943–May 1945* (London: Macmillan, 1984) and Mercuri, *Guerra Psicologica*.
55 C.R.S. Harris, *Allied Military Administration of Italy 1943–1945* (London, HMSO, 1957); F.H. Hinsley, E.E. Thomas, C.F.G. Ransom and R.C. Knight, *British Intelligence in the Second World War: Its Influence on Strategy and Operations, Vol. 3 Part 1* (London: Stationery Office, 1984); R. Bennet, *Ultra and Mediterranean Strategy 1941–1945* (London: Hamish Hamilton, 1989).
56 Pack, *Operation Husky*, pp. 18–21.
57 See Lo Biundo, *London Calling Italy*. Similar anti-German programmes were broadcast by Palmiro Togliatti from Radio Moscow and *Radio Milano Libertà*, a station broadcasting from Moscow on behalf of the Italian Communist Party. See Focardi, *Il cattivo tedesco e il bravo italiano*.
58 BBC WAC, IS, Scripts, s. II, b. 20, F.L.M. Shepley, G. Foa, 7 July 1943, 5.30 p.m.; author's translation.
59 BBC WAC, IS, Scripts, s. II, b. 13, G.R. Foa, *Il Grande tradimento*, 9 November 1942, 4.30 p.m.; author's translation.
60 Focardi, *Il cattivo tedesco*, p. 101.
61 Elena Aga Rossi, *A Nation Collapses: the Italian Surrender of September 1943* (Cambridge: Cambridge University Press, 2000).
62 See Lo Biundo, *London Calling Italy*.
63 BBC WAC, IS, Scripts, s. II, b. 13, L. Shepley, G. Foa, *Axis Conversation n. 60*, 10 December 1942; author's translation.
64 BBC WAC, IS, Scripts, s. I, b. 8, H.R. Stevens, 14 December, 1942, 6.40 p.m.; author's translation.
65 BBC WAC, IS, Scripts, s. II, b. 17, L. Shepley, D. Piani, *Sottovoce n. 71*, 17 April 1943, 5.30 p.m.; author's translation.
66 BBC WAC, IS, Scripts, s. II, b. 18, A. Neugroschel, P. Mortara, *Politica in pantofole n. 53*, 19 May 1943.
67 BBC WAC, IS, Scripts, s. I, b. 9, H.R. Stevens, 21 January 1943; author's translation.
68 BBC WAC, IS, Scripts, s. II, b. 14, A. Neugroschel, P. Mortara, *Politica in pantofole n. 36*, 22 December 1942; author's translation.
69 BBC WAC, IS, Scripts, s. II, b. 16, A. Neugroschel, P. Mortara, G.R. Foa, *Politica in pantofole n. 42*, 2 March 1943; author's translation.
70 Ennio Di Nolfo and Maurizio Serra, *La gabbia infranta: gli alleati e l'Italia dal 1943 al 1945* (Rome: Laterza, 2010).
71 BBC WAC, IS, Scripts, s. I, b. 9, H.R. Stevens, 26 July 1943, ore 6.40 p.m.
72 BBC WAC, IS, Scripts, s. I, b. 8, H.R. Stevens, 30 July 1943, ore 6.40 p.m.

73 BBC WAC, IS, Scripts, s. I, b. 8, H.R. Stevens, 17 August 1943, 6.40 p.m.; author's translation.
74 BBC WAC, IS, Scripts, s. II, b. 21, E. Nissim, *L'uomo qualunque n. 13*, 4 August 1943, 5.30 pm.; author's translation.
75 The expression 'forty-five days' is used to describe the period between the fall of Mussolini's regime (25 July 1943) and the Italian unconditional surrender (8 September 1943).
76 'Repubblichino', *Vocabolario Treccani*, www.treccani.it/vocabolario/repubblichino/, accessed 14 February 2017.
77 Piccialuti Caprioli, *Radio Londra 1940–45*.
78 See Salvatore Lupo, *Il fascismo: la politica in un regime totalitario* (Rome: Donzelli, 2000).
79 BBC WAC, IS, Scripts, s. II, b. 23, Paolo Treves, *Italian Round-up n. 63*, 2 January 1944; author's translation.
80 BBC WAC, IS, Scripts, s. II, b. 32, Elio Nissim, *The Litte Man's interrupted monologue n. 1.*, 3 December 1944; author's translation.
81 BBC WAC, IS, Scripts, s. II, b. 32, Elio Nissim, *The Litte Man's interrupted monologue n. 1.*, 3 December 1944; author's translation.
82 BBC WAC, IS, Scripts, s. II, b. 23, Paolo Treves, Italian Round-up n. 67, 6 January 1944; author's translation.
83 On Mussolini's political career prior to the rise to power of the fascist regime see Renzo De Felice, *Mussolini il rivoluzionario 1883–1920* (Turin: Einaudi, 1965).
84 BBC WAC, IS, Scripts, s. II, Elio Nissim, *Monologue of the Little Man*, 2 April 1944. This is one of the rare English versions of the programmes. In the majority of cases the BBC WAC holds only the Italian transcripts. As a consequence, it is not possible to undertake research on the translation process at the BBC Italian Service.

6

Occupation/liberation

In the previous chapters the dual nature of the BBC Italian Service as both an ally and an enemy radio station has been analysed in the context of the relationship between Italian exiles and the British government (Chapter 4); political interests in the Mediterranean on the occasion of the Ethiopian war and the battle of El Alamein (Chapter 5); and anti-German programmes (Chapter 5).

The correspondence quoted between the BBC and the EIAR in Chapter 4 has demonstrated that the two radio stations exchanged information and material until the Italian entry into the war. In addition, Britain's anti-fascist propaganda only started when the Italian war in Ethiopia put the British colonial interests at risk. This was not in line with the self-representation of Britain as the champion of democracy and anti-fascism. Moreover, despite the BBC's reputation as an impartial source of information, the Italian Service contributed to the distribution of falsehoods about the behaviour of the German troops during the battle of El Alamein.

In this chapter the interpretative key of the occupation/liberation will be applied to some issues relating to the Allies' campaign in Italy: the unconditional surrender of Italy, the problems experienced by Italian civilians in their everyday lives (bombings, food shortages), and the relations between the Allies and the Resistance. The analysis of some programme extracts will show that, in this case also, the rhetoric of the liberation was often in contrast with the actual military interests of the Allied forces.

The forty-five days and Italy's unconditional surrender

As explained in Chapter 5, the period between the Allied landings in Sicily (10 July 1943) and the unconditional surrender of Italy (8 September 1943) is known as the *quarantacinque giorni* (forty-five days). During this time Mussolini's regime was overthrown and a new government established in the south of Italy (Brindisi) by General Marshall Badoglio. Under the new government Italy was still at war on the side of Germany.

The end of the Italian war as a member of the Axis coalition was a cause for debate between Roosevelt and Churchill. The US president wanted Italy's unconditional surrender, whereas the British prime minister preferred a separate peace.[1] A separate peace, said Churchill, would make things easier because it would allow the Allies to rely on Italian institutions and politicians. This would enable them to have a stronger influence on Italian political decisions during the occupation. This solution also implied that Italian institutions would remain the same. Italy would continue to be a monarchy and the king would have to find trustworthy men for the new Italian government. As mentioned in Chapter 5, Badoglio was at first considered a very suitable head of government, since he was anti-fascist but could rely on the support of both the Italian monarchy and army.[2] However, when he actually replaced Mussolini as head of the new government, the Allied authorities began to lose faith in him. During the peace negotiations between the Allies' spokesman, General Eisenhower, and Marshall Badoglio, there was a profound lack of trust. Both parties deceived their counterparts by providing misleading information. In Elena Aga Rossi's words, the armistice between Italy and the Allies was an *inganno reciproco* (mutual deceit).[3]

The fraud was perpetrated by the Allies for two main reasons. First of all, in order to persuade Italy that its unconditional surrender was the most convenient solution, they exaggerated the extent of their military supplies. Therefore, as the Allied authorities claimed, Italian military assistance against Germany was not necessary. This falsehood was supported by British radio propaganda. In the months preceding the Allied landings in Sicily, the BBC constantly repeated that the Allies' military resources were superior in number and strength.[4]

The second reason relates to the existence of a short armistice on military issues, and a long armistice that concentrated on politics. The short armistice included a clause that obliged Italy to commit to the long armistice. However, the long armistice was supposed to remain secret, since it did not offer advantageous conditions to Italy.[5]

On 2–3 September 1943 an agreement was reached in Cassibile: Italy would support Operation Giant 2, as the invasion of Rome was called, and would receive a US airborne division. Badoglio requested that the news of the Italian surrender to the Allies should not be made public until the Allies' arrival because German troops would certainly attack Rome after hearing the news. It was not a coincidence that, after the fall of Mussolini, Germany increased its military garrisons in Italy.

In reality, when Allied troops arrived in Rome on 8 September 1943, no one was defending the city since Badoglio had not mobilised the army against Germany. On the night of 7–8 September General Maxwell Taylor went to Rome to verify that everything was prepared for their arrival. When Taylor realised that Italy was not ready for Giant 2, Badoglio tried to postpone the whole operation. However, Taylor answered that the invasion would still go ahead.[6]

The Allies had obtained what they wanted. While they did not find the military support they were expecting, Italy was out of the conflict. Moreover – and this was another Allied objective – Italy was not an ally but a co-belligerent:

> The local commanders and their political advisers soon discovered that many elements of Italian life – ex-Fascists, non-Fascists, anti-Fascists – wished Italy to become a kind of ally and that they needed Italian help to keep life going behind the lines and to fight the campaign. The result was the idea of 'co-belligerency', 'which means treating the Italians as friends and foes at the same time', as the Foreign Office said disparagingly.[7]

The unconditional surrender of Italy was a controversial topic at the BBC Italian Service. During the forty-five days Radio Londra constantly repeated that it was the only possible solution for Italy. In August 1943 there was no single day on which the unconditional surrender was not mentioned at the BBC Italian Service.

Nevertheless, the documents of Umberto Calosso's archive as well as some correspondence between Colonel Stevens and Bruce Lockhart show that the unconditional surrender caused misgivings and concerns among some members of the Free Italy movement. According to Maura Piccialuti Caprioli, the movement expressed different positions on the surrender of Italy. However, the only member who explicitly mentioned a separate peace in the *Free Italy Talks* was Umberto Calosso.

This is what a *Free Italy* talk from 6 June 1943 said about the end of the war for Italy:

> No, it is not only the President of the United States and the British Prime Minister who say to the tyrants, in Lincoln's words: 'Unconditional surrender'. It is the whole Italian people who want unconditional liberation without compromises, from which everything tinged with Fascism is cast out.[8]

On 18 July *Free Italy* continued to repeat the message that Roosevelt and Churchill's conditions were reasonable.

> Fourth: There is nothing dishonourable in the capitulation asked of the Italian people, because they are asked to give up, not a struggle between equally-matched opponents, but un unequal struggle in which one of the opponents,

morally and materially supported by the whole world, can display overwhelming superiority[9]

A few months earlier, in November 1942, Umberto Calosso had expressed a completely different opinion on the issue. The only fair solution for Italy would be a separate peace instead:

> Pace separata! sia questa la parola d'ordine che la nostra società clandestina raccolta intorno alla radio e a porte chiuse difende intorno a sé, affinché essa diventi un grido travolgente nelle città, nelle campagne e nell'esercito. Pace separata! Pace separata immediata! Basta con le guerre! Quest'inverno non più in guerra.[10]

> Separate peace! May this be the slogan that our secret association, gathered around the radio and behind closed doors, promotes with the aim of turning it into an enthusiastic cry in the cities, in the countryside and among the army. Separate peace! Immediate separate peace! Stop wars! No more war this winter!

A separate peace, continued Calosso in the same programme, would not ruin Italy's military reputation and would clearly show the entire world that there was a difference between valorous Italians and fascists. It would also allow Italy a respectable position in post-war Europe. In February 1943 Calosso was still in favour of a separate peace, which would allow the money spent on the conflict to be invested in more important areas such as education and industry.[11]

A month later, in March 1943, Calosso spoke to Italian soldiers. The message was in line with his previous programmes:

> Pace immediata! E perché questo motto potesse diventare realtà era necessaria la collaborazione dell'esercito: È importante che la storia possa scrivere che l'esercito italiano si è opposto a questa viltà, che il Maresciallo fascista è una cosa e l'esercito italiano è un'altra cosa. Guai a noi se non facesse così. Ma è così, è così.[12]

> Immediate peace! In order to turn this slogan into reality, the collaboration of the army is necessary. It is important that the Italian army make history by opposing this cowardice and showing that the fascist Marshal and the army are two different things. Woe betide us if this were not the case. But this is the case, this is the case.

Calosso also read out some extracts from a clandestine magazine published in Savoy, entitled *Parola del soldato*.

In August 1943, once the military occupation of the Italian mainland was a reality, Calosso's opinion did not change. On 22 August he invited Italians to grab a pencil and some paper and write down a list of Italian priorities. The first item on the list was the peace treaty between Italy and the Allies. A fair treaty should be based on the rights of the people and should follow Mazzini's ideas and the Atlantic Charter.[13]

As these extracts have shown, none of Calosso's programmes mentioned the unconditional surrender as a good option for Italy. Moreover, Calosso was not the only Italian employee who did not support Churchill and Roosevelt's line. In August 1943 Colonel Stevens sent a letter to Bruce Lockhart in which he expressed some concerns about a conversation he had with some Italian broadcasters:

> Dear Bruce Lockhart,
> It came as a great surprise to me a few days ago when I discovered through a chance conversation with an Italian colleague, his reaction to the recent developments. I have since discussed the question with several other Italians who have not much in common except their anti-Fascism and a distinctly pro-English attitude. On one essential I find general agreement: it is roughly this: 'British propaganda has for years differentiated between Fascists and Italian people. It has conveyed to the Italians, especially during the last few months, the message that if they got rid of Fascism they would receive a different treatment. The Italians now find that, though they have got rid of Fascism, so far from being treated differently they are faced, as uncompromisingly as ever, with unconditional surrender. This they feel is a fraudulent trick, which is only aggravated by speaking in the same breath of honourable peace and unconditional surrender.'[14]

Stevens answered these Italians by saying that the British propaganda had only said that Britain and Italy had two enemies in common: fascism and Nazi Germany – but this was not an honest answer. In fact, before the Allied landings in Sicily Radio London did say that the fascist regime and the Italian population were different. Yet Stevens invited Lockhart to take into consideration the opinions of these Italians and address their concerns. Lockhart's response does not seem to be among the Foreign Office records, but Stevens's letter was forwarded to another member of the Foreign Office whose name is not specified. Stevens, said Lockhart in the message to this colleague, was famous for siding with the Italians, and his request should be ignored.[15] This was not the first time that Stevens tried to mediate between the Foreign Office and Free Italy movement. As we have seen in Chapter 4, he defended the movement's interests when the BBC wanted to stop subsidising it. The Italian Service, said Stevens on that occasion, needed some programmes that mirrored Italians' viewpoints on the future of their country. Unfortunately, Stevens's letter includes no detail that allows us to identify the Italian broadcasters he mentions, but it is very likely that these were members of Free Italy.

Evidence of criticism towards the BBC can also be found in another document in Calosso's archive. This document is signed by the Comitato d'azione per l'unione del popolo italiano and discusses several issues relating to British propaganda towards Italy. Some of the arguments used in the British propaganda were regarded as inappropriate by the authors of the text:

> Prendiamo in considerazione un esempio concreto – in questi ultimi giorni è stato spesso ripetuto da Londra agli Italiani: i bombardamenti distruggeranno le vostre città, cessate la vostra resistenza. Ma è esattamente il contrario che si deve dire, non si deve fare appello alla paura, se si vuole che il popolo italiano agisca, ma al coraggio e all'eroismo patriottico. Non è cessate di resistere quello che si deve dire, ma il contrario: rafforzate la vostra Resistenza al governo del traditore Mussolini, passate all'attacco contro questo governo, e così via.[16]

> Let's look at a practical example – in recent days London often repeated to the Italians: bombings will destroy your cities, stop your resistance. But they should say exactly the contrary, they should not appeal to their fear, if they want the Italian population to react, but to bravery and patriotic heroism. They should not be saying 'stop to resist' but, the opposite: 'strengthen your resistance to the government of Mussolini the traitor, go on the offensive against the government of Mussolini the traitor', and so on.

Also in this case it is not possible to ascertain the identities of the individuals who wrote the document on behalf on the Comitato, but it seems that these people were close to Calosso and the BBC since they expressed their disappointment to him. The BBC, they said, was not listening to their advice. Radio London's programmes should be the voice of the Italians rather than the voice of the British.

The next section will focus on the everyday issues experienced by Italian civilians due to the conflict and the ways in which the radio addressed them.

Broadcasting the Italian campaign: bombings, food and cultural heritage

In March 1943 the BBC Italian Service began the so-called 'war of nerves', as one PWE directive to the BBC put it. This strategy consisted of repeating the message that 'the end of the Tunisian campaign would be followed by further blows at the Axis' underbelly without predicting where the blows would fall'.[17] This 'psychological war', consistent with the broader Allied objective of undermining civilian morale, consisted of creating a feeling of uncertainty and danger.[18]

During the same months the PWE concurrently repeated that the BBC should take a friendly approach to attract Italians' interest.[19] In other words, the Allies needed to guarantee the collaboration of civilians, or at least the non-obstruction of their military operations. It was crucial to stress that the British were not fighting against Italy as a country, but were instead combating Mussolini's dictatorship. The Italians and the fascist regime, as the station reiterated until the Allied landings in Sicily, should be considered as two separate entities. Furthermore, if the Italians rejected the fascist regime they would not receive poor treatment at the hands of the occupying troops.

The second step was to convince the population that the British would improve their living conditions by ensuring their safety and providing food. Regardless of their Italian origins, civilians would be treated as if they were British citizens.

In this regard, the bombings of Italian cities as well as the food issue were the object of discussions in many programmes broadcast around the time of the victory at El Alamein, the Allied landings in Sicily and during the actual occupation. Mussolini's regime was usually held responsible for the deaths of many civilians for not planning security measures to protect the Italian population:

> A Genova, in una sola notte, in una sola ora, in un solo rifugio, trovarono la morte in proporzione al numero degli abitanti delle città più vittime che non in due anni di bombardamenti sulla Gran Bretagna. Vittime, non delle bombe britanniche, ma della irresponsabilità e della inefficienza rivelate in circostanze tragiche dal malgoverno fascista.[20]

> In just one raid on Genoa, more people were killed, in proportion to the population of the town, than in two years of bombing Great Britain. It happened in a single shelter, in the course of one brief hour, and the casualties were not caused by the British bombs, but by the Fascist misgovernment – as irresponsible as it is inefficient.

Programmes describing the situation in Britain were also very frequent. Their aim was to point out the differences between fascist mismanagement and the care of the British government for its civilians. British authorities, as these programmes often repeated, supplied their citizens with air-raid shelters and gas masks and evacuated the children before the beginning of the war.

> Volete sapere com'è entrata in guerra l'Inghilterra? Distribuendo, prima di tutto, 46 milioni di maschere antigas. Poi ordinando lo sgombero di tutti i bambini e di tutti gli organismi amministrativi. Costruendo quindi, per coloro che erano rimasti, dei rifugi antiaerei sotterranei in ogni piazza e in ogni parco, e dei rifiuti in cemento armato, in ogni via. Poi è passata ad organizzare le sue difese contraeree; e finalmente ha costruito un numero tale di caccia diurni e notturni, da rendere sempre più precarie e problematiche le incursioni della Luftwaffe. Allora – ed allora solamente, ha pensato ai grossi bombardieri ed alle altre armi offensive che si impongono oggi nei cieli e sui campi di battaglia.[21]

Do you want to know how England went into the war? First of all, by distributing 46 million gas masks. Second, by ordering the evacuation of all children and all administrative institutions. Then in every square and in every park they built underground air-raid shelters for those left behind, and shelters made out of reinforced concrete in every street. Then England went on to organise its air defence; and finally it built enough fighter planes to make the Luftwaffe's air raids more and more difficult and dangerous. Then, and only then, did England build its big bombers and all the other weapons which now dominate the skies and the battlefields.

As Dietmar Süss has noted, the significance of air-raid shelters 'in propaganda terms extended far beyond deep bunkers and sturdy cellars'.[22] From the beginning of the conflict Germany and Britain showed a particular interest in the social structure of air-raid shelters as key to overcoming the fears of the civilians; shelters played a big role in supporting their morale. While it is true that Great Britain had invested in shelters, 'the mass production of individual shelters was preferred over larger tunnels or bunkers above ground'.[23] This measure proved to be insufficient in autumn 1940, when London was heavily bombed for the first time. Hence the British government began opening Tube tunnels to provide public shelters to its citizens.[24] As for Italy, evacuation plans were seen as a cheaper alternative to shelters. Nevertheless, in June 1940, when Italy entered the war, 'Fascist Italy attempted evacuation measures that could not be implemented.' Moreover, for the entire conflict no clear evacuation measures were planned. [25]

Proof of the differences between the British and the Italian security measures, another programme in November 1942 suggested, was the stoical attitude of British civilians towards the unforeseen tragic circumstances brought about by the war. The programme describes a typical day for Mr Smith, the protagonist, during wartime. After hearing the air-raid siren, Mr Smith goes to his allocated air-raid shelter as usual but, unfortunately, the conclusion of that particular day is not so ordinary because his house is destroyed by a bomb. In spite of this disastrous event Mr Smith's self-control is worthy of admiration:

> Casa, mobili, proprietà, il risultato di 20 anni di onesto e onorato lavoro, tutto andato in fumo. Che fare? Disperarsi? Piangere? Neanche per sogno. Il signor Smith, con passo sicuro si reca al Citizens Advice Bureau. C'è una coda di forse 20 persone, tutte destituite come lui, tutte vittime del bombardamento come lui, senza casa, senza averi, senza vestiti, senza soldi. In meno di mezz'ora la coda è scomparsa. Mister Smith ha ricevuto 20 sterline quale soccorso immediato (salvo in pochi giorni avere il resto della cifra stabilita per il compenso degli averi perduti). Ha ricevuto un buono per un vestito, un soprabito, biancheria, scarpe che gli verranno consegnate in poche ore. E, più importante di tutto, ha

ricevuto una carta ove si dice che 'il signor Smith è autorizzato ad occupare immediatamente l'appartamento numero tal dei tali in via tal dei tali'.[26]

His house, furniture, personal belongings, twenty years' worth of honest and honourable work all gone up in smoke. What was he to do? Despair? Cry? Certainly not! Mr Smith, at a brisk pace, went to the Citizens' Advice Bureau. There were about 20 people queuing, all homeless like him, all victims of the bombs like him, no clothes, no money. In less than half an hour the queue disappeared. Mr Smith received £20 for immediate aid … He received a voucher for a suit, an overcoat, underwear and shoes, which were delivered to him a few hours later. And, most importantly, he received a paper upon which it was stated that 'Mr Smith is allowed to occupy a real flat on a real street immediately.'

Before July 1943 the food question was another highly debated issue in Italian Service programmes. In this case too, comparisons were made between Italy and Britain to reinforce the image of the British administration as both reliable and responsible.

The food situation in Britain, as BBC broadcasters often said, was proof of the substantial efforts the British government made to satisfy the essential needs of its population. Fascist propaganda was, however, trying to discredit the British government by misinforming Italians about the distribution of food in Britain:

> Perchè la propaganda fascista si accenna a dimostrare che le condizioni alimentari in Inghilterra sono disastrose? – Come dice un pezzo che vi sarà letto tra pochi istanti? Perchè lo fa? Per tante ragioni: intanto, per il principio antichissimo e proverbiale del 'mal comune mezzo gaudio'. E' un tema che serve egregiamente a far sperare che gli inglesi sian stufi della guerra quanto gli italiani. Dimostrare che c'è scarsezza di cibo in Inghilterra equivale a dimostrare che la campagna marina va a gonfie vele.[27]

> Why is fascist propaganda trying to show that the food situation in England is disastrous? An article, which will be read to you shortly, claims this. Why does it? For many reasons: first of all, for the oldest and proverbial principle that 'trouble shared is a trouble halved'. It is a theme that let [the fascist regime] hope that the English are as tired of the war as the Italians. An attempt to show that there is a shortage of food in England is the same as saying that the marine campaign is going gloriously well.

At the end of the programme, an extract is quoted from an article published by the Italian newspaper *Il Messaggero* on the 'precarious British food situation'. As Isobel Williams notes, before Operation Husky the food situation in Italy was not positive. Italian food production had decreased considerably since the beginning of the conflict, evidenced by the gradual calorific reduction in the average daily diet of Italian citizens (from 2,652 calories in 1936 to

1,733 by 1945). 'Ten percent of Italy's wheat yield was sent to Germany in 1942, as well as supply of 'rice, tobacco, cheese, fruits and vegetables.'[28] This exploitation increased even more during the German occupation. Broadcasts about food rations were therefore a very effective propaganda tool. They also provided the perfect pretext to introduce the theme of the diet of prisoners of war:

> Non voglio dire tutto quello che hanno trovato perché vantarsi di una tavola imbandita è antipatico e volgare, ma hanno trovato che il pane non era razionato, che le patate e le verdure abbondavano, che la pasta non era razionata. Hanno scoperto che al ristorante si possono consumare tutti i pasti che si vogliono senza tagliandi. La carne è in menu tutti i giorni…E gli italiani? Possono chiedere a me, oppure possono chiedere informazioni sulla situazione alimentare in Inghilterra ai prigionieri di guerra italiani recentemente rimpatriati dall'Inghilterra.[29]

> I do not want to mention everything they found, since to boast about a sumptuously decked table is as unpleasant as it is rude, but they found that bread was not rationed, that there were plenty of potatoes and vegetables, and that pasta was not rationed. They found that in the restaurants people could order all the food they wanted without coupons. Meat was on the menu every day … But what about the Italians? They can ask me, or they can ask the Italian prisoners of war who have been recently repatriated from England.

As Isabella Insolvibile's study has shown, there was a huge difference between imprisonment in the Anglo-American and the French, Soviet or Axis camps. Italian prisoners in British or US camps never experienced hunger and malnutrition, not even towards the end of the war, when rations were considerably reduced to help the economies of those countries who were already out of the conflict.[30] Moreover, the Anglo-American authorities tried to adjust the prisoners' diet to their habits in their country of origin. To provide just one example, the diets of German and Italian prisoners were significantly different. The diet for Italians included greater quantities of carbohydrates such as bread and pasta.[31] Therefore, the BBC's reports in relation to prisoners' diets was close to reality. Moreover, as a British informant told the BBC in 1941:

> The average Italian does not care much about abstract justice, nor about honour and principle. He wants his ration of flour or polenta increased and his taxes eased off. If you could persuade him that this would be the result of a British victory, you would do a great deal more than by theorising as who was right or wrong over the Abyssinian campaign.[32]

As the next extracts confirm, this is indeed what the BBC did to persuade Italians that they would benefit greatly from an Allied victory. Whilst the texts examined so far extol the responsible and careful British administration, in July 1943 Radio London talked explicitly about the improved quality of life promised by the Allies. A programme dated 17 July gives an account from a Frenchwoman about the Allies' arrival in Tunis:

> Giorni addietro ho avuto occasione di sentire alla radio una signora francese la quale raccontava che le truppe alleate quando sono giunte a Tunisi avevano portato con loro dei quantitativi di latte in scatola, destinati ai bambini. Lo stesso era avvenuto qualche mese fa a Tripoli, dove ai bambini italiani e arabi era stato distribuito latte condensato e in polvere subito dopo l'occupazione. Se si vuole spiegare questa gentilezza d'animo basta vedere quello che si fa qua in Inghilterra per i bambini, e soprattutto, per la loro alimentazione.[33]

> Days ago, I happened to hear a Frenchwoman on the radio who said that, when the Allied troops arrived in Tunis, they brought large quantities of canned milk for the children. The same had happened some months before in Tripoli, where condensed and powdered milk was distributed to Italian and Arab children after the occupation. If you want to find an explanation for this kindness of heart, you will only have to observe what England does for its children and particularly for their nutrition.

After a detailed description of the food rations for children in Britain, the broadcaster concluded that the experience in Tunis would be repeated in Sicily. Allied troops would provide food and ensure the health of all children. The implied message was that Italian mothers could rest assured that their children would receive good care.

After the Allied landings in Sicily, it certainly became easier for the BBC to talk about the Anglo-American successes. Many programmes dated July 1943 refer to the joy of North Africans and Sicilians and to the warm welcome the Allies received in the conquered territories. It became more difficult, however, to handle topics such as the safety and wellbeing of the population, since the Italian campaign proved to be more difficult and slow than initially expected. While the Allies were now liberating Italy as promised, 'the new invaders soon discovered that between the abstract ... and the physical realities of Southern Italy in late 1943, there lay a world and more of difference'.[34]

AMGOT was now the Anglo-American institution in charge of administering the conquered territories. As such, it was central to emphasise what its Control Commission was doing to support the reconstruction of Italy. Moreover, there were now two Italys and it was crucial to demonstrate that Southern Italy, in the hands of the occupation troops, was better administered than the North. As Calosso said in March 1944, six months after the unconditional surrender of Italy, conditions in Southern regions were already changing:

> Despite the pompous statements during twenty years of Fascist misrule, the South was still much poorer than the North: the industries were still concentrated

in the Valley of Po; the motor-roads in the North were built at the expense of the railway in the south; illiteracy, which comprised 4% of the population in Piedmont rose as high as 48% in Calabria. Despite all that, Southern Italy has got somewhere in six months. If the Allies behaved like Fascism which had a ruinous hypnotic effect on the nerves of the Italians before their harsh awakening, it would be easy to gag the press and the parties, beat the big drum and announce that Southern Italy is the land of plenty ... And for the first time, an important thing, Southern Italy has taken the lead over the rest of the country and is making itself heard all over oppressed Europe, of which it is the first free corner.[35]

The Italian Service started claiming that the Allies were doing their best to distribute provisions. However, the war was difficult and there were many obstacles to overcome before Italy could remedy its shortage of supplies.[36] The importation and distribution of food were mainly obstructed by military operations and German attacks on the main communication routes.[37] Also, it would take some time before Italian factories could access all the raw materials, machinery, transport, power and fuel required to begin producing properly again. Nevertheless, as Colonel Stevens claimed in November 1944, the Allied forces were gradually rehabilitating Italian industry, as the increased production of essential goods in liberated Italy showed.[38]

As for bombings, it may not be a coincidence that the number of broadcasts about bombs decreased in 1944–45. Information about bombings in Italy was still aired, but became less common in the BBC schedule. As Gabriella Gribaudi notes, at the end of the Second World War the Allies refused to accept their responsibility for deaths caused by their bombings. Their bombs were to be regarded as different from the Axis bombs because they were dropped to defeat Nazi-fascism.[39] The theme of the casualties caused by air raids was certainly difficult to handle during the Italian campaign. When bombs were included in the programme themes, the BBC adopted a mild approach and references to human victims in Italy were almost entirely absent.

With reference to the damage caused by air raids, Radio London began mentioning the measures taken by the Allies to protect and restore historical monuments instead, as several programmes show:

> La guerra ha le sue esigenze, ma nei limiti del possibile, le forze alleate, consapevoli dell'importanza delle opere d'arte e degli edifici storici nel quadro della civiltà europea, si preoccupano di sottrarli agli orrori della guerra, o comunque di limitare i danni. Questo ha dichiarato ieri alla camera dei comuni il Ministro della guerra Sir James Grigg, il quale ha pure dato particolari precisi sulle misure prese dagli Alleati per salvaguardare il patrimonio artistico nelle zone d'operazione.[40]

The war has its toll, but, as far as possible the Allied forces are aware of the importance of artwork and historical buildings. With regard to European civilisation, they are trying to spare everyone from the horrors of war, or at least to limit the damage. This was declared yesterday in the House of Commons by the Minister of War Sir James Grigg, who also provided detailed information on the measures taken by the Allies to safeguard artistic heritage in the operational zones.

Under the supervision of expert archaeologists, the text continues, special divisions were already working in the liberated territories, restoring the most damaged buildings and protecting items of cultural value that had been passed down through thirty centuries of history.

A month later, Radio Londra said that the British authorities had started to collaborate with the Sovrintendenza alle Belle Arti Italiana (Secretariat of Italian Fine Arts) to rescue numerous monuments from destruction.[41] From February 1944 the Allied air forces tried to find a compromise between military needs and respect for monuments and sites of historical and artistic value. As a consequence, heritage sites were divided into three groups: 'those that were absolutely to be avoided', 'those that were to be avoided if possible' and 'those that could be bombarded and attacked without any qualms'.[42]

The theme of the protection of heritage sites recurred several times in the BBC's Italian programmes during 1944, especially in those cases where the Allies were operating close to cities which had valuable cultural treasures. For example, the day before the liberation of Rome the Italian Service transmitted a declaration from General Maitland Wilson, the Supreme Allied Commander in the Mediterranean theatre, on the cultural prominence of the city:

> Le autorità alleate tengono presente che ROMA è la sede pontificia e che essa include lo Stato neutrale della Città del VATICANO. E' perciò ferma intenzione dei governi alleati e delle autorità militari alleati di continuare (compatibilmente con le necessità militari) a prendere ogni precauzione possibile per salvaguardare la popolazione di ROMA e i monumenti storici e religiosi della urbe.[43]

> Allied authorities know very well that ROME is the Pope's residence and that the City includes the neutral State of VATICAN City. It is, therefore, the firm intention of the Allies and their military authorities to take all measures possible to safeguard the population of Rome as well as the historical and religious monuments in the city.

But, as another programme stated, the role of the Allied forces also included helping the country to reconstruct its political life. The Anglo-Americans were collaborating with local authorities, aiming for an independent and free Italy as soon as possible. However, Radio Londra claimed, there was still a substantial obstacle to Italian democracy: the German forces. The programme once again opened with talk of the 'hard and difficult war'. Only by destroying Hitlerism could the Allies finally rebuild 'a world where the governors keep the governors in check, a world where authority, work and money are shared as equally as possible'.[44]

'Patriots builders of the future': a second Risorgimento and a new democratic Europe

The previous section of this chapter has analysed the ways in which the Allied authorities and their gradual occupation/liberation of Italy have been described by the BBC. This section will concentrate on a key aspect of the biennial 1943–45: the partisan Resistance. Between 1943 and 1945 the Italian Service broadcast many programmes about the Italian partisans. The aim of these programmes was either to provide operational information to the partisan brigades or to praise their actions. Also in this case relations between the Allies and the partisan Resistance were ambiguous. As Claudio Pavone writes in relation to the Allied coalition:

> As the Resistance came to be recognised by the Allies – for whom, it should be noted, recognition was the best way of controlling it – there were increasing manifestations of intolerance of their presence and of the way they provided their help, which, nevertheless, the Allies knew they could not do without.[45]

But the same reasoning, continues Pavone, referring to the work of Henri Michel, applies to the Resistance:

> As Henri Michael has written, towards the Allies the entire European Resistance 'manifests both gratitude and unease, a faith that weathers the worst trials and a desire for self-determination, that is to say for revolt' – all the more so in the case of the Italian Resistance, which had to reckon with an 'enemy ally'.[46]

While the Allies and the partisans shared the common aim of defeating Nazi-fascism, the troops of the Allied coalition were still perceived as enemies. The Italian Resistance has been described by Pavone as a patriotic war against two foreign forces (Germany and the Allied occupation forces);[47] a civil war against fascist Italy; and class war against capitalist elites. It is on the patriotic aspects of the Resistance that the next pages will focus.

The Italian Resistance has been often described as a second Risorgimento. The Risorgimento led to Italian independence from the Hapsburg Austrian Empire. Similarly, the aim of the Resistance was liberation from Germany. The expression 'Second Risorgimento' was commonly used in newspapers and magazines published after 1945.[48] Both fascist and anti-fascist personalities made use of the Risorgimento rhetoric to refer to their present:

> More or less all the political and ideological positions of the Resistance movement, and indeed of the Fascists too, chose their special bit of the Risorgimento

to refer to. The two largest movements – the Garibaldi brigades militarily, the Action Party politically –gave themselves names that evoked the Risorgimento veins which, in the struggle for hegemony in the new state, had succumbed to the liberal-moderate monarchic solution.[49]

Mussolini, for example, made comparisons with the Risorgimento on more than one occasion: with reference to the conditions imposed on Italy by the Treaty of Versailles at the end of the First World War; and over the German *Anschluss* and the creation of the Axis coalition.

The parallelism between the Risorgimento and Resistance, as noticed by Philip Cooke, continues to animate Italian political debate. The tracks of this *topos* can be found in urban spaces, films, and public celebrations on the occasion of national anniversaries.[50] Given the widespread use of the Risorgimento–Resistance rhetoric, suggests Cooke, the word *topos* is perhaps more appropriate than the expression 'historical parallelism': We are dealing with a rhetorical topos that is very ofen used in various historiographic and cultural contexts, and by many politicians including Pertini, Saragat, Spadolini, Veltroni, Ciampi and even Umberto Bossi who, in 1991, shouted to the ecstatic public in Varese: 'We will be the leaders of a second Risorgimento', even though this has nothing to do with the Resistance.[51]

As the next pages will show, despite the ambivalent relationship between the Allies and the Resistance fighters, the BBC Italian Service contributed to the creation of this *topos*. In several programmes the partisans were compared to Garibaldi and Mazzini.

One example is a programme broadcast on 9 May 1944 on the anniversary of Mazzini's death. During the programme a message written by Mazzini in November 1848 was read out. The broadcaster, Aldo Bergamasco, introduced the quotation by saying that Mazzini's lines inspired him in his years of exile in London. With these lines, the broadcaster continued, Mazzini spoke to young men:

> It is for the people to remake the country with their money and their blood. The men of the national party must make the people understand this truth which is too often forgotten, namely that a nation can only be regenerated by its own efforts, by the sweat of its brow, by prolonged sacrifice and deep awareness of its rights and its duty.
>
> I call men of the national party all those who have not sold their gifts and their souls to a ministry, a sect, a prince or a reigning house of their own ends, but have religious beliefs in the nation and its sovereignty and order their thoughts, acts and teaching in such a way that the country, free and not subject to any disruptive, vicious, immoral influence, may decide its own destiny legally and after nature consideration ... That is what Mazzini wrote 96 years ago, although his words could describe the position today. The words he

addressed to the Italian fighters and workers of 1848 still apply to the workers and fighters of 1944.[52]

After 96 years the Italian political situation was very similar. The new 'sellers of their souls' to a ministry or a prince, the programme suggests, were those who supported Hitler and the RSI. At the end of the programme, more detailed comparisons between events from the Risorgimento and the Resistance were made:

> The list of places where the people won themselves sovereignty in 1848 is almost exactly the same as such a list today. The Milan strikers of 1944 are worthy descendants of the Milanese who fought on the barricades in 1848. The volunteers of 1848 who defied the mightiest reactionary armies of Europe with a handful of cartridges have been imitated by their descendants fighting in the partisan units ... The Italian people fighting against Nazi-Fascist tyranny are the best memorial to Mazzini ... This year Mazzini is being remembered in the fighting lines. If each one does his duty, in years to come we shall celebrate the triumph of Mazzini's ideas.[53]

A similar programme was broadcast on the occasion of the anniversary of Garibaldi's death on 2 June 1944. Uberto Limentani opened the programme by saying that the name and the symbol of Garibaldi were still alive in Europe; Garibaldi's memory was inspiring those who believed in freedom and fought against tyranny. In this case also the programme refers to key places of the Risorgimento, but this time the cities mentioned are British:

> La coincidenza d'ideali col popolo inglese, la calda corrente di reciproca simpatia acquistarono all'Eroe, per così dire, diritto di cittadinanza in Inghilterra. Con sentimento di profonda commozione chi vi parla torna spesso ad un parco del Buckinghamshire, in raccoglimento davanti a un albero piantato da Garibaldi, oggetto di religiose cure e di devoto pellegrinaggio. Fu qui a Londra che Garibaldi ricevette, nel 1864, l'accoglienza più entusiastica che la capitale avesse mai tributato a un ospite. Fu a Newcastle che l'esule, dieci anni prima riceveva in dono dagli operai di quel porto una spade dall'elsa d'oro, e che, attraverso le loro parole e la loro fiducia, si sentiva eletto a campione di una causa santa.[54]

> The shared values with and warm mutual fondness for the English made the Hero gain, so to speak, English citizenship. It is with a feeling of deep emotion that the person who is talking to you often goes back to a park in Buckinghamshire, meditates before a tree planted by Garibaldi, which is now religiously taken care of, and visited by devoted pilgrims. It was in London in 1864 that Garibaldi received the warmest welcome a guest had ever experienced in the capital. It was in Newcastle that, ten years before, the exile had been given a sword with a golden hilt by the workers at those docks. Thanks to their words and trust, he felt he was the chosen champion of a holy cause.

Once again workers were at the centre of a BBC programme. British and Italian workers, as will be explained in the next chapter, were often compared, with the aim of creating empathy among the citizens of the two countries. Another interesting element of this extract is the use of the expressions *religiose cure*, *devoto pellegrinaggio* and *causa santa* to refer to Garibaldi and his followers. As we have seen in Chapter 2, the BBC often appealed to religion to engage with the Italian people. This was certainly true on the occasion of festivities such as Christmas and Easter, but religion was always a good propaganda tool for addressing Italians. As the next extract will show, this is not the only case where religious rhetoric is associated with the Resistance.

Another BBC reference to the Italian Risorgimento was the use of the word 'patriot' to describe the partisans. In a programme dated 5 January 1941, Paolo Treves explained who the patriots were. At the beginning of the programme Treves said that neo-fascists were trying to stop the patriots by announcing reprisals against them. Yet, this was a vain attempt since the patriots' actions were already demonstrating that their bravery could not be easily defeated:

> Perché coloro che hanno fatto giustizia a Milano, in Corso Ventidue Marzo il 30 dicembre, del milite Pietro Del Buffo sono patrioti. E patrioti sono coloro che asseragliati nelle montagne si battono contro la Wehrmacht inviata in spedizione punitive. E patrioti sono quei coraggiosi che hanno dato al console tedesco a Torino Franz e al rappresentate del partito nazista Bekert l'occasione di seguire il funerale del fascista Aldo Morey.
>
> E patrioti sono quei vicentini che hanno tolto di mezzo il generale Antonio Faggioni al servizio dei tedeschi, e patrioti sono quei moltissimi che subiscono rappresaglie e le persecuzioni, quelli che a Milano languiscono e soffrono la tortura nelle celle di San Vittore, dietro le pesanti grate di ferro, là dove i bracci sboccano nella grande raggiera, e una volta sorgeva un'immagine sacra. Patrioti, e niente altro, niente di diverso, perché tutti testimoni, con la loro opera oggi, col loro sangue domani, della grande religione della patria, quindi della libertà, perché come scriveva il Machiavelli con infrangibile sequenza, 'il nome della libertà è assai gagliardo, il quale forza alcuna non doma, tempo alcuno non consuma, e merito alcuno non contrappesa'.[55]

> Because those who did justice to the soldier Pietro Del Buffo in Milan, in *Corso Ventidue Marzo* on 30 December, are patriots. And patriots are those who, barricaded in the mountains, are fighting the *Wehrmacht* that was sent there on a punitive expedition. And patriots are those brave people that gave the German consul in Turin, Franz, and the representative of the Nazi Party, Bekert, the chance to go to the funeral of the fascist Aldo Morey.
>
> And patriots are those people from Vicenza who got general Antonio Faggioni, working for the Germans, out of the way; and patriots are those beyond number who are victims of reprisals and persecution, those who languish and

are tortured in the cells of San Vittore, behind heavy iron grilles from which their arms protrude and in cells where holy images used to hang on the wall. Patriots and nothing else, nothing different, because they are all witnesses, with their present actions and their future blood, to the great religion of the motherland, therefore of freedom. As Machiavelli wrote in an eternal phrase, 'the word freedom is extremely powerful, it exerts no power, it wastes no time, it is beyond merit'.

The efforts of the patriots had already resulted in the death of many fascist personalities. As a consequence, several patriots had been arrested and subjected to torture. In this extract partisans are called 'witnesses of the great religion of the motherland' and there are references to a holy image that previously hung on the wall of the partisans' cells. The programme implies that partisans were waging their war against Nazi-fascism with the same devotion and dedication of a deeply religious person.

Moreover, as Candidus said in another programme, there was a key difference between the partisans and the neo-fascists. While Radio Rome and Radio Monaco were continuously launching appeals to persuade Italians to continue to fight on the side of Germany, there was no need to exhort patriots. They were supporting the cause of liberation voluntarily:

> Si osservi il radicale contrasto tra il reclutamento Tedesco fascista e quello dei patrioti. Per reclutare i patrioti non c'è bisogno di melodrammatici appelli radiofonici, nè di incitamenti giornalistici; non c'è bisogno di allettarli con alte paghe e trattamento speciale; non c'è bisogno di promettere assemblee costituenti o surrogati di socialismi scoperti ad hoc e che tradiscono basse manovre demagogiche; non c'è bisogno di gonfiarli con appellativi eroici; non c'è bisogno di intimorirli con oscure minacce. Sono volontari in tutta l'estensione della parola, volontari della causa italiana, ed esclusivamente italiana, e che in questo momento si esprime in funzione antitedesca e antifascista.[56]

> Let's observe the radical contrast between the recruitment of German-fascists and that of the patriots. In order to recruit patriots there is no need for melodramatic radio calls, nor journalistic incitements; there is no need to persuade them with high salaries and special treatment; there is no need to promise constituent assemblies or special surrogates of socialism that are the expression of demagogic strategies; there is no need to flatter them with heroic epithets; there is no need to scare them with dark threats. They are volunteers, as per the literal meaning of the word, volunteers for the Italian – and exclusively Italian – cause that is the expression of anti-German and anti-fascist feeling.

Another difference, the programme continued, was the amount of military equipment at the disposal of the two groups. While the fascists fighting in the North could rely on the support of Germany, patriots were not protected by the Allied forces, who were still in Southern Italy. Moreover, while fascists could access regular daily rations, partisans did not have access to guaranteed meals. Yet, the partisans had a better support: 'the hospitality of the Italian homes, and the support of the population who offers them food, woollen clothes and comfort'.[57]

Similar considerations on the differences between fascists and partisans were expressed in March 1945 by Nissim's *omo qualunque*:

> Pigliamo l'esempio dei nostri patriotti, dei patriotti italiani ... che hanno fatto e fanno meraviglie dove senton puzzo di tedeschi ... Dunque, se pensiamo a loro ci accorgiamo subito della differenza, che è questa: i patrioti, i guerriglieri italiani, come i loro fratelli di tutta la Europa, hanno un gran fegato ... ma sapete dove lo prendono? ... lo prendono dal loro amor di patria, dall'amore per il loro paese, nella volontà che il loro paese sia LIBERO. E' lo stesso coraggio che ispirava .... i nostri vecchi ... quelli che andaron con Garibaldi, che è stato diciamo così, l'inventore della guerriglia ...[58]

> Let's talk, for example, about our patriots, the Italian patriots ... who did and are doing amazing things wherever they smell Germans ... So, if we think about them, we immediately realise that there is this difference: the patriots, the Italian fighters, like their other brothers all over Europe, have a big gut ... but do you know where they get it from? ... from the love for the motherland, love for their country, the wish for their country to become FREE. This is the same bravery that inspired ... our elders ... the ones who joined Garibaldi who was, we might say, the inventor of guerrilla fighting.

The Italian Service's programmes often praised the actions of the partisan groups fighting in other European countries. This was the case with a programme dated 13 January 1945. The programme focused on accounts of women who contributed to the Resistance in other European countries, including France, Yugoslavia and Norway. As this interview with a Yugoslav woman shows, the populations of many European countries supported the partisans:

> Yugoslav W: Quando nella primavera del 1941 il nostro paese fu invaso, il popolo resistette. E' stato il popolo, e la gente più povera che ha armato l'esercito di liberazione e che ha provveduto al suo vettovagliamento. Sono andati scalzi per dare scarpe ai soldati, hanno dato il bestiame per l'esercito. In Jugoslavia non c'è più bestiame. Il popolo ha esaurito tutte le sue risorse tanto di viveri che di vestiario. E ora di pieno inverno, il problema del vestiario è ancora più acuto, è ancora più immediato di quello dei viveri.[59]

> Yugoslav W: When our country was invaded in spring 1941, the population resisted. It was the population, and the poorest people, who armed the liberation army and provided it with supplies. They went barefoot to give their shoes to the soldiers, they gave their cattle to the army. In Yugoslavia there are no more cattle. The population has run out of food supplies and clothing. And now, in the middle of winter, the clothing issue is even more serious and even more urgent than that of the supplies.

These last two extracts introduce the concept of a European identity based on the Resistance and the partisan fight against tyranny. As we have seen, the *omo qualunque* called the partisans of other countries 'brothers from all over Europe' of the Italian patriots. Similarly, the interviews with those European women who helped the partisans suggest that the fight against Nazi-fascism was creating the basis for a new unified Europe. In this new Europe totalitarian regimes would no longer be accepted. This message was at the centre of many programmes broadcast by the Italian Service between 1944 and 1945. This was the case with a broadcast entitled *Italian Partisans* and dated 20 July 1944. At the beginning of the programme Livio Zino Zencovich, the broadcaster, declared that only a tiny percentage of the heroic actions of the partisans would find space in the British press, since the guerrilla was, by definition, opposed to publicity. Nevertheless, the partisans would certainly be happy to hear that they embodied the hope of Italians as well as that of the entire world. This world belonged to ordinary people:

> E il mondo è composto in fondo di quella gente semplice e talora umile, che tornando a casa la sera, incontro nell'autobus o nella ferrovia sotterranea immersi nella lettura di un giornale. E questa gente, che non ha di rado sfiorato la minaccia dei siluri volanti per compiere il proprio dovere, apprende che già in Italia – in quell'Italia che fino a poco tempo fa veniva superficialmente bollata dall'etichetta del Fascismo – vi sono degli uomini e delle donne che compiono lo stesso dovere per gli stessi fini: fini che appaiono così chiari agli uomini della strada; il diritto di vivere una vita tranquilla e in pace, senza l'incubo di crudeltà, di persecuzioni e soprusi; e un vincolo di solidarietà nuova si stabilisce immediatamente tra l'uomo qualunque che dietro al suo giornale, sta viaggiando verso uno dei tanti suburbi di Londra, e il partigiano che ad Arezzo o a Livorno sta lottando contro i tedeschi.[60]

> And the world, after all, belongs to these simple and humble people I meet on the bus or the Tube, immersed in reading a newspaper, when I return home in the evening. And these people, who to do their duty often risked death from flying doodlebugs, are learning that in Italy – the Italy that not long ago was superficially labelled a fascist country – there are some men and women who do their duty with the same purpose: a purpose that seems crystal clear to the man in the street; the right to live a quiet and peaceful life, without fear of cruelty, persecution and oppression; and a new bond of solidarity immediately unites the ordinary man who, behind his newspaper, is travelling to one of the many London suburbs, and the partisan who is fighting against the Germans in Arezzo or Livorno.

The international nature of the Resistance was further confirmed by some news broadcast by Allied Radio Bari and mentioned in a BBC programme entitled *Patriots: Builders of the Future*. The officials who coordinated the French and Italian Resistance, respectively, were planning future joint actions.

Moreover, the Comitato Nazionale Italiano di Liberazione per l'Italia Settentrionale had just concluded an agreement with Marshal Tito and the Committee for the Liberation of Slovenia, with the aim of creating a unified international fighting group.[61]

> Sono accordi di fatto, intervenuti fra coloro che combattono sul fronte della resistenza, e che quindi conoscono meglio di chiunque le esigenze militari, psicologiche e ambientali della lotta, e quindi hanno, per amor di collaborazione e per necessità spirituale, il diritto di mettersi al di sopra di ogni differenza politica, di superare le barriere territoriali e di ignorare le rigide limitazioni e convenzioni giuridiche; anche se ciò possa dispiacere ad alcuni per i quali il principio nazionalista e le formule della sovranità sono ancora dei tabù, e quindi non sanno rinunciare a risentimenti per passate occorrenze, nutrono dispettose suscettibilità, e magari vorrebbe vedere i futuri rapporti fra i popoli regolati dalle stesse norme ed entro gli stessi schemi che furono in vigore fino al 1939. E non sanno quello che anche il più umile patriota combattente sa – che nulla e nessuno al mondo potrebbe più ripristinare le condizioni di allora, e che del resto nessuno di noi vorrebbe veder resuscitate. Per fortuna questa guerra sta già abolendo il vecchio significato delle frontiere fra nazione e nazione, almeno per quanto concerne l'Europa; sta già sterilizzando il vecchio nazionalismo espansionista e sopraffattore, degenerazione dello spirito nazionale e cancro di molti paesi continentali; ha già dato ai popoli europei un primo ma potente barlume di coscienza unitaria.

> These are factual agreements between those who fight on the resistance fronts, and therefore know better than anyone else the military, psychological and environmental requirements of the fight. As a consequence, they have, for the sake of collaboration and spiritual need, the right to go beyond all political differences and territorial borders, the right to ignore strict limitations and laws; even though some people who still think that the nationalist principle and sovereignty are still taboo subjects might feel sorry and are still resentful about past events. These people are spitefully oversensitive and perhaps would like the relationships between populations to be ruled by the same norms and mental schemes as before 1943. And they do not know what even the humblest fighting patriot knows – that nothing and no one in the world would be able to reinstate the rules of the time and that, after all, none of us would like to see them again. Luckily, this war is already abolishing the old meaning of borders between nation and nation, at least as far as Europe is concerned; it is already neutralising the old expansionist and despotic nationalism, which is the degeneration of the national spirit in many countries of the continent; it has already given the European populations a first but powerful glimmer of unitary consciousness.

As these last extracts have shown, Radio Londra often pointed out that the outcome of the long war against Nazi-fascism would be a new democratic Europe. This Europe was the legacy of the Italian Risorgimento and the

European Resistance. In both cases, Britain contributed to their success. This powerful rhetoric is perhaps the best example of the BBC's duplicity. While, as mentioned in the introduction, Radio Londra is mainly remembered as the expression of anti-fascism and the Resistance, the actual relationship between the Allies and the partisans was far more controversial.

This chapter has focused on three key aspects of the Allied campaign in 1943–44: the Italian unconditional surrender, the issues experienced by the Italian civilians due to the conflict, and the partisan Resistance.

The archival documents analysed have revealed that, in spite of the declarations by the Italian broadcasters regarding the objectivity of the corporation, some themes were more delicate than others. The future of Italy worried Calosso and other Italian broadcasters, who did not consider the unconditional surrender to be an honourable solution for their country. Once again, the Foreign Office's authorities did not take seriously Italian refugees' concerns and Stevens's attempts to act as a mediator between these broadcasters and the PWE were ignored by Bruce Lockhart.

The relationship between the partisan Resistance and the Allies was another controversial element of the Italian campaign. As Ellwood and Pavone's work has shown, on the one hand they needed to operate jointly in order to be successful; on the other, they still regarded each other as enemies. Despite this, the programmes on bombings, food and the partisans show the BBC's capability to cope well with its ambiguous role. As the next chapter will show, through its programming the corporation obtained the trust of many civilians who asked Stevens to intercede with the Allied authorities on their behalf on more than one occasion.

Notes

1. Di Nolfo and Serra, *La gabbia infranta*, p. 26.
2. Di Nolfo and Serra, *La gabbia infranta*, p. 21.
3. Elena Aga Rossi, *L'inganno reciproco: l'armistizio tra l'Italia e gli angloamericani del settembre 1943* (Rome: Ministero per i Beni Culturali e Ambientali, 1993).
4. Lo Biundo, *London Calling Italy*.
5. Aga Rossi, *L'inganno reciproco*, pp. 42–47.
6. Di Nolfo and Serra, *La gabbia infranta*, pp. 49–50; Aga Rossi, *L'inganno reciproco*, pp. 33–55.
7. Ellwood, *Italy 1943–45*, p. 2.
8. BBC WAC, IS, Scripts, s. II, b. 19, *Unconditional surrender, A Free Italy talk*, 6 June 1943.
9. BBC WAC, IS, Scripts, s. II, b. 20, *The Message: What it Means, A Free Italy talk*, 18 July 1943.

10 Centro Piero Gobetti, Fondo Umberto Calosso (hereafter CPG, FUC), *Interventi di Umberto Calosso da Radio Londra*, Umberto Calosso, *Separate Peace*, 28 November 1942, 23.30; author's translation.
11 CPG, FUC, *Interventi di Umberto Calosso da Radio Londra*, Umberto Calosso, *A Programme for Italy*, 28 February 1943.
12 CPG, FUC, *Interventi di Umberto Calosso da Radio Londra*, Umberto Calosso, *To the Soldiers*, 28 March 1943; author's translation.
13 CPG, FUC, *Interventi di Umberto Calosso da Radio Londra*, Umberto Calosso, *A Question*, 22 August 1943.
14 NA, FO371/37251, Colonel Stevens to Bruce Lockhart, 7 August 1943. Another copy of this letter can be found at the BBC WAC.
15 NA, FO371/37251, Bruce Lockhart's letter, 9 August 1943.
16 CPG FUC, *Documenti Antifascismo 1941–52*; author's translation.
17 NA, FO371/37249, PWE Weekly directive for BBC Italian Service, week beginning Thursday 18 March 1943.
18 The expression 'psychological war' has been used by historian Lamberto Mercuri to refer to the Anglo-American propaganda in Italy between 1942 and 1946. Mercuri, *Guerra psicologica*.
19 NA, FO371/37249, PWE Special directive for BBC Italian Service, 14 January 1943.
20 BBC WAC, IS, Scripts, s. II, b. 8, H.R. Stevens, 19 November 1942; author's translation.
21 BBC WAC, IS, Scripts, s. II, b. 8, London Diary n. 177, 24 November 1942; author's translation.
22 Dietmar Süss, 'Wartime Societies and Shelter Politics in National Socialist Germany and Britain', in Baldoli et al., *Bombing States and Peoples in Western Europe*, p. 23.
23 Süss, 'Wartime Societies', p. 26.
24 Süss, 'Wartime Societies', p. 27.
25 Baldoli and Knapp, *Forgotten Blitzes*, p. 144.
26 BBC WAC, IS, Scripts, s. II, b. 14, Mario Forti and Piero Mortara, *Piovon le bombe*, 1 December 1942; author's translation.
27 BBC WAC, IS, Scripts, s. II, b. 18, 5 May 1943; author's translation.
28 Williams, *Allies and Italians Under Occupation*, p. 171.
29 BBC WAC, IS, Scripts, s. II, b. 18, L. Shepley, *Food in Britain*, 1 May 1943; author's translation.
30 Insolvibile, *Wops*, p. 79.
31 Insolvibile, *Wops*, p. 80.
32 BBC WAC, E2/191/1, Foreign Gen, European Intelligence papers. Survey of European Audiences: Enemy countries, 194; BBC Monthly Surveys of European Audiences. Enemy Countries. 17 February 1941.
33 BBC WAC, IS, Scripts, s. II, 17 July 1943; author's translation.
34 Ellwood, *Italy 1943–45*, p. 49.
35 BBC WAC, IS, Scripts, s. II, Umberto Calosso, *The two Italys*, 19 March 1944.
36 The topic is discussed in Ellwood, *Italy 1943–45*; Williams, *Allies and Italians*.
37 BBC WAC, IS, Scripts, s. II, b. 28, Paolo Treves, *Allied Control Commission Conference*, 25 August 1944.

38 BBC WAC, IS, Scripts, s. I, b. 12, H.R. Stevens, 20 November 1944.
39 Gabriella Gribaudi, 'Tra discorsi pubblici e memorie private. Alcune riflessioni sui bombardamenti e la loro legittimazione', in Nicola Labanca (ed.), *I bombardamenti aerei sull'Italia: politica, Stato e società, 1939–1945* (Bologna: Il Mulino, 2012), pp. 305–321. See also Gribaudi, *Guerra totale*. Drawing on accounts from many civilians who experienced the conflict in Southern Italy, the book focuses on the ways in which the war affected their lives. Particularly interesting is the fact that many civilians recall differences between the US and British bombs. According to their accounts, the British bombings always aimed at military targets and tried to spare the lives of Italian civilians.
40 BBC WAC, IS, Scripts, s. II, b. 23, Uberto Limentani, *La distruzione di opera d'arte in Italia e in Europa e le dichiarazioni di Sir James Grigg*, 2 January 1944; author's translation.
41 BBC WAC, IS, Scripts, s. II, b. 24, Uberto Limentani, *War damage to historic monuments*, 7 February 1944.
42 Marta Nezzo, 'The Defence of Works of Art from Bombing in Italy during the Second World War', in Baldoli et al., *Bombing States*, p. 113.
43 BBC WAC, IS, Scripts, s. II, *Allied statement on Rome*, 3 June 1944; author's translation.
44 BBC WAC, IS, Scripts, s. II, April 1944.
45 Pavone, *A Civil War*, p. 233.
46 Pavone, *A Civil War*, p. 233.
47 Pavone, *A Civil War*, p. 214.
48 Claudio Pavone, 'Le idee della Resistenza. Antifascisti e fascisti di fronte alla tradizione del Risorgimento', *Passato e Presente*, 7 (1959), 850–918; 850.
49 Pavone, *A Civil War*, p. 217.
50 Pavone, *A Civil War*, 854.
51 Philip Cooke, 'La Resistenza come secondo Risorgimento: un *topos* retorico senza fine?', *Passato e Presente*, 86 (2012), 62–81; 63. Author's translation.
52 BBC WAC, IS, Scripts, s. II, A. Bergamasco, *Italian Fighters and Workers programme, Re-reading Mazzini*, 9 March 1944.
53 Bergamasco, *Italian Fighters*.
54 BBC WAC, IS, Scripts, s. II, Uberto Limentani, *Nel settantaduesimo anniversario della morte di Giuseppe Garibaldi*, 2 June 1944; author's translation.
55 BBC WAC, IS, Scripts, s. II, b. 23, Paolo Treves, *Italian Round-up n. 66*, 5 January 1944; author's translation.
56 Candidus, *Patriots*, 7 January 1944, s. II, b. 23, BBC WAC.
57 Candidus, *Patriots*. Author's translation.
58 BBC WAC, IS, Scripts, s. II, b. 35, Elio Nissim, *Monologue of the Little Man*, 18 March 1945; author's translation.
59 BBC WAC, IS, Scripts, s. II, b. 33, Pat Baker & Giovanna Foa, *Women's Programme: International Women Service Groups*, 13 January 1945; author's translation.
60 BBC WAC, IS, Scripts, s. II, b. 27, L. Z. Zencovich, *Italian Partisans*, 20 July 1944; author's translation.
61 BBC WAC, IS, Scripts, s. II, b. 27, Candidus, *Patriots Builders of the Future*.

7

Who tuned in to the BBC? The Italian Service: its target audiences and listeners

The analysis of the radio transcripts in Chapters 5 and 6 has confirmed that the BBC played an ambiguous role in Italy. In order to win the war, it was crucial to demonstrate that the Allied coalition was a superior military force. As the BBC often repeated, the Allies would not treat the Italians as enemies if they got rid of fascism and the Nazi occupiers. However, they could also bomb their cities. This implied that the BBC, as we have seen, manipulated the truth during key moments of the conflict, such as El Alamein, and the unconditional surrender of Italy. While this is not surprising in a war context, these data contrast the widespread opinion according to which Radio Londra was the voice of freedom and anti-fascism. The contradictory role of the Italian Service has also emerged from Chapters 3 and 4. The Italian exiles working for the BBC experienced several issues with the British Foreign Office and were not always free to express their political opinions. However, despite this, their memoirs refer to the BBC as a second home.

By analysing the BBC's target Italian audiences and the reception of the programmes, this chapter aims to understand how the myth of Radio Londra was constructed. By focusing on the work of radio historians and scholars, the first part of the chapter looks at the difficulties in obtaining reliable quantitative estimates about radio listeners in the 1930s and 1940s. The second part concentrates on the categories of Italians that the BBC hoped to reach and analyses some programme extracts. The third and fourth sections concentrate, respectively, on some indirect and direct sources of qualitative information on the listeners: the BBC surveys on the audiences of enemy countries and the letters sent by listeners to the Italian Service to Colonel Stevens.

Audience and methodological issues

Il problema del pubblico è, come ormai si sa, il grande paradosso di qualunque studio sui moderni mezzi di comunicazione: al pubblico è attribuito un ruolo centrale...ma esso appare al tempo stesso inafferrabile, conoscibile solo per grandi aggregati e congetturalmente; vasto al punto da coincidere con l'intera società, il pubblico della radio e della TV è al tempo stesso frammentato fino all'inverosimile, all'interno di singole case, ed ora delle singole stanze di una casa.[1]

The issue of the public is, as we are now aware, the great paradox of any study about modern media: the public is given a central role ... but at the same time it appears ungraspable, you can only make conjectures about large groups of audiences; radio and TV audiences are large enough to represent society as a whole, yet are also extremely fragmented.

Understanding audiences is arguably one of the biggest challenges for scholars and radio producers. As Tiziano Bonini states in the introduction to a recent volume on radio audiences, this was particularly difficult in the interwar period, but similar methodological issues applied to later decades. It was only with the birth of social networking websites that media scholars could more easily access qualitative information on radio audiences and analyse the comments that listeners left on the public pages of radio stations, famous broadcasters or disc jockeys.[2]

If studying contemporary radio audiences is already a challenging operation, how can we understand what kind of programmes listeners liked or disliked in the 1920s, 1930s and 1940s? This is even more difficult in the case of the BBC Italian Service during the Second World War. Radio Londra was a foreign radio station broadcasting under war conditions to a country governed by a totalitarian regime. Did Italian listeners tune in to the BBC to seek more objective information on the conflict or for entertainment purposes? Listening to the BBC as well as to other foreign radio stations in fascist Italy was illegal. The royal decree n. 765 passed on 16 June 1940 established that all private radios should be dismantled and given to the fascist authorities in charge of public security. As a consequence, Italians listening to the BBC could face heavy fines, arrest or imprisonment. The penalties for those who did not respect the law varied over the years of the conflict. From April 1941 a person who listened to the BBC risked spending up to eighteen months in jail and a fine of L.30,000. In January 1942 both the length of imprisonment and the amount of the fine were increased: listeners to foreign programmes could be imprisoned for up to three years and pay a fine between L.4,000 and L.40,000.[3] The reports of the fascist police, analysed by Maura Piccialuti Caprioli in her inventory, show that these laws were not respected by many Italians. These documents relate to people who had been reported to the police by Italians who acted as spies for the regime:

> Dall'estate 1940 i rapporti dei fiduciari contengono sovente denunzie di privati o di esercizi pubblici presso i quali si ascoltano radio straniere; qualche rara

volta si fa il nome, fra gli ascoltatori, di persone meno oscure, e allora seguono inchieste, di solito di esito negativo. Si riporta sempre più spesso che la gente parla dell'ascolto anche in luoghi pubblici, senza remore o cautele di sorta. Sempre più spesso i fiduciari sono costretti ad ammettere una 'morbosa curiosità' per le stazioni radio straniere, e 'andare alla stazione per avere notizie' è l'espressione usata dagli ascoltatori più cauti, quando per istrada, al caffè o dove altro si possa esser sorvegliati senza che ci si accorga, si vuol fare intendere a qualcuno che si ascolta Radio Londra.[4]

Since summer 1940 financial reports have often included declarations against private individuals or businesses where people listened to foreign radio stations; on some rare occasions the names of slightly better known people are mentioned, leading to investigations which are usually inconclusive. The reports often refer to people who even talk in public, with no hesitation or caution, about the fact they listen to these stations. More and more often informants are forced to admit that they developed a 'morbid curiosity' for foreign radio stations, and 'going to the station' is the most common expression used by the most cautious listeners on the street, at a café or in places where they might be watched and want to suggest to someone that they listen to Radio Londra.

The BBC, said the reports, had an audience of both rich and poor people. It was reported from Padua in March 1941, a year after the penalties were introduced, that Radio Londra was listened to more than EIAR bulletins. In the same month, a Milanese told the Italian police that people listened to the BBC because they no longer trusted the fascist news. The measures to prevent listening to foreign radio stations were interpreted as proof that the EIAR lied about the conflict. What emerged from the reports is that fascists also regularly listened to the BBC, as this extract shows:

Anche molti fascisti o per meglio dire, molti che portano il distintivo del P.N.F. perché a questo regolarmente iscritti, hanno il piacere di ascoltare la radio inglese e taluni si fanno anche un dovere di informare gli ignari di quanto apprendono da quella fonte... Nell'attesa il popolo ragionante si chiede se, non essendo possibile impedire a chi ha una radio di ascoltare le voci dal mondo, non sia possibile prendere per il collo quelli che tali voci riferiscono.[5]

Also many fascists or, rather, many people who wear the PNF badge because they officially joined the organisation, like listening to English radio stations, and some of them even feel they have a duty to pass on the information they have heard from that source to those who are unaware of it ... Meanwhile, intelligent people wonder whether, given that you cannot forbid those who own a radio to listen to voices from all around the world, it is not possible to punish those who report what these voices say.

These reports are certainly important, attesting to the fact that many Italians did not respect the law. However, as Piccialuti Caprioli remarks, it seems that there are no longer records for the period from November 1941 onwards.[6]

While fascist police documents have not been consulted for the purpose of this research, it might be useful to provide some data on the numbers of people who were actually punished for listening to the BBC. Also in this case, Piccialuti Caprioli's work is invaluable. A sample corresponding to one quarter of the documentation shows that from 10 June 1940 to 25 July 1943 only 44 Italians out of 4,500 were imprisoned, 31 of whom were explicitly punished for tuning in to the BBC.[7] It was extremely difficult for the fascist authorities to control and punish listeners to foreign radio stations. Yet, if caught, Italians still risked severe penalties. This leads us to the conclusion that the BBC was certainly more than a simple form of entertainment for Italians. Yet it was not a simple source of news either. As this chapter will show, for many Italians the BBC was concurrently a moral support, an alternative source of information on the conflict and a window onto a foreign country and culture.

When analysing the audiences of radio stations operating in the Second World War, another issue arises. How can we access quantitative data on the numbers and social backgrounds of the listeners? One criterion used at the time to obtain such data was to analyse the numbers of people who owned a radio set and a radio licence. However, this method could only be used by the home services. As for the services broadcasting to enemy countries, how to access such numbers and statistical data? For the BBC Italian Service, it was certainly not easy since, as we have seen in Chapter 5, this information could only be provided by fascist institutions. While information exchanges between the BBC and the EIAR took place in the 1930s, things changed after June 1940.

Moreover, even the numbers of radio owners in Italy does not tell us anything about the stations these people listened to. Additionally, given that only a few people could afford to buy a radio set, group listening was very common. In the Italian case there was also another issue: Radio Londra broadcast in standard Italian. Given the variety and diversity of dialects spoken in Italy at the time and the low level of literacy, how many people could actually understand the BBC programmes? It is likely that the gatherings of clandestine BBC listeners were attended by at least two categories of people, those who could actually understand Italian and those who could only obtain second-hand information from other listeners.

While these premises already show that it is not possible to obtain reliable quantitative information about listeners to the Italian Service, it can be obtained from BBC audience surveys and the letters sent by many Italian listeners to the BBC. These letters were the expression of the thoughts and feelings of many Italians and are evidence that Radio Londra's programmes were well received by many Italians. An indirect source of information about listeners to the Italian Service are the programmes themselves. While they cannot tell us who the actual listeners were, they can at least inform us about the audiences that the BBC wanted to reach. The content of the programmes, the surveys and the letters will be discussed later in this chapter. In this section the work of other scholars will be analysed with the aim of providing a better understanding of the difficulties faced by historians working on radio audiences in the 1930s and 1940s.

In an article about the reactions of listeners to the BBC Empire Service, Simon Potter claims that it is 'difficult, perhaps impossible, to find direct and convincingly representative evidence for how listeners in the British diaspora reacted to the Empire Service in the 1930s'.[8] However, there are also different and indirect ways of researching the audience of the Empire Service. For example, as suggested by Potter, 'we can at least examine how those running public broadcasting organisations in Britain and the Dominions perceived audiences to be responding'.[9] In the case of the Empire Service the situation is particularly complex, because audiences differed widely depending on the specific dominion. Similarly, it is extremely difficult to establish who listened to Radio Bari, another colonial radio station broadcasting in the 1930s. As Arturo Marzano suggests, in the case of Radio Bari there are three main elements that make an evaluation of its impact problematic: the quality of the signal, the high cost of radio sets and the number of people who could understand Arabic, since many people only spoke dialect. In this case also it is only possible to access indirect sources such as correspondence between diplomats operating in North Africa, the press and listeners' comments published in a magazine called *Radyo Bari*.[10] The listeners' comments are, in this case, the only direct source of information. Nevertheless, *Radyo Bari* was the printed voice of the fascist radio station and would not have published any negative comment.

As for fascist broadcasts in Italy, the sources that have been extensively analysed by historians of fascist radio are the results from radio surveys. The first survey dates from 1925 and was launched through the magazine *Radiorario*. The survey asked the listeners to Radio Roma what their favourite radio genres were. This was followed by another survey, launched in 1927 for the listeners of Radio Roma, Radio Milano and Radio Napoli. The Italians were asked what programmes they wished to listen to, what kind of music they preferred, whether they wanted more cultural programmes and talks and what existing programmes could be improved and developed.[11] Yet the questions were so generic that the answers were not as useful as hoped. Hence the EIAR ended up relying more on the listeners' letters.[12] Despite this, surveys continued to be a common practice, but the first and most exhaustive was that launched in 1927. From this it emerged that the middle and upper classes started to regard radio as a medium for taking part in the political and cultural life of their country.[13]

Another interesting survey for the purpose of this work is the one that took place between 1939 and 1940. From this survey we can see which social classes could potentially listen to the BBC and what their preferences were at the outbreak of the Second World War. One of the reasons for the fascist government launching a new survey was the fear that the regime could no longer rely on the support it had previously. Hence the decision to ask the Italians what they thought about the EIAR, one of the main instruments of the political and cultural propaganda of the regime. As Anna Lucia Natale has noted, the idea of launching a new survey to test the stability of the regime 'sembrerebbe rivelare un'accresciuta consapevolezza da parte dell'EIAR, dell'utilità di tale strumento nello stabilire un rapporto di collaborazione con il pubblico' ('would seem to reveal an increased awareness on the part of the EIAR of the usefulness of such a tool in establishing a collaborative partnership with the public').[14]

The survey was quite successful: 901,386 radio licence holders out of 1,194,849 took part in the questionnaire. As mentioned earlier, the numbers of licence holders and actual listeners did not match. However, according to Natale, the survey covered around six million potential listeners, including people who did not own a radio set. Natale has applied Sylos Labini's categories of *ceti superiori, medi* and *inferiori* (upper, middle and lower classes) to the outcomes of the survey. It emerged that the highest percentage of radio subscribers was in the North of Italy and the majority of them belonged to the upper classes. In central Italy there was a slightly lower percentage of radio subscribers and the lowest percentage of radio subscribers was in the South, about half of that of northern Italy. Moreover, there were many more subscribers in the cities than in rural areas.[15] As regards the fascist regime, it emerged that the highest percentage of dissent was among students and the upper classes, who contested the cultural ideas behind the EIAR's programming; there was moderate dissent among the middle classes and housewives, who expressed balanced opinions on most of the programmes; among lower classes there was high appreciation of the programmes. Their negative comments only related to some specific broadcasts that were not considered interesting, such as programmes teaching foreign languages. It was also clear from the survey that the peak listening hours were 1–2 p.m. and 8 p.m., whereas on Sundays and holidays the majority of listeners tuned in to the BBC in the early hours of the morning. This is not surprising, since these hours corresponded with Italian lunch and dinner times, when Italians were not at work.

As noticed by Gianni Isola, in general, all social classes liked the same programmes and listened to the radio at the same times. On the eve of the

Second World War radio was already part and parcel of the everyday life of many Italians and created new forms of interaction:

> Un dato confermato da certe percentuali d'ascolto per le fasce orarie meridiane e serali: anch'esse, mediamente superiori al 90%, fanno pensare che la radio abbia costituito un vero e proprio cuneo inserito nella tradizione, nei rapporti sociali e interpersonali ed abbia reso omogenei tempi e modi di vita di ceti sociali detentori di abitudini diverse e spesso contrastanti.[16]

> Some data are confirmed by the listening percentages for the afternoon and evening time slots: these, too, are over 90 per cent and suggest that radio has become a real part of tradition, and has levelled out the schedules and lifestyles of social classes whose daily habits used to be different, not to say entirely opposite.

These last data about the standardisation of daily habits are particularly relevant in the context of this book about the BBC Italian Service, as the following pages will explain in more detail. In this regard, as Monticone has noticed, Antonio Gramsci's considerations about the *romanzo d'appendice* (feuilletons) can be applied to radio as well:

> Si può supporre che i lettori del romanzo di appendice non fossero diversi dai primi radioascoltatori, almeno da quelli (ed erano la stragrande maggioranza) delle aree urbane. In ambedue i casi infatti si è di fronte al consumo di un materiale culturale subalterno, né vale obiettare che la radio, per esempio per quanto riguarda la musica, trasmettesse brani di autori consacrati dalla cultura ufficiale, perché la riproducibilità tecnica dell'espressione musicale, sottraendo l'esperienza dell'ascolto al luogo privilegiato e classista della sala da concerto, ne scambiava il valore d'uso.[17]

> It can be assumed that the readers of feuilletons were not so different from the first radio listeners, at least from those (the great majority) living in urban areas. In both cases we are dealing with consumers of inferior cultural material. We cannot even object that radio, as far as music was concerned, for example, broadcast pieces by officially recognised composers, since the fact that live music was no longer a privilege for the rich who could afford to go to a concert hall reduced its use-value.

For many readers, as Gramsci wrote in 1930, feuilletons became the new literature for ordinary people. While for the cultured upper classes knowledge of one's national literature was almost a social duty, for the lower classes it was really important to follow the episodes in newly published serialisations. These were more accessible than traditional literature and created new trends and topics of discussion. Similarly, radio made music more accessible, since people who could not afford tickets to go to music halls could now listen to concerts on the radio.[18]

As David Forgacs and Stephen Gundle claim in their book about mass culture in Italy, radio played a big role in creating a popular culture 'even before the arrival of mass consumption toward the end of the 1950s'.[19] It contributed, for example, to the growing popularity of sport and light music. Moreover, from the interviews that the two authors carried out with Italian listeners it emerged that radio had changed the lives of many Italians. Even those who could not afford to buy their own sets recalled weekly visits to relatives to listen to the radio. A woman who worked as a housekeeper for a rich family remembered that, as soon as her employers bought a set, radio broadcasts became a key part of her working day. Other people linked their memories of particular historical events with the moment when they heard the news on the radio.[20]

We can therefore affirm that, despite only few Italians being actually able to afford a set, ordinary people were familiar with the new medium as well. As the last parts of this chapter will confirm, even people without direct access to radio broadcasts were constantly updated by neighbours or friends. The next section will explain the arguments and strategies used by the BBC to engage with different categories of Italians.

Broadcasting the Italians and the British: stereotypes as cultural bridges

The BBC programmes addressed various categories of Italians with the aim of engaging with a large number of civilians. As Franco Monteleone has noted, this was also true for another Allied station, Radio Moscow. Palmiro Togliatti's broadcasts from Moscow were accessible to everyone, regardless of their social origins or political beliefs.[21]

As mentioned in Chapter 2, the BBC broadcast in Italian for the first time in September 1938, though the Italian Service was properly established when Italy entered the war. The first directives for Italian propaganda dated back to September 1940 and were written by Ion Munro and his assistant, Gerald Sharp. Munro was a press officer at the British Embassy in Rome. When preparing propaganda for Italy it was crucial to take into consideration that Italians had a great sense of humour. They were also logical, jealous, frivolous and melodramatic. These features were to be borne in mind when seeking the best approach for the programmes.[22] In addition, as suggested by a Lieutenant-Colonel H.M. Moran, British propaganda should focus on civilians, especially women. During the First World War women had shown that they loved their families more than the state. They had blocked railway tracks to stop the trains that would take their husbands and sons to the front. Moreover, continued Munro, there were two Italys, represented respectively by convinced fascists on the one hand and the majority of the population on the other. The civilian population included many people who were forced to join the Fascist Party, but there were also many Italians who still loved Mussolini. For this reason, Mussolini should not be attacked directly, though attacks on Mussolini would be certainly more effective in a later stage of the conflict. That later phase soon arrived. On Christmas Eve 1940, Churchill gave his aforementioned speech, in which Mussolini was accorded sole responsibility for Italian involvement in the conflict against Britain.[23] Even after the fall of Mussolini, as this chapter will show, it was crucial to speak to ex-fascists to obtain their support.

While the BBC aimed to reach all civilians during the entire conflict, its target audiences differed according to the military and political objectives of the different phases of the war. By examining the content of the broadcasts it is possible to identify at least two main goals of British political warfare between 1943 and 1945.

As already mentioned in Chapters 5 and 6, after the decision to land in Sicily, it became vital to prepare Italian public opinion for the arrival of the Allies. It was, moreover, necessary to weaken consent for the fascist regime. Another goal was to persuade the Italians that Mussolini was responsible for Italian participation in the conflict. Every single Italian was important; everybody could contribute to the Allies' cause by supporting their arrival. During this phase of the war the BBC aimed at reaching a wide range of Italians, including women, workers, soldiers, 'little men', and people from the upper classes such as lawyers and intellectuals. Hence, the BBC created a programme for each of these categories.

After the Italian surrender and the beginning of the partisan Resistance, the BBC began to transmit operational information and special coded messages for the partisan groups. The operational information included, whenever possible, details on the military advance of both the Allied and Axis forces. Obviously, this operational information could be listened to and understood by anyone, including the enemy. Therefore, as already mentioned in Chapter 7, the information provided was never too detailed. Programmes for ordinary people continued to be broadcast after the Italian surrender, especially in the last months of the conflict. In this phase cultural programmes, language courses and broadcasts dedicated to listeners' letters became more common features on British radio.

One of the most frequent strategies used was that of cultural stereotypes. The idea was to show that the British and the Italians actually had many more things in common than they thought. In other words, as Kay Chadwick wrote to refer to the French Service, the aim was to give 'a human face to Britain which endeavoured to establish France and Britain as connected communities of ordinary citizens facing corresponding ordeals, and with shared hopes and goals'.[24]

One of the stereotypes about Italy was that Italian women only cared about family and fashion. In 1941 Britain introduced military conscription for women, so all unmarried women and childless widows between the ages of 20 and 30 were liable to be called up.[25] The decision to extend conscription to women was obviously supported by British propaganda. Posters encouraging women to work in factories or join the voluntary military services, such as the Women's Royal Naval Service and Women's Auxiliary Forces, were very common. The BBC Italian Service also supported these campaigns.

On 29 June 1943 a broadcast entitled *English Women in War Time* was aired. British women's contribution to the war effort was used as a pretext to suggest that Italian women should follow their example. 'As a consequence of their emancipation', women were invited to support their country. However, the arguments used in the programmes showed that women were considered incapable of understanding political issues.

> Le uniformi, giubbetto e gonnella di colore coloniale per l'esercito e azzurro per l'aviazione sono ormai parte della vita inglese. Più popolare di ogni altra, l'uniforme del Servizio femminile della marina: giubbetto e gonnella blu, con un grazioso berretto alla marinara.[26]

> The uniforms, a khaki jacket and skirt for the army and sky-blue for the air force, are now part of British life. The most popular of all is the uniform for the Women's [Royal] Naval Service: a navy-blue jacket and skirt, with an attractive sailor hat.

In order to engage with Italian women, the BBC appealed to their sense of fashion by describing the beauty of the uniforms and the brightness of their colours. The fabrics and colours of women's uniforms were at the centre of another programme, broadcast on 6 January 1945:

> Si incontrano spesso in Gran Bretagna donne di ogni età e ceto sociale il cui elegante vestito o tailleur è fatto di una morbida stoffa di lana di un caratteristico colore verde petrolio. Un osservatore superficiale potrebbe a prima vista ritenere che si tratti di una nuova mania cromatica o dell'introduzione di un nuovo colore 'tipo'. Ma un più attento esame rivelerà che non si tratta di una moda ma di un uniforme.[27]

> In Britain one often meets women of all ages and social classes whose elegant dresses and suits are made from a soft woollen material, typically in a petrol-green colour. At first glance, the casual observer might think this was a new colour fad, or the introduction of a new fashion shade. A more careful examination, however, will reveal that this is not a fashion, but a uniform.

The uniform mentioned in the programme is that of the Women's Voluntary Service (WVS). This military body included all the women who volunteered for Britain during the war. The services provided by the WVS included the distribution of information about what to do in case of military air raids.

The first line of the extract, which refers to women of all ages and social classes, is particularly interesting. As the analysis of other programmes will show, the BBC Italian Service often pointed out that the outbreak of the conflict had abolished social differences. Everyone was constantly at risk of being harmed or killed by enemy bombings. Similarly, anyone could contribute to the war effort, regardless of his or her social origin.

Whether they decided to participate in the war or not, fashion was also used as a tool to create connections between Italian and British women. On 2 February 1945 the Italian Service broadcast an interview with an Italian woman who moved to Britain after marrying a Scottish man. The topic of the interview was the clothing issue during the war:

> L. Observer: E in fatto di moda ha trovato differenza tra qui e l'Italia?
> Mrs Cuff: Oh grande differenza. Vede, in Italia la donna è vestita in modo molto più civettuolo. Qui fa freddo – e naturalmente bisogna mettersi molta roba di lana.
> L.Observer: E c'è la neve.
> Mrs Cuff: Già e questo spiega le calzature abbastanza pesanti e coi tacchi bassi. In compenso i colori sono più vivaci. In tempo di guerra, io trovo, si ha bisogno di colori violenti, come reazione ai colori grigi dell'uniforme. Il rosso specialmente. Del resto anche in Italia si porta questo colore: un rosso papavero.[28]

> [Broadcaster]: As regards fashion, have you found a difference between here and Italy?
> Mrs Cuff: Oh, a great difference. You see, in Italy women dress in a much prettier way. Here, it's cold, and of course one has to wear a lot of woollen stuff.
> [Broadcaster]: Also, there's the snow.
> Mrs Cuff: Yes, and that's why the shoes are rather heavy and have low heels. To make up for this, the colours are brighter. In wartime, I find, one needs striking colours, as a reaction to the grey colours of the uniform. Red, especially. Moreover, people wear this colour in Italy too: a poppy red.

The aim of this interview was to show that the British government took care of its citizens by providing decent clothing and taking people's personal circumstances into consideration. Mrs Cuff was Italian. Since she came from a warm country, she did not have the appropriate clothes to face the Scottish winter. Hence the British government offered her a special coupon to obtain more clothes.[29] After identifying the difference between Italy and Britain in terms of fashion, the woman and the broadcaster agreed on the fact that there was a common element associating the two countries: a passion for the colour red. This element might be considered insignificant;

however, it is representative of British propaganda strategy. By referring to similarities between British and Italian habits, the BBC aimed at making the Italians feel closer to Britain.

Another common stereotype was that of the Italian woman as a good mother and thoughtful wife. The Italian woman was often represented as a mother whose son or husband had been killed in bombing raids. In April 1944 a programme about women's rights was broadcast. However, these rights did not relate to their position in society, but to their roles in the family:

> These rights seem to us Italian women to be the elementary right of every woman to have her own home, her own fireside; the right to bring up her children; the right not to see her husband, father or brother snatched away at any moment to satisfy the ambitions of the heads of government in useless and senseless wars.[30]

The other side of the coin was the attachment of Italian sons to their mothers. This was evident from the *Italian Soldiers Programme*. This programme was launched in December 1944 and its aim was to deliver messages from Italian prisoners or soldiers in Britain to their families. In the first programme of the series some songs were broadcast, sung by Italian soldiers. The first song, *Mamma mia*, was interpreted by soldier Giovanni Acerboni from Treviglio. The song was introduced by the BBC broadcaster with the following words: 'Il primo pensiero di ogni soldato italiano è per la mamma lontana che pensa a lui e attende sue notizie' ('The first thought of every Italian soldier is for the distant mother who thinks of him and awaits news from him').[31] This introduction was followed by a comic monologue by Lance Corporal Abele Venosti from Naples and two songs entitled respectively *Nostalgia napoletana* and *Violetta*. These glimpses of daily life conveyed a clear propaganda message: Italian families should be reassured about the well-being of their family members in Britain. Their relatives were healthy and were making friendships with other Italians. The protagonists of the *Italian Soldiers Programme* were the embodiment of good, ordinary Italians who loved singing, telling jokes and laughing.

Similar programmes were broadcast for those in the British prisoner-of-war camps. Programmes about the everyday life of the prisoners were an excellent propaganda tool. By showing that the foreigners in the camps were receiving good treatment, Britain was portrayed as a generous and charitable country. The French Service broadcast similar programmes, speaking about the warm welcome given to French refugees in Britain.[32] Prisoners could also provide useful information for use in the programmes. Many radio sets were installed in the camps so that the prisoners could listen to both the BBC and the news from Rome. 'This was granted for the purpose of monitoring the reactions to Italian war bulletins, as well as to reduce the spread of rumours

– and the manufacturing of illegal radio receivers.'[33] At the beginning of 1941 many Italian soldiers who had been captured in North Africa were transferred to Britain, where they could be used as a workforce in the service of the British economy.[34]

These prisoners contributed to Britain's food production by working on farms. For this reason, the PID and the PWE claimed, the prisoners should be treated well, since a tired worker was useless: 'inoltre, raccomandava il PID, bisognava dare ai prigionieri una buona impressione della Gran Bretagna, e questo era compito di tutti i militari addetti ai campi. Si trattava, comprensibilmente, di una questione di propaganda' ('moreover, the PID recommended, prisoners had to be given a good impression of Britain, and this was the task of all the military personnel in the camps. It was understandably a question of propaganda').[35] It is not a coincidence that Colonel Stevens visited the camps on more than one occasion. On 23 September 1941 he visited Royston camp; during his visit some Italian prisoners shared their difficulties and issues with him. One of their main concerns related to correspondence with their families in Italy. They complained about the difficulties in receiving news from home; they suspected that their letters to Italy were never delivered. During the visit Stevens asked the prisoners whether they wanted the BBC to broadcast their names over the radio, which could help them re-establish contact with their families.[36]

There are no references to politics in the programmes for the prisoners. As mentioned earlier, Italian women were not regarded as being engaged with the political life of their country. The same reasoning applied to the average Italian man, embodied by Nissim's *omo qualunque*.

As the previous chapters have shown, the *omo qualunque* was portrayed as a man with very little culture. However, regardless of his level of education, it was evident to him that his life was affected by the war. In a special programme in the series entitled *Il carosello dell'omo qualunque*, he was in conversation with various characters. Among them was the female announcer who used to read the messages from the Italians in Britain in the series called *Piccola Posta della Voce di Londra*. She had a message for the Italian *omo qualunque* on behalf of the British 'little man' who wished to meet him. Later in the programme the meeting between the Italian and the British 'little man' takes place:

O.Q.I: Voglio dire solidari con gli italiani …
O.Q.: Naturale … fra omini qualunque ci s'intende sempre
O.Q.I: Vero. Io fumo la mia pipa …
O.Q.: E io i 'mezzo toscano
O.Q.I: Io sono … diciamo così insulare …
O.Q.: E io … peninsulare. Dunque siamo quasi parenti. Ah, ah.[37]

Omo qualunque inglese (OQI): I want to express my solidarity with the Italians ...
Omo qualunque (OQ): Of course ... common people can always get along.
OQI: That's true. I smoke my pipe ...
OQ: And I my Tuscan cigar.
OQI: I'm ... let's say 'insular' ...
OQ: And I'm ... 'peninsular'. So, we're almost related. Ha-ha![37]

As mentioned earlier, a passion for the colour red associated the Italian Mrs Cuff with British women. Also in this case small aspects of everyday life created connections and empathy between the Italian and the British man. Both were surrounded by the sea and they both smoked. As the programme suggested, there were more similarities than differences between the two countries. At the end of the programme, when the British *omo qualunque* left, the Italian commented on the meeting with the following words: 'un brav'uomo però ... lui chiacchiera poco ... ma fa le cose per benino, con cura, con precisione ... e con diligenza'.

Many programmes focused instead on the differences between Britain and Italy, with the aim of explaining why such differences existed. In other words, these programmes offered keys to understanding British culture and lifestyle. As this work has shown, many broadcasters were Italians and wrote their own programmes. As a consequence, many broadcasts revealed much about how the British were viewed by the Italian exiles. The British Foreign Office did exert its control over both the programmes and the lives of the Italian refugees; however, this was mainly in the area of military and political issues. On cultural aspects most of the Italian broadcasters seemed to be free to decide programme content. Therefore, the Italian Service's broadcasts were expressions of both British views on Italy and Italian opinions on Britain. In the programme just analysed the British *omo qualunque* is described by the Italian as a man who does not talk so much. Likewise, in a programme by Paolo Treves entitled *Mr. Smith*, the British were represented as reserved people. The programme was part of the series *L'Uomo della settimana*. Each week the focus was on a different character to be blamed or praised for his actions. Mr Smith was the symbol of the average British man and was portrayed by Paolo Treves as an admirable person:

> Potreste incontrarlo, al termine del suo lavoro, in una qualunque casa d'Inghilterra, calmo e posato, il volto raso, spesso la pipa in bocca, pochi gesti e voce uguale. Se gli parlate, vi risponderà cortese, senza troppo interesse, almeno apparente. E' difficile che il signor Smith vi domandi i fatti vostri, si occupi di ciò che non lo riguarda. Forse il signor Joe Smith non ha molta immaginazione, non indulge a troppo sottili analisi psicologiche. Fa il suo dovere senza risparmiarsi, sa benissimo che il suo lavoro è indispensabile alla vita della nazione –ma non ne parla molto. Probabilmente non ne parla neppure

con se stesso, nelle soste della sua fatica, o la domenica quando ama coltivare i cavoli e le carote nel suo pezzetto di giardino. Legge il giornale con attenzione, ascolta puntualmente la radio, alle nove tutte le sere, si compiace se le notizie sono buone, e se sono cattive è sempre sicuro che le cose potrebbero andar peggio, e che presto la situazione migliorerà.[38]

You might find him, after his working day, in an average British house, calm and composed, shaved, often gripping a pipe in his mouth, making few gestures and maintaining a steady voice. If you speak to him he will answer politely and, at least apparently, with limited interest. It's unlikely that Mr Smith will ask you about your business or busy himself with things that don't concern him. Perhaps Mr Joe Smith doesn't have much imagination, and doesn't over-indulge himself in complex psychological analysis. He does his duty without sparing himself, knowing very well that his work is indispensable to the life of the nation, but he doesn't talk about it much. He probably doesn't even talk to himself about it, in the breaks from his toil, or on Sundays when he enjoys growing cabbages and carrots in his little piece of garden. He reads the paper carefully, and listens to the radio attentively, at nine o'clock every evening; he's happy if the news is good, and if it's bad he's always sure that things could be worse, and that the situation will soon improve.

In both cases – the British *omo qualunque* and Mr Smith – there are references to the uncommunicative and apparently cold nature of the British. Of particular interest is the reference to the cabbages grown in Mr Smith's garden. Gardening was a very popular hobby in Britain, but the metaphor was also an effective way of alluding to the individualism of British society. However, the appearances were misleading. Mr Smith was actually a man with great civic sense, and his apparent disinterest was actually trust. Mr Smith was calm and steady because he trusted his government. Even bad news did not worry him because he was certain that things would soon change. The implicit message of this programme was that the Italians did not share the same privilege because they could not rely on the irresponsible fascist regime.

The programmes analysed thus far targeted Italians who were not familiar with politics and had little culture. However, the programmes for intellectuals and upper classes seemed to suggest that the category of ordinary Italian also included them. Education and income are usually the key criteria for distinguishing social classes. It is really interesting instead to read what Paolo Treves said about the *italiano medio* (average Italian):

Un italiano qualunque, l'italiano medio. Milioni oggi pensano a lui in tutti i paesi del mondo libero, milioni immaginano il suo volto, cercano di seguire i suoi pensieri, al di là di quella nebbia tremula che gli vela lo sguardo... Conosciamo le mani oneste segnate dalla fatica, e anche le mani bianche e fini dell'intellettuale che tra il pollice e l'indice congiunti sembra trattenere un pensiero segreto.³⁹

> An ordinary Italian, the average Italian. Today, millions think about him in all the countries of the free world; millions imagine his face and try to understand his thoughts, behind that shifting mist that veils his glance ... We know the honest hands marked by toil, and also the fine pale hands of the intellectual, who seems to be holding a secret thought between his thumb and his index finger.

Again here, it was more important to talk to the Italians as human beings rather than as peasants, lawyers or students, since war united all social classes. From the factory worker to the intellectual, everyone shared the same uncertain destiny.

As has been said in Chapters 3 and 6, when discussing the Free Italy movement, workers were often the focus of the BBC programmes. The Italian Risorgimento against the Austrians was often mentioned to incite workers to rebellion against the Nazi-fascists. The history of the Italian workers and the so-called *biennio rosso* (two red years) in 1919–20 had already shown that factory workers could be a subversive force. Moreover, by working in factories, they were more likely to be killed in enemy air raids. Also in the case of the Second World War, workers protested against the regime by striking in March 1943. This was evidence that part of the Italian population had begun to oppose the regime prior to September 1943.⁴⁰ The theme of socialist proletarian internationalism was particularly appropriate for piquing their interest:

> Italians! The eyes of the world are turned on our country at this time. Not only the chancelleries, but the factories, the trade unions, the villages of the whole world are watching Italy. Here in England, in the Mechanical Workers' Union, the largest union in the world, everyone wants to know something about Italy. The English mechanics want to know what the Italian mechanics have done in the past, what they are doing now and what they can do.⁴¹

In March 1944, a year after the factory riots in Turin and Milan, workers were once again on strike. Arthur Deakin, the assistant general secretary of the Transport and General Workers Union, congratulated the people in charge of Italy's transport for their remarkable work:

> We know that your underground struggle against Fascism never ceased. The mass strike in Turin and Milan one year ago, which were among the main causes of the overthrowing of Fascism, proved to us that in spite of savage oppression you had succeeded in keeping alive a most efficient net of underground trade unions and factory committees ... The railwaymen and tramwaymen, the transport workers of all categories, as well as the engineers and workers of the electric power stations are in front, but with them are not only the

workers of all other industries, and the agricultural population, but even the shopkeepers, municipal and civil servants and students.[42]

Italian workers were not alone; they could count on the support of other workers. The programme ended with the promise that British workers would do everything in their power to support their Italian comrades.

Another category targeted by the BBC was the political and cultural elites. The number of programmes for such Italians increased between the spring of 1943 and the unconditional surrender of Italy. This was predictable, considering the war's developments. Every Italian could contribute to the overthrow of the fascist regime; however, the people to refer to when reorganising the Italian state were the intellectuals and politicians. In the months preceding the Allied landings new programmes were launched. Among these was *Un italiano dai capelli grigi* by Aldo Cassuto, whose protagonist was a cultured, elderly anti-fascist man, and *Lettera ad un italiano* by Paolo Treves. In this programme Treves sent fictional letters to acquaintances and friends and the addressees of these letters included anti-fascist intellectuals. Among these were Benedetto Croce, who was finally able to be published again in Italy.[43]

In the majority of cases, however, Treves wrote to ex-fascists who had changed their minds about Mussolini and his regime. The language used in the programmes aimed at creating an intimate dialogue between Paolo and his correspondents. Paolo spoke to his addressees in a paternalistic tone and played the role of an old friend who wanted to give his dear friends some wise advice:

Caro Carlo,
avrei voluto scriverti da tempo, appena ho saputo del tuo stato d'animo attuale, della tua inquietudine davanti ai problemi della situazione. Non credere che non capisca la tua preoccupazione. So che la tua buona fede è assoluta, che hai creduto nel fascismo, nelle parole che da tanti anni ti sono state dette, fin dai tempi del ginnasio…E adesso che tutto sembra precipitare intorno a te, non trovi più nel fascismo quel mondo in cui tu credevi, e proprio perché sei un ragazzo onesto non osi pensare che i tuoi maestri abbiano avuto torto, anzi, che molti di essi ti abbiano consciamente imbrogliato.[44]

Dear Carlo,
I've been wanting to write to you for a while, having heard about your current state of mind and your worries about the problems of your situation. Please don't think that I don't understand your concerns. I know that your good faith is absolute, and that you believed in fascism, in the words spoken to you for so many years, right from secondary school. … Now that everything seems to be collapsing around you, you no longer find in fascism that world that you believed in; because you are an honest young man, you hardly dare think that your teachers were wrong, or even that many of them knowingly misled you.

Unlike the programmes analysed in Chapter 5, in which ex-fascists were ridiculed, in this extract the former fascist is regarded as a person who has genuinely changed political sides. This is unsurprising: on the one hand, it was crucial to warn the Italians and inform them that the newly formed RSI was not different from the previous regime; on the other, however, ex-fascists could become new supporters of the Allied forces. This is why it was extremely important to gain the trust of those who might genuinely have changed their opinions. Paolo appreciated that Carlo's political ideas were nourished in the context of fascist indoctrination. Therefore, he made clear that he was not trying to reproach him. From the education received in a fascist school to journals such as the previously mentioned *Gerarchia*, to the fascist corporations, Paolo demolished, letter by letter, all the lies and institutions with which Carlo had identified himself up to the spring of 1943. Carlo was not the only addressee of these letters. Each letter was directed at a fascist from a different generation. From the extract it emerges that Carlo was still in education, since Paolo refers to his fascist *maestri* (mentors) who had betrayed him; Carlo is also called *ragazzo* (young man).

Another addressee is an elderly lawyer whose name is not specified. The lawyer may have been in his sixties, as he had witnessed the crisis of the Italian liberal state. The reason why fascism had taken power in 1922, as Paolo warned him, was fear of the people, which led to repressive measures against any form of dissent. He should consider this to avoid further mistakes in the present. New forms of fascisms would not be allowed. At the same time, Paolo said to reassure him, this would not lead to the institution of 'Soviet e i tribunali operai per giudicare sommariamente i capitalisti' ('Soviet and workers' courts to judge the capitalists summarily').[45] As confirmed by an audience survey, the BBC was aware that there were conflicting feelings in Italy about communism and Britain's alliance with the Soviet Union:

> The witnesses give conflicting pictures of what Italians are thinking about Bolshevism. The general effect is that, as one might expect, the cultured and middle classes are afraid of it, mostly because they fear a repetition of 1919, while, in general, the working classes are not afraid of Bolshevism and there are some communists.[46]

While many peasants and shopkeepers said that Bolshevism 'could not be worse than the regime', there were also many Italians who 'thought of the Russians as [a] horde of savages which would bear down on Italy and burn all her churches'.[47] This was undoubtedly an element to consider when preparing the programmes for Italy.

The next section will focus on how the Italians responded to the BBC programmes. While it is not possible to obtain detailed information for each of the categories previously mentioned, there is copious evidence that was listened to and appreciated by people of all social classes.

BBC audience surveys

As we saw in Chapter 1, the BBC's duty, according to its first director, John Reith, consisted of educating and entertaining the British population. Despite this, as David Hendy has noted, 'it's true that many broadcasters, most notably the BBC under its founding father John Reith, were notoriously reluctant to pander to audience tastes. As Reith himself saw it, the BBC's historic task was to lead and to shape public attitudes, not to follow them.'[48] But in reality, continued Hendy, archival evidence shows that the BBC was 'often pathologically concerned with the minute-by-minute opinions of its listeners'.[49]

The same reasoning applies to the Italian Service. BBC audience surveys of enemy countries show that the British station was constantly in search of information on its listeners and their habits. To win the war, it was essential to know what Italian listeners thought about the conflict and the Allied propaganda. The surveys are based on the information provided by British people who had lived or travelled in Italy. There are also references to letters sent by listeners in these documents. Many of the informants were former internees in Italian camps, who had returned to Britain. Some lived in other countries such as Portugal, where they had the opportunity to exchange information with travellers from Italy. The informants were often called 'witnesses' or 'travellers' and their identity was never revealed. Percentages of listeners to the Italian Service can be found in these reports. However, these data are not the outcome of reliable and verifiable investigation. One example is an extract from a paper on European audience estimates from 26 July 1943:

> The release of a large number of British civilians from internment in Italy early in 1943 provided a source of copious direct evidence on listening to the BBC. Coming from various places all over Italy, the witnesses interviewed had all been able to get news from the BBC during their period of internment and all gave examples of many different classes and types of Italian who listen. Group listening in underground cellars, back rooms of shops, etc. was reported from 6 different places. All our witnesses confirmed the widespread diffusion of BBC news and said that all Italians, even if they did not admit listening, appeared to be well informed of news which they could only have got from the BBC. A British prisoner-of-war who left Italy on 13th April 1943 said that nothing would stop the Italians listening to the BBC except the introduction of the death penalty; he estimated that 70% of his Italian contacts listened to the BBC.[50]

This survey does tell us that the BBC was listened to in secret by groups of people who gathered in the basements of houses. However, the percentage provided by the former British prisoner is only his personal estimate. Moreover, while the word 'class' is mentioned here, there are no further details that allow for the identification of such classes.

Since the data contained in the surveys are based on word of mouth, it is extremely difficult to establish the boundaries between reality and the personal interpretation of the informants. Yet these monthly reports included important details on the reception of Radio Londra, its audience and listening conditions, since jamming enemy radio frequencies was common. The information contained in the surveys, moreover, confirmed that stated in reports from the fiduciaries of the fascist regime, analysed by Maura Piccialuti Caprioli: Radio Londra was listened to by Italians of all social classes and backgrounds.

Since 1941 the BBC was well aware that its news commentaries and talks were listened to in spite of the fascist censorship laws, as confirmed by a sub-section of a survey from January 1941, entitled *BBC News Gets Through*:

> The Italian press is no longer content with attacking the 'few misguided people' who indulge in clandestine listening, and the steady flow of sentences proclaimed against transgressors of the ban do not seem to have obtained any appreciable result. A leader appearing on the front page of the <u>Corriere della Sera</u> (5.2.41), after emphasising the bad effect which enemy radio propaganda can have on the public, laments that there is no absolute defence against this weapon: 'Since jamming can only partly disturb reception the best thing is to counteract the effects by propaganda in the opposite direction. This is a grim battle of every day, indeed of every hour, and it calls for the waste of intellectual forces which might be better employed elsewhere'.[51]

As this extract shows, enemy radio propaganda was publicly described in the fascist press as a very dangerous weapon. This was an indirect admission of weakness, since these declarations confirmed that fascist laws were not respected.

Another interesting fact, reported by an American informant in 1942 and confirmed by other surveys, is that Italians listened to the BBC in their own language as well as in others such as French and English. This group of listeners included people from the upper and middle classes as well as merchants, sailors and people connected with foreign trade. Among these listeners were also Italians who had lived in English-speaking countries and a 'number of ordinary educated people whose knowledge of English allow[ed] them to pick up the gist of broadcasts in English'.[52] In the same report another important category of listeners to the BBC in English is mentioned: this group was formed of people who could not understand foreign languages but received indirect news from the BBC from other listeners.

BBC news travelled from mouth to mouth not only horizontally among people of the same social class, but vertically into other classes often in unexpected ways. Servants would pick up the conversations of their masters, news originating from the BBC. The shopkeepers and the market place of the district heard it the morning after.[53]

In the case of news distributed by word of mouth, the directive suggested, the original source of information was often forgotten as the stories were relayed. Moreover, along the way, the news often acquired distortions and exaggerations in the telling. A few months later, on 11 May 1942, another survey confirmed the same data: 'The neutral who left Rome last November found that all the people with whom she came in contact listened to the BBC or had received second hand information from that source.'[54] Moreover, this informant added:

> The thirst for news among Italians of all classes was considerable, and described her daily embarrassment at being publicly asked for Radio Londra news by the shopkeepers, who would also discuss events with a total disregard for danger. The attitude of disbelieving Axis claims until they were confirmed by the BBC was prevalent, and she recalled that, when the Italian papers announced the first bombing of London, many people waited for the BBC to authenticate the report.[55]

Reference to the fact that the BBC was listened to by people of all social classes was common in the BBC surveys throughout the years of the conflict. This was confirmed, said one survey, by the fact that Italians were aware of all their military defeats despite the regime hiding the truth from them: 'every day servants asks for the latest news which they spread among the masses. In this way, news items in one day have reached every circle. This oral information is now more important than the news given by the daily paper.'[56]

By the end of 1941 the BBC was also aware that fascist politicians and Italian churchmen were among its listeners. In a survey dated 28 August 1941 a fascinating episode is reported by a resident of Lisbon who often had the chance to interview travellers from Italy:

> The Lisbon correspondent then proceeds to tell a charming story (or should it be called 'legend'?):
> Some little time ago, the major of a certain town was informed that his son had fallen in the field of honour. This misfortune was to be celebrated by a Requiem Mass attended by all the civil and military authorities, as well as all the local notables. The major, however, had just time to listen to London before donning his weeds and heard with mingled joy and dismay that the young man was an unwounded prisoner. He was in a frightful fix for if he stopped the Mass everyone would have known he had heard. Fearful penalties are attached to listening in to foreign broadcasts and he, the major, had done

it. So he decided to carry on. When he reached the Church there was not a single soul there, not even the priests!⁵⁷

This anecdote is very similar to that of Colonel Stevens, mentioned in the introduction. How can we be sure that the phrase 'Hooray for Colonel Stevens' was actually written on the walls of Sicilian houses? Similarly, it is impossible to verify whether the story of the Mass was real. Another interesting aspect is the language used in the BBC report to introduce the anecdote, which is described as a 'charming story' and a 'legend'. The story was also commented on in the following way: 'The woman who told it, swore it was true ... Se non è vero ... Even if the Italians invented or adopted this story, it is significant.' As mentioned in the introduction, many legends circulated in Italy during the Second World War. These included the story of Pippo, the alleged Allied aircraft that was believed to monitor Italian civilians every night.⁵⁸ What is especially interesting in this report is that in 1941 the BBC was already aware of the circulation of legendary stories about its programmes. In the same report the woman from Lisbon said that the BBC was called 'the Angel's Voice' by many Italians: 'Everyone listens to the BBC in Italian, which they call "the Angel's voice". Colonel Stevens is particularly admired though he says some pretty plain things to them'.

Other fascinating anecdotes related to precautionary measures taken by Italians when exchanging information about BBC programmes. This is what was reported by a woman who had been in Genoa in the summer of 1941:

> During my journey a little fact amused me very much. A great number of Italians were talking about their dreams ... 'I dreamt', said the Neapolitan restaurant owner, 'I dreamt that the Russians have bombed Berlin', said the hairdresser from Rome. Finding such an unusual amount of dreamers abnormal, I finally asked an old friend of mine in Rome, why so much dreaming was going on in Italy. ' You see, Madame', explained my friend to me, 'here to dream means to listen in to a foreign wireless station'.⁵⁹

Another traveller reported that, during his internment in a hotel at an Alpine resort, he was constantly informed about the BBC news by the hotel proprietor. Everybody, said this former British internee, listened to the BBC, especially in the evenings. Yet it was difficult to obtain details on listening habits because people always pretended not to listen:

> Prudence led some people to adopt precautionary measures. People meeting in the street, for instance, would talk of the BBC only after dealing with some other topic so that, if questioned, they could always fall back on a harmless subject of conversation without fear of one or the other inadvertently giving the game away.⁶⁰

The easy access to BBC news was also confirmed by another survey from April 1943. 'Out of 27 travellers from Italy', said the report, 'only one had been without news from the BBC during the period of internment.' The person who could not listen to the BBC was a woman who had been interned in a concentration camp. The other internees had their own radios or listened with friends. The least fortunate could obtain second-hand information. The same survey confirmed the reports of the informants of the Italian police:

> None of them had ever heard of special police patrols hunting for black listeners – only one witness from Milan remembered a rumour that the Carabinieri were checking up on people's sets, but this had been many months ago and she had heard nothing more about it. It was the general impression that detection was due to spying done by servants, neighbours, or anyone with a private grudge.[61]

Some of the informants provided the BBC with their own advice on how to approach Italians. This was the case of a British woman who had left Italy on 10 June 1940, when Mussolini declared war on France and Great Britain. This woman had met many Italians under the age of 30 and suggested that British propaganda should be 'factual or amusing or interestingly presented and camouflaged' since Italians were suspicious, 'propaganda-proof and propaganda tired'. They certainly did not want 'ideological and rhetorical talks'.[62] Moreover, continued the informant, the Italians were convinced that the British were 'gentlemen'. This conviction should not be disregarded. The woman seemed to be particularly far-sighted because this was true of Colonel Stevens, whose elegant style was warmly appreciated by many Italians.

The next and last section of this chapter will analyse some extracts from letters sent to Colonel Stevens. The letters show that the reports of British witnesses and the content of this correspondence had many common features.

Dear Colonel Stevens ... listeners' letters to the BBC

According to David Hendy, 'in our own age of interactivity, we're sometimes too ready to assume that "the listener" has been discovered – or rather empowered – for the first time'.[63] In reality, he continues, 'the numbers of people communicating with their favourite radio stations, seeking to express an opinion or challenge its decisions, have always been staggering'.[64]

This is certainly true for the BBC Italian Service during the Second World War, as many listeners sent letters to London to express their opinion on the programmes they listened to. Unlike the BBC audience surveys, which are mostly based on the experience of British witnesses in Italy, this correspondence is a more direct source of information on the Italian audience. Moreover, unlike surveys, Peppino Ortoleva has written, letters and oral sources can tell us about the subjective listening experience of individuals.[65] In the case of this research on the Italian Service, the letters are also a source of information on the emotions and feelings of several Italians during the Second World War.

The correspondence is not representative of the entire Italian population for various reasons. Not all listeners decided to send their thoughts to the BBC. In addition, the percentage of people who could actually read and write in standard Italian was low. This meant that many listeners could not write to the BBC even if they wanted to. Among the authors of the letters were doctors, lawyers and professors. Moreover, it is very likely that, given the war conditions, many letters did not reach their destinations or were destroyed by bombs. The BBC Written Archives Centre holds only a few boxes of listeners' letters. Nevertheless, the correspondence from Italy must have been larger. In 1944 alone, 4,000 letters were received by the BBC from Italians. The majority of these letters related to enquiries about Italian prisoners of war in Britain or praised the BBC for its programmes. It is not a coincidence that in 1944 the Italian Service launched a programme to thank its listeners and answer requests for information received from Italy. Many letters, however, provided useful feedback on programmes and commentators.[66] As for the backgrounds of the letter writers, the majority belonged to the middle classes (professionals, teachers, white-collar workers and students). But letters were also sent by blue-collar workers, railwaymen, housewives and unskilled labourers. Noteworthy data related to the numbers of female listeners:

> Out of the 80 letters containing the most detailed comments on our broadcasts 21 are women. Two of these women, one a young girl of 21 and the other middle-aged have been interested enough to answer in some detail questions on listening asked in a special broadcast for Italy in the Listeners' information bureau series on 27.8.44. This is rather surprising, since it was thought that in this part of Italy, where the old prejudice that 'the woman's place is in the home' is still very much alive, few women would be interested in listening to our broadcasts or be sufficiently versed in political matters to follow the commentaries ... It is surprising, too, that a good many of these letters are from women of the middle or lower middle classes.[67]

As we have seen in the first section of this chapter, women were addressed by the BBC as mothers and wives because they were not considered capable of engaging with political issues. In reality, as we will also see shortly, there were many women among the letter writers, some of whom were constantly in touch with the radio during the years of the conflict. One element to consider is that, with the exception of a couple of letters, there is almost no trace of criticism towards the BBC. According to Briggs, in 1940 the BBC received several hostile letters from Italy.[68] However, these letters no longer appear to exist. Despite all these preliminary considerations on the impossibility of obtaining representative estimates about the audience from the letters, it must be said that they do provide very important qualitative information on the reception of the BBC in Italy.[69] The last section of this chapter will concentrate on the content of this correspondence.

Communications with the BBC were certainly difficult and dangerous for Italians living under the fascist regime. The majority of letters sent prior to the Allied landings arrived from neutral territories. The various branches of the BBC could often be listened to in several countries. Therefore, it could happen that speakers living in countries other than Italy listened to Radio Londra. Some letters, for example, were sent from Commonwealth territories by British listeners who understood Italian. The great majority of these letters were sent to Colonel Stevens. Stevens was thanked for providing reliable information on the conflict, but it was his moral support that was appreciated above all. According to a British informant:

> Colonel Stevens' immense popularity which, he declared, was probably due to 'his serious way of presenting news comments and to his pleasant voice. He conveys the feeling to his listeners that he has pondered deeply over what he says and that he is always aware of the responsibilities of his job.[70]

A high percentage of listeners expressed their embarrassment writing to someone they had never met in person. What allowed them to overcome such awkwardness, said many of the letters, was the desire to thank him and the other BBC employees for their work. Many listeners wrote that they wanted to do something in return for the great benefits that Stevens's programmes brought them. It emerged from the correspondence to the Italian Service that Stevens was becoming an icon for many Italians. Several listeners did not call themselves listeners but *ammiratori* (fans). Among the names of other broadcasters mentioned in the letters are Candidus (John Marus), Umberto Calosso and the *omo qualunque*.[71]

On 16 June 1942, Mr P.H. from Lugano wrote to Stevens to ask for some favours: he wanted a signed photograph and transcripts of the texts of his talks and wished to meet him and shake his hand at the end of the conflict. The man also invited Stevens to spend a well-deserved holiday at his home in Lugano.[72] Mr P.H. was not the only listener who asked for Stevens's photo and programme texts. Clearly, these listeners wanted to be able to put a face to the voice that kept them company during those difficult days. As for the transcripts of his broadcasts, some selected programmes were published during the war with the title *E' al microfono il colonnello Stevens*. The listeners' letters might have encouraged this publication. Moreover, the BBC Written Archives holds some copies of these short pamphlets with

Stevens's dedications and signature. It is therefore possible that some of the listeners' requests were granted.

Stevens's distinctive trademark was the greeting that opened and ended all his talks. A woman writing from Malta said that the best moment of her day was 8.30 p.m., when she could tune in to the BBC and return Stevens's *buonasera*: 'your beautiful and lovely Italian, your great sense of humour and wit appeals to me so greatly and your very clever talk – I always answer your "Buonasera" and I add "tante e tante grazie" (many and many thanks)'.[73] This woman was not the only case, in many letters there are references to the habit of reciprocating the presenter's 'good evening'.

Italian fans of the BBC also regarded the station as an authority to contact in order to resolve practical issues in their home towns. An example of this is a letter sent by A.G., a citizen of Nola, near Naples. This man wrote to Stevens for the first time in the summer of 1944 to ask him to intervene with the Allied authorities on his behalf because there was no electricity in Nola. After hearing from some friends that Stevens mentioned Nola at the BBC, A.G. sent him another letter of thanks:

> La Sua cortese risposta a mezzo de "LA VOCE DI LONDRA" dei giorni 8 e 9 luglio u.s. mi è stata riferita di molti amici di Napoli e la notizia del Suo gentile interessamento perché la nostra zona possa ottenere la concessione dell'energia elettrica, si è sparsa per tutta la plaga nolana provocando un coro di rallegramenti e di speranze. A mio mezzo, la popolazione tutta, La prega di accogliere i più sinceri ringraziamenti ed i più vivi voti di gratitudine.[74]

> Your courteous answer via 'LA VOCE DI LONDRA' of 8 and 9 July was reported to me by many friends in Naples and the news of your kind intervention to get electricity for our area has spread in the Nola region and made people happy and hopeful. On behalf of the entire population, I would ask you to accept our warmest thanks and our vivid expression of gratitude.

This may not have been the only case of this kind, since Stevens answered the man that he did not hold the kind of authority and power that people often attributed to him:

> Mi sento in dovere di spiegare che io non dispongo di quell'influenza e, tantomeno, di quei poteri che spesso mi vengono attribuiti dagli ascoltatori italiani con I quali, per tramite del microfono, ho avuto la fortuna di forgiare il legame che tuttora ci stringe nell'amicizia e nella stima reciproca. Se le mie parole alla radio portano qualche volta ad un risultato benefico – come pare sia avvenuto in quest'occasione- io, per conto mio, ne son felicissimo. Ma non posso onestamente farmene un vanto che non sarebbe meritato.[75]

> I feel I must explain that I am not as influential and powerful as Italian listeners – with whom I had the pleasure of forging solid bonds of friendship and mutual esteem that still exist – often believe. If my words on the radio might

lead to positive outcomes – as it seems happened on this occasion – I can only be very happy. But, honestly, I cannot boast about something I have not done.

These requests for help to resolve problems increased once the Allies were occupying Italy, because Italians were now free to contact London. Several Italians asked Stevens to make enquiries about their missing relatives in British territories.

In many cases Stevens did contact the relevant offices and authorities to obtain the requested information. This is evident from his answers to these letters and the aforementioned programme titled *La Piccola Posta della Voce di Londra*. The programmes in the series often referred to happy cases in which the missing relatives were found.

Other requests related to military issues. On 19 July 1943 a woman, most probably British, asked Stevens to intercede with the Allied authorities to stop the bombing of Rome. Did the British not know, she asked, that bombs could destroy the 'eternal city' and centuries of history?[76]

Bombing was the subject of another letter, sent by a Milanese man. The beginning of the letter praises Stevens. However, in the second part, the man complains about the bombing of Milan. The Allies, suggested the writer, should focus on other targets such as Vatican City, Venice, Naples or Cremona. The listener ended this letter with the following words: 'Per l'amor di Dio mi lasci stare Milano' ('for God's sake, don't touch Milan'), otherwise, he would have to turn against Stevens.[77]

Stevens was also asked smaller favours by some Italians who were curious about Britain and wanted to know more about it. This is the case with a letter sent in December 1945 by an Italian woman, who had heard that Stevens was ill and sent him her good wishes for a prompt recovery. The woman started her letter by referring to the usual Christmas message that Stevens sent to Italians during the conflict. At the end of the letter, she asked for a British Christmas card:

> E ora perdonatemi se vi chiedo un piccolo favore: mi risponderete? E, in tale caso, potreste inviarmi una di quelle belle cartoline di Natale che si usano da voi e che – come ha detto Radio Londra – in questi giorni riempiono le mensole dei vostri caminetti? Sarebbe un grato favore che mi fareste: come se mi permetteste, per un attimo, di far capolino nelle vostre case in festa. Non posso ricambiarVi la gentilezza: in questo paesino chiuso tra i monti, dove da diversi anni lavoro, non c'è nulla che possa degnamente portare un omaggio dall'Italia. Non avendo di meglio Vi mando, qui, i più sinceri auguri per il nuovo … e vogliate scusarmi se Vi ho rubato un pò di tempo.[78]

> And now forgive me if I ask you a little favour: will you answer? And if that's the case, could you please send me one of those beautiful Christmas cards that are common in England and that – as Radio Londra said – at this time

of the year sit on the shelves above your fireplaces? This favour would be appreciated: it would be like allowing me to enter your festively decorated houses for a moment. I cannot return the favour: in this small town in the mountains, where I have worked for many years, there is nothing from Italy that can worthily pay you homage. Since I have nothing better to offer, I will send you my most sincere wishes for the New Year ... and sorry again for taking some of your time.

As the extract shows, the woman lived in a small town in the mountains. Hence her wish to discover a new country and gain an insight into the British festive atmosphere. A BBC survey from December 1944 further confirmed that many Italians were interested in knowing more about British culture and traditions. Some listeners wrote to the BBC that they wanted to know how British political parties and democracy worked. Moreover, there was 'a tremendous demand for books by British authors and books about Britain. Several writers of letters have expressed their eagerness to learn English and have asked for books and dictionaries to help them in their studies.'[79]

Other listeners praised Colonel Stevens by sending small presents such as poems written in his honour, postcards from Italy and little paintings. A priest wrote on behalf of many other churchmen to bless the Allies' arrival and attached a holy picture to his letter.[80] The son of an industrialist and former colonel from Tunis sent Stevens a poem he had composed for him.[81]

As previously mentioned, although the BBC WAC does not seem to hold many letters with negative feedback, there are a couple of examples of complaints. One, from a British man called Mr A.W.M. and written on 11 June 1943, complained that the BBC should stop saying that the Italians had been dragged into the war by Mussolini. After three years of British propaganda in Italy the regime was still there. According to Mr A.W.M this was evidence that Italians liked fascism.[82]

Another group of Stevens's 'admirers' were Italian prisoners of war interned in British camps. As we have seen, Stevens visited the camps several times during the conflict. And it appears from the letters that Stevens was regarded as a moral support.[83] On June 1943 a prisoner interned in camp n. 56 told Stevens that he had not been able to listen to his news commentaries in a long time. He was writing on behalf of the other prisoners to say that they were all very sorry to no longer be receiving the BBC news: 'since a long time I have been one of your regular listeners; since the first months of 1940. I felt that you cared about my country. Not only for propaganda purposes as the fascists wanted us to believe.'[84]

Some listeners were in contact with Stevens throughout the entire conflict. The most representative case in this regard is the correspondence between Stevens and Ms Gabriella C. from Vacallo-Chiasso in Switzerland. Gabriella was a young woman in her early twenties.[85] The first letter from this lady was sent to the BBC in 1941. Judging from the content of the letters, which show a high level of education, we can presume she belonged to the upper-middle class. She was studying English and sometimes asked Stevens to send her English books she could not obtain in her country due to the war.

Stevens always granted Gabriella's requests. The young girl became an informant for the BBC since she often referred to political events happening in Switzerland and Italy. One interesting story she mentioned in a letter related to some ex-fascists who lived in Switzerland. In 1942 they were called up, but refused to go because, they said, the BBC had opened their eyes. Many of them, said Gabriella, were fired by their companies after the intervention of the Italian consulate in Switzerland. Others experienced more serious issues when their residence permits expired.

In another letter, dated 31 August 1942, Gabriella said that some Serbian children had told her that in Yugoslavia some Italians were fighting against the Germans. Her information, said the letter, was reliable, since one of the children was an anti-German spy working for Serbia.[86] Towards the end of 1942, after noticing the copious correspondence between Stevens and Gabriella, Michael Roberts of the BBC's General Intelligence Office suggested that Stevens should ask his fan for more information.[87] Hence Stevens asked whether she or her friends could provide data on the audience of Radio Londra in Switzerland.

But what is most interesting in the correspondence between Gabriella and Stevens is the human aspect of this exchange. The passion and determination of a young woman who wanted to contribute to the end of the war, a war that had a terrible impact on her private life, clearly emerges from the letters. Over time Stevens became her mentor. Gabriella often expressed her political thoughts on topics such as the Atlantic Charter and awaited Stevens's opinions.

In one of the letters she even invited Stevens to her wedding, which was to take place at the end of the war. Stevens answered to say that he would be delighted to attend and invited Gabriella to London in return: 'in attesa dell'invito ufficiale voglio rallegrarmi con Lei di augurarle nel Suo matrimonio tanta felicità quanta ne hanno goduto Colonel e Mrs Stevens; i quali si promettono di inviarLe, in una diecina d'anni all'incirca, l'invito alle loro nozze d'oro!' ('while I am waiting for the official invitation, I wish you as much happiness as Colonel and Mrs Stevens have enjoyed in their marriage, and who promise to send you, in about ten years' time, an invitation to their Golden Wedding').[88]

The happy news of Gabriella's wedding was, however, followed by a dreadful letter in which she announced the death of her fiancé:

Nella mia lettera di ieri l'altro mi è mancato il coraggio di dichiararle la verità; anche con lei come con tutti, ho voluto dimostrare un'allegria spensierata che mi sono imposta quale metodo di vita. Mi pento di aver agito slealmente nei suoi confronti e la prego di scusarmi. Gli auguri che ella così gentilmente mi ha voluto porgere per il mio matrimonio non giovano più; da due mesi e mezzo ho perso il mio fidanzato, è morto e non c'è più. Glielo scrivo per debito di coscienza, non perché desidero conforto; nessuno me lo può dare, nemmeno Iddio che toglie tutto; non per trovare sollievo nella narrazione, questo racconto è per me molto doloroso e preferirei tacerlo. Non ho mai trattato questo argomento nemmeno con i più intimi per non dare spettacolo di un dolore che non può veramente sentire.[89]

In the letter I wrote you the day before yesterday I was not brave enough to tell you the truth; I wanted to show you, as well as anyone else, that light-hearted cheer that I imposed upon myself as a lifestyle. I regret having been disloyal to you and I beg you to forgive me. Your kind wishes for my wedding are no longer a reason to be happy; more than two and a half months ago I lost my fiancé, he died and is no longer here. I am writing this to you to clear my conscience, not because I want to be comforted; no one can do it, not even God who takes everything away; I am not doing it because I draw comfort from the narration, this story for me is very painful and I would rather not be telling it. I have not even spoken about it with my close relatives and friends because I did not want to turn a sorrow that no one can really understand into a show.

The tone of this letter clearly shows that for many Italians, Colonel Stevens was more than simply a radio broadcaster. Yet he was not merely a star either. In her letter Gabriella felt the need to apologise for her delay in telling Stevens the truth about the loss of her future husband. Moreover, she told Stevens something that – she claimed – she did not dare to share with her close relatives and friends. Gabriella's case could be considered exceptional, given her youth and the continuity of the exchange. However, the messages sent by many other listeners demonstrate that Stevens was considered *uno di famiglia* (a family member) by his fans. Some of the cases mentioned show that there were also listeners who sent him Easter or Christmas wishes or those who wrote to him to receive news of his health after the BBC announced that he would be on sick leave for a while. This was the case in a telegram sent on 31 October 1943 in which 'Your faithful listeners at the café Svizzero Locarno' sent him their best wishes for a speedy recovery.[90]

In many cases there is evidence that Stevens did answer the letters from his fans. In other circumstances someone at the BBC answered on his behalf.

As the correspondence with Gabriella C. has shown, the BBC was particularly interested in maintaining contact with its listeners, since they could provide useful information on the programmes' reception. Other letters were simply answered out of politeness.

At the end of the conflict Stevens continued to receive correspondence from Italy. Many of these letters, sent in 1945–46, referred to listeners' memories of the programmes and wishes that these memories would leave a legacy in Italy; as one listener wrote in December 1946: 'dovrà restare nella mente e nel cuore di tutti gli italiani che furono sereni, onesti e fervidi cospiratori, per il conforto che esse hanno tratto nei foschi giorni della tragedia sciagurata che insanguinò e mortificò il nostro paese' ('The memories of your radio programmes will remain in the minds and hearts of all those Italians who were honest and fervid conspirators, as they have comforted them in the grim days of the grievous tragedy that covered with blood and mortified our country').[91]

It was evident that the influence and importance of the BBC Italian Service in Italy did not end with the liberation of the country and the conclusion of the Second World War.

The programmes analysed in this chapter have shown that the BBC aimed at reaching various categories of Italians. These included intellectuals and politicians. Their contribution was extremely important as they could help the Allies' reconstruction of Italy. The same reasoning applied to ex-fascists, who could become new supporters of the Allied coalition. However, ordinary men and women were the main target audience of BBC programming. Among the key ingredients for the success of Radio Londra was the attention to the details of Italians' everyday lives during the war. The employment of stereotypes about the British and Italians was an effective propaganda tool. This apparently simple strategy was actually a very successful way of creating connections between the two countries. As the letters and surveys confirm, many Italians started developing an interest in Britain's culture and society due to the BBC programmes. Other broadcasts that made Italians tune in to the BBC were the programmes for prisoners and the *Piccola posta della voce di Londra*. Through these kinds of programme many Italians could obtain information about their relatives in Britain or answers to letters they had sent to the BBC.[92]

Despite the complexity of the sources regarding audiences, the BBC surveys, listeners' letters and the reports of the fascist police, analysed by Piccialuti Caprioli, confirm this data: Radio Londra was listened to by many Italians regardless of their social background and their political beliefs. Moreover, while it is almost impossible to judge whether British propaganda had an actual impact on the Allied victory, the letters clearly show that the BBC was very successful among many Italians. This is evident from the tone of this correspondence: Stevens was considered a trusted and familiar person and the BBC was seen as an authority to contact over issues in their home towns.

As this chapter has shown, there were many fascists among the BBC's listeners. These people listened to the radio either to spy on their enemy or to obtain information that they could not get from their home service. The case of the Mass organised in honour of the Italian official is, in this regard, exemplary.

The majority of listeners, however, were Italians who were tired of the war and hoped to obtain more reliable information. It is in the fears, weariness and hopes of those difficult days that the myth of Radio London was created. The absence of freedom in Italy turned the BBC into 'the Angel's Voice' that told the truth about the conflict. Words of mouth and oral information exchanged by Italians played an important role too, since these caused distortions and exaggerations.

Notes

1. Franco Monteleone and Peppino Ortoleva (eds.), *La radio storia di sessant'anni, 1924–1984* (Turin: ERI, 1984), p. 54; author's translation.
2. Tiziano Bonini and Belén Monclús (eds.), *Radio Audiences and Participation in the Age of Network Society* (New York: Routledge, 2018).
3. Piccialuti Caprioli, *Radio Londra 1939–45*, pp. lxiii, lxx, lxxiv.
4. Piccialuti Caprioli, *Radio Londra 1939–45*, p. lxv; author's translation.
5. Report from Genoa, 21 July 1941, quoted in Piccialuti Caprioli, *Radio Londra 1939–45*, p. lxxi; author's translation.
6. Piccialuti Caprioli, *Radio Londra 1939–45*, p. lxxiii.
7. Piccialuti Caprioli, *Radio Londra 1939–45*, p. lxxvi. The archive in question, analysed by Caprioli, is called *Ministero dell'Interno, Direzione generale di pubblica sicurezza, Divisione affari generali e riservati, Confinati politici* and is held at the *Archivio Centrale dello Stato* in Rome.
8. Simon Potter, 'Who Listened when London Called? Reactions to the BBC Empire Service in Canada, Australia and New Zealand, 1932–1939', *Historical Journal of Film, Radio and Television*, 28 (2010), 475–487; 475.
9. Potter, *Who Listened when London Called?*, 476.
10. Marzano, *Onde fasciste*, pp. 381–417.
11. Gianni Isola, *Abbassa la tua radio, per favore ... Storia dell'ascolto radiofonico nell'Italia fascista* (Florence: La Nuova Italia, 1990), p. 85.
12. Isola, *Abbassa la tua radio*, p. 86.
13. Natale, *Gli anni della radio*, p. 75.
14. Natale, *Gli anni della radio*, p. 75.
15. Natale, *Gli anni della radio*.
16. Isola, *Abbassa la tua radio*, p. 100.
17. Franco Monteleone, *Storia della radio e della televisione in Italia: società, politica, strategie e programmi* (Venice: Marsilio, 1992), p. 46.
18. Monteleone *Storia della radio*, p. 46.

19 David Forgacs and Stephen Gundle, *Mass Culture and Italian Society from Fascism to the Cold War* (Bloomington: Indiana University Press, 2007), p. 62.
20 Forgacs and Gundle, *Mass Culture*, p. 55.
21 Monteleone, *Storia della radio*, pp. 149–50.
22 Sponza, *La BBC 'in bianco' e 'in nero'*, p. 4.
23 Sponza, *La BBC 'in bianco' e 'in nero'*, p. 4.
24 Kay Chadwick, 'Our enemy's enemy', *Media History*, 21:4 (2015), 37.
25 'Conscription: the Second Word War', *UK Parliament*, www.parliament.uk/about/livingheritage/transformingsociety/privatelives/yourcountry/overview/conscriptionww2/, accessed 30 May 2017.
26 BBC WAC, IS, Scripts, s. II, b. 19, L. Zencovich, *English Women in War Time*, 29 June 1943; author's translation.
27 P. Baker, F.L. Shepley, *Women's Programme: the W. V. S.*, 1 January 1945, Scripts, s. II, b. 33, BBC WAC; author's translation.
28 BBC WAC, IS, Scripts, s. II, b. 34, L.Z. Zencovich (basic script by Renata Cuff), *Interview with Mrs Cuff*, 2 February 1945; author's translation.
29 See Summers, *Fashion on The Ration*.
30 *Women's Rights*, 10 April 1944, Scripts, s. II, b. 24, BBC WAC.
31 BBC WAC, IS, Scripts, s. II, G.R. Foa, D. Piani, *Italian soldiers programme*, n. 1, 3 December 1944.
32 Kay Chadwick, 'Our enemy's enemy', 38.
33 Sponza, *Divided Loyalties*, p. 135.
34 Insolvibile, *Wops*, p. 43.
35 Insolvibile, *Wops*, p. 72.
36 BBC WAC, IS, s. Colonel Stevens, b. Prisoners of War Letters 1941–46, Colonel Stevens's notes on a visit to an Italian prisoner of war, 23 September 1941.
37 BBC WAC, IS, Scripts, s. II, E. Nissim, *Il carosello dell'omo qualunque*, 10 December 1944; author's translation.
38 FFT, FPT, Paolo Treves, *Talks dati BBC e altri MS inglesi (1940–1943)*, b.12, *L'uomo della settimana: Mr. Joe Smith*, 3 July 1943. Paolo Treves's considerations on Britain and his impressions on the county can be found in *England: The Mysterious Island*; author's translation.
39 FFT, FPT, Talks dati BBC e altri MS inglesi (1940–1943), B. 12, Paolo Treves, *L'uomo della settimana: Un Italiano qualunque*, n.d.; author's translation.
40 Claudia Baldoli, 'Bombing the FIAT: Allied Raids, Workers' Strikes, and the Italian Resistance', *Labour History Review*, 77 (2012), 75–92.
41 BBC WAC, IS, Scripts, s. II, b. 18, *The True Voice of Italy, A Free Italy talk*, 19 May 1943.
42 BBC WAC, IS, Scripts, s. II, b. 24, *Message from Arthur Deakin to Italian Workers*, 11 March 1944.
43 BBC WAC, IS, Scripts, s. II, b. 21, Paolo Treves, *Lettera a Benedetto Croce*, 11 August 1943.
44 FFT, FPT, *Talks dati BBC e altri MS inglesi (1940–1943)*, b. 12, Paolo Treves, *Lettera ad un italiano*, 31 May 1943; author's translation.
45 FFT, FPT, *Talks dati BBC e altri MS inglesi (1940–1943)*, b. 12, Paolo Treves, *Lettera ad un italiano n. 5*, 12 and 23 August 1943.

46 BBC WAC, E2/195, BBC Surveys of European Audiences, Italy, 25 May 1943.
47 BBC WAC, E2/195, BBC Surveys of European Audiences, Italy, 25 May 1943.
48 David Hendy, preface to Bonini and Monclús, *Radio Audiences*, p. xii.
49 Hendy, preface to Bonini and Monclús, *Radio Audiences*, p. xii.
50 BBC WAC, E2/184, *European Intelligence paper, European audience estimates, Italy 1943–44*, July 1943.
51 BBC WAC, E2/191/1, Survey of European Audiences: Enemy Countries, 1941.
52 BBC WAC, E2/191/2, BBC Monthly Surveys of European Audiences. Enemy Countries. Germany and Italy, 17 January 1942.
53 BBC WAC, E2/191/2, BBC Monthly Surveys of European Audiences. Enemy Countries. Germany and Italy, 17 January 1942.
54 BBC WAC, E2/191/2, Surveys of European Audiences: Enemy Countries 1942–Jan 1943, 11 May 1942.
55 Surveys of European Audiences: Enemy Countries 1942–Jan 1943, 11 May 1942, E2/191/2, BBC WAC.
56 BBC WAC, E2/191/1, BBC Monthly Surveys of European Audiences: Enemy Countries, Germany and Italy, 15 April 1941.
57 BBC WAC, E2/191/1, BBC Monthly Surveys of European Audiences. Enemy Countries. Germany. Italy, 28 August 1941.
58 Baldoli and Knapp, *Forgotten Blitzes*.
59 BBC WAC, E2/191/1, BBC Monthly Surveys of European Audiences, Enemy Countries. Germany and Italy, 8 November 1941.
60 BBC WAC, E2/191/2, Surveys of European Audiences: Enemy Countries 1942–Jan 1943, 23 October 1942.
61 BBC WAC, E2/195, BBC Surveys of European Audiences. Italy, 5 April 1943.
62 BBC WAC, E2/191/1, BBC Monthly Surveys of European Audiences: Enemy Countries, Germany and Italy, 10 June 1941.
63 David Hendy, preface to Bonini and Monclús, *Radio Audiences*, p. xii.
64 Hendy, preface to Bonini and Monclús, *Radio Audiences*, p. xii.
65 Monteleone and Ortoleva, *La Radio*, pp. 55–56.
66 BBC WAC, E2/195, BBC Surveys of European Audiences, 8 December 1944.
67 BBC WAC, E2/195, BBC Surveys of European Audiences, 8 December 1944.
68 Briggs, *The War of Words*, p. 167.
69 Due to copyright rules at the BBC WAC data protection laws, the names of the letters' authors cannot be revealed. Their initials or first names will be used to refer to them. All the letters quoted directly or mentioned are held at the BBC WAC in the following folders: S107, Colonel Stevens, Letters 1941; 1941–42; 1943; 1944; 1945–46.
70 BBC WAC, E2/191/2, Surveys of European Audiences: Enemy Countries 1942–January 1943, 11 May 1942.
71 Elio Nissim is not mentioned with his real name, but with the name of his character, the *omo qualunque*.
72 BBC WAC, 1941/2, S107, Colonel Stevens, Letters, Letter from Lugano, June 1942.
73 BBC WAC, 1941/2, S107/9/1, Colonel Stevens Letters 1941, Letter from Malta, 28 January 1941.

74 BBC WAC, S107, Colonel Stevens, Letters 1944, Letter from Nola, 9 October 1944. This letter was written on 18 July 1944 and received on 9 October 1944; author's translation.
75 BBC WAC, S107, Colonel Stevens, Letters 1944, Colonel Stevens to A.G. 24 November 1944; author's translation.
76 BBC WAC, S107, Colonel Stevens, Letters 1943, Letter from 19 July 1943.
77 BBC WAC, S107, Colonel Stevens, Letters 1941/2, Letter from 2 June 1942.
78 BBC WAC, S107, Colonel Stevens, Letters 1945/46, Letter from Pistoia, 27 December 1945author's translation.
79 BBC WAC, E2/195, Surveys of European Audiences, Germany and Italy, 8 December 1944.
80 BBC WAC, S107, Colonel Stevens, Letters 1941–2, Letter from St John's Seminary, 17 March 1942.
81 BBC WAC, S107, Colonel Stevens, Letters 1943, Letter from Tunis, 16 June 1943.
82 BBC WAC, S107, Colonel Stevens, Letters 1943, Letter from Pound Lane, Pool, 11 June 1943.
83 BBC WAC, S107, Colonel Stevens, Prisoners of War Letters 1941–46, Letter from a British PoW camp, 8 February 1946.
84 BBC WAC, S107, Colonel Stevens, Prisoners of War Letters 1941–46, Letter from PoW camp n. 56, June 1943; author's translation.
85 BBC WAC, S107, Colonel Stevens, Letters 1943, Stevens to Major Harrison, 9 June 1943.
86 BBC WAC, S107, Colonel Stevens, Letters 1941/2, Letter from Vacallo-Chiasso, 31 August 1942.
87 BBC WAC, S107, Colonel Stevens, Letters 1941/2, Internal circulating memo, Italian-speaking Switzerland, 9 October 1942.
88 BBC WAC, S107, Colonel Stevens, Letters 1943, Colonel Stevens to G.C. from Vacallo-Chiasso, 12 May 1943, BBC WAC.
89 BBC WAC, S107, Colonel Stevens, Letters 1943, Letter from Vacallo-Chiasso, 12 June 1943; author's translation.
90 BBC WAC, S107, Colonel Stevens, Letters 1943, Letter from Locarno, 31 October 1943.
91 BBC WAC, S107, Colonel Stevens, Letters 1945–46, Letter from Genoa, 27 December 1946; author's translation.
92 Kay Chadwick refers to a similar situation at the French Service, since the content of the letters sent to the BBC by French Service was broadcast back home to show that the French had positive view about Britain. Chadwick, 'Our enemy's enemy', 39.

Conclusion: Radio Londra between myth and reality

As John Foot states in *Italy's Divided Memories*, myths are 'almost always linked to actual events, but they also extrapolate from those events and modify their meaning'.[1] However, continues Foot, it is in this process of distortion of reality that we can find important information on the ways in which history and collective memory are created, since myths often end up as a substitute for reality.

Similar considerations had been made in 1921 by the famous co-founder of *Les Annales d'histoire économique et sociale*, Marc Bloch, who applied these reflections to the war experience. False rumours, claimed the French historian, disclose hidden meanings in a society. The fact itself that a rumour is widespread means that there are favourable conditions for its reception.[2]

These ideas can be applied to this study on the BBC Italian Service during the Second World War. As mentioned in the introduction, despite Radio Londra being the propaganda tool of an enemy country, the BBC is often associated with the partisan Resistance and remembered as the voice of democracy and freedom. If we consider that the BBC broadcast in a country governed by a totalitarian regime, this data is unsurprising. However, it should be noted that seventy-two years after the end of the Second World War this positive portrait of the BBC is still part of the legacy of the conflict in Italy as well as in other European countries that were subject to Nazi occupation.

As many scholarly publications quoted in this work have shown, the dichotomy between the Allied liberators on one side and the Axis coalition responsible for the conflict on the other has been challenged by past and more recent historiography.[3] In line with these studies, this research aimed at analysing the role of the BBC from a new perspective and understanding how and when the myth of Radio Londra was created. In so doing, the work intended to contribute to rewriting the history of the BBC from a transnational point of view and understanding how the corporation became a leading global broadcaster during the conflict.

The book has focused on the actual programmes to comprehend what the BBC said to Italians and how it coped with its dual position as concurrently the voice of a military occupier and liberator of Italy from the Nazi yoke. On the other hand, listeners' reactions to the programmes have been studied with the aim of understanding whether the myth is linked to the reception of the BBC programmes at the time. Another aim of this project was to discover whether the Italian broadcasters working at the BBC were allowed to work independently from the British Foreign Office.

The archival sources analysed have revealed that the BBC did hold an ambivalent position and delivered conflicting messages with the aim of defeating the Axis coalition and winning the war. 'Breaking up' and 'making up' civilian morale was the main goal of British propaganda in Italy, since it was vital to encouraging forms of resistance to Nazi-Fascism and persuading the Italians to surrender to the Allied forces.[4]

Chapters 5 and 6 have demonstrated that, in order to pursue this goal, the British radio station manipulated the truth on more than one occasion. This was particularly true in the case of the battle of El Alamein, when the station misinformed Italians about the retreat of General Rommel's troops; and over the unconditional surrender of Italy, which was presented as an honourable solution, although in reality this option would not allow Italy to play a role in the peace negotiations.

The theme of the unconditional surrender, as we have seen, caused misgivings and concerns among some Italian broadcasters who disagreed with the BBC's political agenda. Radio Londra, they said, lied by associating the concepts of honourable peace and unconditional surrender. These two options were extremely different and would have opposite consequences for Italy, and Italians needed to be aware of this.

This is not the only issue that the Italian refugees experienced during their exile in London. As Chapter 4 has shown, in June 1940, many Italians living in Britain were interned in British camps as enemy aliens. Even those undisputed anti-fascist Italians faced a harsh internment. Some of them were already working for the BBC, but this did not guarantee them better treatment. Clearly, the anti-fascist cause was not a British priority. This is further confirmed by the fact that the BBC also employed ex-fascist sympathisers or refugees whose political positions were ambiguous.

Evidence of the BBC's controversial position can also be found in the correspondence between the BBC and the EIAR presented in Chapter 5. This correspondence demonstrates that the British station only distanced itself from the fascist regime when Italy declared war on France and Britain. While in the 1930s the BBC Arabic Service was attacking fascist Radio Bari in the Middle East and North Africa, the BBC Home Service and the EIAR exchanged material, artists and advice.

Other sources have, however, shown another side of the relationship between the corporation and the Italians. In Chapter 3 we have seen that the BBC was regarded by many of its Italian employees as a second home. The memoirs of Paolo Treves, Uberto Limentani and Elio Nissim have also revealed that, in spite of all the issues they experienced, they felt free to express their opinions in their programmes. They also referred to the BBC as an objective source of news. The possibility of fighting fascism from abroad and supporting the morale of their compatriots must have contributed to softening memories of their difficult relationships with British governmental institutions.

Finally, by analysing letters from Italian listeners and BBC audience surveys, Chapter 7 has explained the context in which the myth of Radio Londra was created. It is in the reception of the programmes that many legends about the BBC are rooted. The fascist laws forbidding Italians from listening to foreign radio stations had a counterproductive effect, turning the BBC into the source of otherwise inaccessible news. Many Italians thought that the fascist regime was denying them access to foreign news to hide the truth. Moreover, the clandestine nature of these programmes turned listening to the BBC into a daily ritual that united all the transgressors. The difficulties in accessing a radio set also played a significant role because information was often circulated by word of mouth. As the news was passed around, it became distorted and exaggerated. In many cases, as the story of the Mass in Chapter 7 has shown, it was very difficult to recognise the boundaries between myth and reality.

Another important factor contributing to the success of the BBC Italian Service was the context of the war itself. People feared they might be killed by a bomb at any moment and the Italian Service's broadcasters, as the programmes analysed have shown, were particularly good at addressing the fears of civilians.

Programmes for everyone

As we have seen in Chapter 1, one common feature that characterised the propaganda of several countries during the Second World War was its aim of reaching ordinary men and women. The propagandist needed to know intimately the thoughts, feelings and fears of civilians in foreign countries in order to find the most convincing approach for speaking to them.

As explained in Chapter 7, it is almost impossible to obtain reliable quantitative data about the listeners of the Italian Service. It is also extremely difficult to judge whether British propaganda had any actual impact on the Allied victory. Nevertheless, the surveys and the letters have shown that the BBC Italian Service did manage to engage successfully with many Italians.

One of the main reasons for the corporation's success was its ability to target different audiences. The creation of specific programmes for soldiers, prisoners, women, intellectuals and ex-fascists constructed an almost intimate relationship between the BBC and its listeners. Stevens was invited to a wedding, to spend a holiday in Italy at the end of the conflict, was sent poems and paintings, and was blessed by a priest who attached a holy image to his letter. Moreover, it is clear from the tone of the letters that he was seen by many Italians as a 'family member'.

Another reason for the BBC's success in Italy was its reassuring role. By delivering information about missing relatives and sending messages from their family members in the British prisoner-of-war camps, Radio Londra provided useful services to Italian civilians in those difficult times. The letter from the man in Nola who asked Stevens to intercede with the Allied authorities to restore his town's electricity demonstrates that several civilians regarded the station as an important point of reference.

Yet another significant reason for the BBC's success in Italy radio was the novelty that foreign radio programmes represented in the 1940s for ordinary people around the world.

Transnational programmes and international listeners: the creation of European audiences

As we have seen in Chapter 1 and 5, British colonial interests in North Africa and the Middle East, followed by the outbreak of the Second World War, led to the creation of the BBC's foreign-language programmes. Transnational radio broadcasts revolutionised war propaganda, since they created new forms of interaction with civilians of enemy countries. This interaction, as the letters have shown, was bi-directional.

But transnational radio programmes also created an opportunity for exchanges between British people and foreign communities living in Britain. The BBC World Service, as the European Service was renamed in 1965, was created and developed as a result of this cooperation between immigrants and multilingual British journalists. It was not simply a matter of speaking another language; the aim was rather to understand other cultures and approach them in the most appropriate ways. According to Marie Gillespie and Alban Webb, 'the BBC World Service has derived much of its intellectual, creative and diplomatic significance from the diasporic broadcasters who have been at the heart of the BBC's foreign language services'.[5]

As Simon Potter has written in relation to the BBC Empire Service, 'a distinctive type of "British" programming was required, different to that supplied to audiences in the UK, or indeed in Canada, and reflecting peculiarly

Australian and New Zealand conceptions of Britishness'.[6] Similarly, the programmes in Italian and other European languages needed to be different from the programmes of the Home Service. They needed to adjust to the mentality and culture of the civilians of other European countries and find the right approach for exporting British history, politics and lifestyle abroad. Moreover, while the Empire Service aimed at creating a British global community – but failed to do so –[7] the Italian Service was intended to make Italians feel closer to the British. A common strategy, as explained in Chapter 7, was comparing everyday British and Italian habits in order to forge connections between ordinary people in the two countries. The Italian Service appears to have been quite successful in this regard, as shown by the letters in which Italian listeners asked for information about the British political system or for English books in order to learn the language. The case of the Italian woman who asked Colonel Stevens for a Christmas card is especially interesting. As she wrote, this card would allow her to experience the British Christmas atmosphere from her little town in the mountains.

The station also intended to strengthen the idea that Italy was part of a new democratic Europe built with the help of the Allied forces, as the programmes on the partisan Resistance in Chapter 6 illustrate. In this new Europe national boundaries would no longer divide the peoples of different countries. This new shared identity was rooted in the Resistance to Nazi-fascism that had involved cooperation between partisan brigades of several countries and civilians who offered them food, clothes and protection. Whether these messages were conveyed for mere propaganda purposes or not, it is undeniable that they did leave a legacy in Italy, a legacy which continued to live in the memories of many Italians as well as in post-war programming. The BBC Italian Service would broadcast in Italian until the early 1980s, when Margaret Thatcher's government closed several European branches of the BBC.

Notes

1 John Foot, *Italy's Divided Memory* (Basingstoke: Palgrave Macmillan, 2009), p. 18.
2 Marc Bloch, *Réfléxions d'un historien sur les fausses nouvelles de la guerre* (Paris: Allia, 1999).
3 A few examples include Ellwood, *Italy 1943–45*; Pavone, *A Civil War*; Gribaudi, *Guerra totale*; Focardi, *Il cattivo tedesco*; Insolvibile, *Wops*.
4 Overy, 'Making and Breaking Morale'.
5 Gillespie and Webb (eds), *Diasporas and Diplomacy*, p. 1.
6 Potter, 'Who Listened when London Called?', p. 480.
7 Potter, *Broadcasting Empire*, p. 1.

Bibliography

Archival sources

Amsterdam, Institute for Social History (ISH), Paolo Treves's Papers (PTP)
Caversham, BBC Written Archives Centre (BBC WAC), Italian Service (IS)
Florence, Fondazione Filippo Turati (FFT), Fondo Paolo Treves (FPT)
London, Danny Nissim's Private Archive (DNPA), Elio Nissim's Papers (ENP), Foreign Office (FO), National Archives (NA)
Manchester, International Department, Labour Party (ID, LP), John Rylands Library (JRL), *Manchester Guardian* Archive (MGA), People's History Museum (PHM), William Gillies's Papers (WGP),
Pisa, Fondo Arnaldo Momigliano (FAM), Scuola Normale Superiore di Pisa (SNSP),
Turin, Centro Studi Piero Gobetti (CSPG), Fondo Umberto Calosso (FUC)

Printed primary sources

British Broadcasting Corporation, *Ecco Radio Londra*, Wembley, 1945.
Chi è Candidus, 1944.
'I was Anderson's Prisoner', *Tribune*, 9 August 1940.
Lockhart, Bruce R.H., *Comes the Reckoning*, London, Putnam, 1947.
Marus, John, *Parla Candidus: Discorsi dal 13 Aprile 1941 al 3 dicembre 1944*, Milan, Mondadori, 1945.
Nissim, Elio, *Il pappagallo del nonno: Ricordi anglo-fiorentini*, Udine, Campanotto, 2001.
Orestano, Francesco, 'La vita religiosa nella nuova Europa', *Gerarchia*, December 1942, 476–484.
Pentad, *The Remaking of Italy*, Hardmondsworth, Penguin,1941.
'Saying it with Music. BBC to Italy', *Daily Telegraph*, 9 January 1941.
Reith, John, *Broadcast Over Britain*, London, Hodder & Stoughton, 1924.
Treves, Paolo, *What Mussolini Did to Us*, London, Victor Gollancz, 1940.
Treves, Paolo, *Sul fronte e dietro il fronte italiano*, Rome, Sandron, 1945.

Books

Aga Rossi, Elena, *L'inganno reciproco: l'armistizio tra l'Italia e gli angloamericani del settembre 1943*, Roma, Ministero per i Beni Culturali e Ambientali, 1993.

Aga Rossi, Elena, *A Nation Collapses: the Italian Surrender of September 1943*, Cambridge, Cambridge University Press, 2000.
Albanese, Giulia and Pergher, Roberta, *In the Society of Fascists: Acclamation, Acquiescence, and Agency in Mussolini's Italy*, Basingstoke, Palgrave Macmillan 2012
Baldoli, Claudia, *Exporting Fascism: Italian Fascists and Britain's Italians in the 1930s*, Oxford, Berg, 2003.
Baldoli, Claudia and Knapp, Andrew, *Forgotten Blitzes: France and Italy under Allied Air Attack, 1940–45*, London, Continuum, 2012.
Baldoli, Claudia, Knapp, Andrew and Overy, Richard (eds), *Bombing States and Peoples in Western Europe, 1940–45*, London, Continuum, 2011.
Balfour, Michael, *Propaganda in War, 1939–1945: Organisations, Policies and Publics in Britain and Germany*, London, Routledge & Kegan Paul, 1979.
Bennet, R., *Ultra and Mediterranean Strategy 1941–1945*, London, Hamish Hamilton, 1989.
Bernabei, Alfio, *Esuli ed emigrati Italiani nel Regno Unito, 1920–40*, Milan, Mursia, 1997.
Bloch, Marc, *Réfléxions d'un historien sur les fausses nouvelles de la guerre*, Paris, Allia, 1999.
Bloom, Emily, *The Wireless Past: Anglo-Irish Writers and the BBC, 1931–1968*, Oxford, Oxford University Press, 2016.
Bonini, Tiziano and Monclús, Belén (eds), *Radio Audiences and Participation in the Age of Network Society*, New York, Routledge, 2018.
Briggs, Asa, *The Birth of Broadcasting*, Oxford, Oxford University Press, 1961.
Briggs, Asa, *The War of Words*, Oxford, Oxford University Press, 1970.
Cannistraro, Philip, *La fabbrica del consenso: Fascismo e mass media*, Rome, Laterza, 1975.
Cavaleri, Walter, *Tre punti e una linea*, L'Aquila, Consiglio Regionale d'Abruzzo, 2007.
Cavarocchi, Francesca, *Avanguardie dello spirito: il fascismo e la propaganda culturale all'estero*, Rome, Carocci, 2010.
Costa Ribeiro, Nelson, *BBC Broadcasts to Portugal in World War II: How Radio Was Used as a Weapon of War*, Lewiston, NY, Edwin Mellen, 2011.
Cruickshank, Charles, *The Fourth Arm: Psychological Warfare 1938–1945*, London, Davis-Poynter, 1977.
De Grazia, Vittoria and Luzzatto, Sergio (eds.), *Dizionario del fascismo*, Turin, Einaudi, 2010.
De Felice, Renzo, *Mussolini il rivoluzionario 1883–1920*, Turin, Einaudi, 1965.
Delmer, Sefton, *Black Boomerang: An Autobiography*, London, Secker & Warburg, 1962.
De Luna, Giovanni, *L' occhio e l'orecchio dello storico: le fonti audiovisive nella ricerca e nella didattica della storia*, Scandicci, La Nuova Italia, 1993.
Delzell, Charles, *Mussolini's Enemies: The Italian Anti-Fascist Resistance*, New York, Howard Fertig, 1974.
Di Donato, Riccardo (ed.,) *Ritorno al Risorgimento: Conversazioni a Radio Londra 1941–1945*, Pisa, Archivio Arnaldo Momigliano, 2013.
Di Nolfo, Ennio, *Le paure e le speranze degli italiani: 1943–53*, Milan, Mondadori, 1986.
Di Nolfo, Ennio and Serra, Maurizio, *La gabbia infranta: gli alleati e l'Italia dal 1943 al 1945*, Rome, Laterza, 2010.
Dionisotti, Carlo, *Ricordo di Arnaldo Momigliano*, Bologna, Il Mulino, 1989.

Eliot, Simon and Wiggam, Marc (eds), *Allied Communication to the Public during the Second World War: National and Transnational Networks*, London, Bloomsbury, 2020.

Ellwood, David, *Italy 1943–45* Leicester, Leicester University Press, 1985.

Föllmer, Golo and Badenoch, Alexander (eds), *Transnationalizing Radio Research: New Approaches to an Old Medium*, Bielefeld, transcript Verlag, 2018.

Focardi, Filippo, *Il cattivo tedesco e il bravo italiano: la rimozione delle colpe della seconda guerra mondiale*, Rome, Laterza, 2013.

Foot, John, *Italy's Divided Memory*, Basingstoke, Palgrave Macmillan, 2009.

Footitt, Hilary and Kelly, Michael, *Languages at War: Policies and Practices of Language Contacts in Conflict*, Basingstoke, Palgrave Macmillan, 2012.

Footitt, Hilary and Tobia, Simona, *War Talk: Foreign Languages and the British War Effort in Europe, 1940–1947*, Basingstoke, Palgrave Macmillan, 2013.

Forgacs, David, *Italian Culture in the Industrial Era 1880–1980: Cultural Industries, Politics and the Public*, Manchester, Manchester University Press, 1990.

Forgacs, David and Gundle, Stephen, *Mass Culture and Italian Society from Fascism to the Cold War*, Bloomington, Indiana University Press, 2007.

Friedmann, Otto, *Broadcasting for Democracy*, London, Allen & Unwin, 1942

Garnett, David, *The Secret History of PWE: The Political Warfare Executive, 1939–1945*, London, St Ermin's, 2002.

Gillespie, Marie and Webb, Alban (eds), *Diasporas and Diplomacy: Cosmopolitan Contact Zones at the BBC World Service (1932–2012)*, Routledge, London, 2013.

Gillman, Peter and Gillman, Leni, *'Collar the Lot!' How Britain Interned and Expelled its Wartime Refugees*, London, Quartet, 1980.

Gribaudi, Gabriella, *Guerra totale: tra bombe alleate e violenze naziste: Napoli e il fronte meridionale, 1940–44*, Turin, Bollati Boringhieri, 2005.

Hale, Julian, *Radio Power: Propaganda and International Broadcasting*, London, Elek, 1975.

Harris, C.R.S., *Allied Military Administration of Italy 1943–1945*, London, HMSO, 1957.

Havers, Richard, *Here is the News: The BBC and the Second World War*, Stroud, Sutton, 2007.

Hendy, David, *Radio in the Global Age* (Malden, MA: Polity Press, 2000).

Hibberd, Matthew, *Il grande viaggio della BBC: Storia del servizio pubblico britannico dagli anni venti all'era digitale*, Rome, Rai-ERI, 2005.

Hinsley, Francis Henry, *British Intelligence in the Second World War*, London, HMSO, 1993.

Hobsbawm, Eric, The *Age of Extremes: The Short Twentieth Century, 1914–1991*, London, Abacus, 1995.

Horten, Gerd, *Radio Goes to War: the Cultural Politics of Propaganda during World War II*, Berkeley, University of California Press, 2001.

Inghilterra e Italia nel '900. Atti del convegno ai Bagni di Lucca. Ottobre 1972, Florence, La Nuova Italia, 1973.

Insolvibile, Isabella, *Wops: i prigionieri italiani in Gran Bretagna (1941–1946)*, Naples, Edizioni Scientifiche Italiane, 2012.

Isnenghi, Mario (ed.), *I luoghi della memoria: simboli e miti dell'Italia unita*, Rome, Laterza, 1998.

Isola, Gianni, *Abbassa la tua radio, per favore ... Storia dell'ascolto radiofonico nell'Italia fascista*, Florence, La Nuova Italia, 1990.

Istituto Socialista di studi storici del Piemonte e Valle d'Aosta (ed.), *Umberto Calosso antifascista e socialista*, Venice, Marsilio, 1981.
Kirkpatrick, Ivonne, *Mussolini: Study of a Demagogue*, London, Odhams, 1964.
Labanca, Nicola (ed.), *I bombardamenti aerei sull'Italia: politica, Stato e società, 1939–1945*, Bologna, Il Mulino, 2012.
Lanotte, Gioachino, *Il 'quarto fronte': musica e propaganda radiofonica nell'Italia liberata, 1943–1945*, Perugia, Morlacchi, 2012.
Lanotte, Gioachino, *'Segnale radio': musica e propaganda radiofonica nell'Italia nazifascista, 1943–1945*, Perugia, Morlacchi, 2014.
Launchbury, Claire, *Music, Poetry, Propaganda: Constructing French Cultural Soundscapes at the BBC during the Second World War*, Berne, Peter Lang, 2012.
Leishman, Marista, *My Father – Reith of the BBC*, Edinburgh, Saint Andrew, 2006.
Limentani, Uberto, 'Radio Londra durante la guerra', in *Inghilterra e Italia nel '900: atti del convegno di Bagni di Lucca* (Florence: La Nuova Italia, 1973), p. 205.
Lo Biundo, Ester, *London Calling Italy: La propaganda di Radio Londra nel 1943*, Milan, Unicopli, 2014.
Lodhi, Aasiya and Wringley, Amanda (eds), *Radio Modernisms: Features, Cultures and the BBC*, London, Routledge, 2020.
Luneau, Aurélie, *Radio Londres: les voix de la liberté, 1940–1944*, Paris, Perrin, 2005.
Luneau, Aurélie, *Je vous écris de France: lettres inédites à la BBC, 1940–1944*, Paris, L'Iconoclaste, 2014.
Lupo, Salvatore, *Il fascismo: la politica in un regime totalitario*, Rome, Donzelli, 2005.
Lupo, Salvatore, *The Two Mafias: a Transatlantic History, 1888–2008*, Basingstoke, Palgrave Macmillan, 2015.
Macmillan, Harold, *War Diaries: Politics and War in the Mediterranean, January 1943–May 1945*, London, Macmillan, 1984.
Mansell, Gerard, *Let Truth be Told: 50 Years of BBC External Broadcasting*, London, Weidenfeld & Nicolson, 1982.
Marzano, Arturo, *Onde fasciste: La propaganda araba di Radio Bari (1934–43)*, Rome, Carocci, 2015.
Menduni, Enrico, *I linguaggi della radio e della televisione: teorie, tecniche, formati*, Rome, Laterza, 2006.
Menduni, Enrico (ed.), *La radio: percorsi e territori di un medium mobile e interattivo*, Bologna, Baskerville, 2002.
Mercuri, Lamberto, *Guerra psicologica: la propaganda anglo-americana in Italia, 1942–1946*, Rome, Archivio Trimestrale, 1983.
Monteleone, Franco, *La radio italiana nel periodo fascista: studio e documenti 1922–1945* Venice, Marsilio, 1976.
Monteleone, Franco, *Storia della radio e della televisione in Italia: società, politica, strategie e programmi* (Venice: Marsilio, 1992).
Monteleone, Franco and Ortoleva, Peppino (eds), *La radio storia di sessant'anni, 1924–1984*, Turin, ERI, 1984.
Monticone, Alberto, *Il fascismo al microfono: radio e politica in Italia 1942–45*, Rome, Studium, 1978.
Muracciole, Jean-François and Piketty, Guillaume (eds), *Encyclopédie de la seconde guerre mondiale*, Paris, Robert Laffont–Ministère de la défense, 2015.
Natale, Anna Lucia, *Gli anni della radio: 1924–1954: contributo ad una storia sociale dei media*, Naples, Liguori, 1990.
Orlando, Ruggero, *L'Inghilterra è un castello in aria*, Milan, Bompiani, 1956.

Orlando, Ruggero, *Qui Ruggero Orlando: Mezzo secolo di giornalismo*, Milan, Sugarco, 1990.
Pack, S.W.C., *Operation Husky: The Allied Invasion of Sicily*, Newton Abbot, David & Charles, 1977.
Pallotta, Gino, *Il Qualunquismo e l'avventura di Guglielmo Giannini*, Milan, Bompiani, 1972.
Pavone, Claudio, *A Civil War: A History of the Italian Resistance*, trans. Peter Levy and David Broder, London, Verso, 2014.
Peresso, Giorgio, *Giuseppe Donati and Umberto Calosso – Two Italian Anti-Fascist Refugees in Malta*, Malta, Gudja SKS, 2015.
Petrella, Luigi, *Staging the Fascist War: The Ministry of Popular Culture and Italian Propaganda on the Home Front, 1938–1943*, Berne, Peter Lang, 2016.
Piccialuti Caprioli, Maura, *Radio Londra 1939–45*, Rome, Laterza, 1979.
Piccialuti Caprioli, Maura (ed.), *Radio Londra 1940–45: inventario delle trasmissioni per l'Italia*, Rome, Ministero per i Beni Culturali e Ambientali.
Piffer, Tommaso, *Gli Alleati e la Resistenza italiana*, Bologna: Il Mulino, 2010.
Pizarroso Quintero, Alejandro, *Stampa, radio e propaganda: gli alleati in Italia, 1943–1946*, Milan, Franco Angeli, 1989.
Portelli, Alessandro, *The Death of Luigi Trastulli and Other Stories: Form and Meaning in Oral History*, Albany, State University of New York Press, 1991.
Potter, Simon, *Broadcasting Empire: the BBC and the British World, 1922–1970*, Oxford, Oxford University Press, 2012.
Potter, Simon, *Wireless Internationalism and Distant Listening: Britain, Propaganda, and the Invention of Global Radio, 1920–1939*, Oxford, Oxford University Press, 2020.
Rhodes, Anthony, *Propaganda. The Art of Persuasion: World War II*, London, Angus & Robertson, 1976.
Rigby, Charles A., *The War on the Short Waves*, London, Lloyd Cole, 1944.
Rolo, Charles, *Radio Goes to War*, London, Faber & Faber, 1943.
Sebastiani, Pietro, *Laburisti inglesi e socialisti italiani: dalla ricostituzione del PSI (UP) alla scissione di Palazzo Barberini, da Transport House a Downing Street, 1943–1947*, RomE, FIAP, 1983.
Sechi, Maria, and Pisano, Agnano (eds), *Fascismo ed Esilio II: la patria lontana: testimonianze dal vero e dall'immaginario*, Pisa, Giardini, 1990.
Setta, Sandro, *L'Uomo qualunque: 1944–48*, Rome, Laterza, 1975.
Sponza, Lucio, *Divided Loyalties: Italians in Britain During the Second World War*, Berne, Peter Lang, 2000.
Stenton, Michael, *Radio London and Resistance in Occupied Europe* Oxford, Oxford University Press, 2000.
Street, Sean, *Historical Dictionary of British Radio*, Lanham, MD, Scarecrow Press, 2006.
Summers, Julie, *Fashion on the Ration: Style in the Second World War*, Profile Books, 2015.
Treves, Paolo, *England: The Mysterious Island*, Trans. D. Forbes, London, Victor Gollancz, 1948.
Varsori, Antonio, *Gli Alleati e l'emigrazione democratica antifascista (1930–1943)*, Florence, Sansoni, 1982.
Webb, Alban, *London Calling: Britain, the BBC World Service and the Cold War*, London, Bloomsbury, 2014.

Whittington, Ian, *Writing the Radio War: Literature, Politics, and the BBC, 1939–1945*, Edinburgh, Edinburgh University Press, 2018.
Williams, Isobel, *Allies and Italians Under Occupation: Sicily and Southern Italy 1943–45*, Basingstoke, Palgrave Macmillan, 2013.
Williams, Manuela A., *Subversion in the Mediterranean and the Middle East, 1935–1940*, London, Routledge, 2006.
Zanella, Antonio (ed.), *Sentivamo radio Londra: l'odissea di due fratelli ampezzani in Bulgaria nel corso della seconda guerra mondiale, dal diario di Oreste Ghedina*, Cortina d'Ampezzo, Cooperativa di Cortina, 1992.

Journal articles and special issues

Baldoli, Claudia, 'Bombing the FIAT: Allied Raids, Workers' Strikes, and the Italian Resistance', *Labour History Review*, 77 (2012), 75–92.
Berrettini, Mireno, '"To Set Italy Ablaze!" Lo Special Operations Executive e i reclutamenti di agenti tra enemy aliens e prisoners of war italiani (Regno Unito, Stati Uniti e Canada)', *Altreitalie*, 40 (2010), 5–25.
Chadwick, Kay, 'Our enemy's enemy', *Media History*, 21:4 (2015), 426–442.
Cooke, Philip, 'La Resistenza come secondo Risorgimento: un topos retorico senza fine? *Passato e Presente*, 86 (2012), 62–81.
Costa Ribeiro, Nelson and Seul, Stephanie (eds), 'Revisiting Transnational Broadcasting: The BBC's Foreign Language Services During the Second World War', *Media History*, 21:4 (2015), 365–377.
Cronqvist, Marie, and Hilgert, Christoph, 'Entangled Media Histories: The value of Transnational and Transmedial Approaches in Media Historiography', *Media History*, 23:1 (2017), 130–141.
Cronqvist, Marie and Hilgert, Christoph, 'Entangled Media Histories: Response to the Responses', *Media History*, 23:1 (2017), 148–149.
Hilgert, Christoph, Cronqvist, Marie and Chignell, Hugh, 'Tracing Entanglements in Media History', *Media History*, 26:1 (2020), 1–5.
Hilmes, Michelle, 'Entangled Media Histories: A Response', *Media History* 23:1 (2017), 142–144.
Lo Biundo, Ester, 'The War of Nerves: Le Trasmissioni di Radio Londra da El Alamein all'Operazione Husky', *Meridiana: Rivista di Storia e Scienze Sociali*, 82, Sicilia 1943 (2015), 13–35.
Lo Biundo, Ester, 'Voices of Occupiers/Liberators: The BBC's Radio Propaganda in Italy between 1942 and 1945', *Journal of War and Cultures Studies*, 9:1 (2016), 60–73.
McHugh, Siobhán, 'The Affective Power of Sound: Oral History on Radio', *Oral History Review*, 39:2 (2019), 187–206.
McLuhan, Marshall, 'Radio: The Tribal Drum', *AV Communication Review*, 12:2 (1964), 133–145.
Nicholas, Siân, 'Media History or Media Histories? Re-addressing the history of the mass media in inter-war Britain', *Media History*, 18:3–4 (2012), 379–394.
Overy, Richard, 'Making and Breaking Morale: British Political Warfare and Bomber Command in the Second World War', *Twentieth Century British History*, 26:3 (2015), 370–399.
Passerini, Luisa, 'L'archivio sonoro', *Rivista di Storia Contemporanea*, 3 (1987), 438–441.

Pavone, Claudio, 'Le idee della Resistenza. Antifascisti e fascisti di fronte alla tradizione del Risorgimento', *Passato e Presente*, 7 (1959), 850–918.
Potter, Simon, 'Who Listened when London Called? Reactions to the BBC Empire Service in Canada, Australia and New Zealand, 1932–1939', *Historical Journal of Film, Radio and Television*, 28 (2010), 475–487.
Ribeiro, Nelson, 'BBC Portuguese Service during World War II: Praising Salazar while defending the Allies', *Media History*, 21:4 (2015), 397–411.
Seul, Stephanie, '"Plain, unvarnished news"? The BBC German Service and Chamberlain's Propaganda Campaign Directed at Nazi Germany, 1938–1940', *Media History*, 21:4 (2015), 378–96.

Online resources

'BBC: Radio Londra 1941–42', http://anpi-lissone.over-blog.com/article-37158365.html, 2009, accessed 29 May 2017.
'Conscription: the Second World War', www.parliament.uk/about/living-heritage/transformingsociety/private-lives/yourcountry/overview/conscriptionww2/#:~:text=The%20National%20Service%20(Armed%20Forces,farming%2C%20medicine%2C%20and%20engineering, accessed 2 March 2022.
De Toffoli, Dario, 'Giochi: il festival a Modena tra Turing e Radio Londra', www.ilfattoquotidiano.it/2014/04/09/giochi-il-festival-a-modena-tra-turing-e-radio-londra/945492/, 2014, accessed 29 May 2017.
'History of the BBC, Overseas Programming', www.bbc.co.uk/historyofthebbc/research/general/overseas, accessed 25 August 2016.
'Le radio proibite dal fascismo: Radio Londra, http://anpi-lissone.over-blog.com/article-le-radio-proibite-dal-fascismo-radio-londra-37122724.html, 2009, accessed 29 May 2017.
'Orlando, Ruggero', *Dizionario Biografico degli Italiani*, 79 (2013), www.treccani.it/enciclopedia/ruggero-orlando_(Dizionario-Biografico)/, accessed 21 October 2016.
'Radio Londra. 1939–1945', www.anpi.it/libri/76/radio-londra-1939–1945, 2011, accessed 29 May 2017.
'Repubblichino', *Vocabolario Treccani*, www.treccani.it/vocabolario/repubblichino/, accessed 14 February 2017.
Sponza, Lucio, *La BBC 'in bianco' e 'in nero'. La propaganda britannica per l'Italia nella seconda Guerra mondiale*, Storiamestre, 18 December 2013, http://storiamestre.it/2013/12/bbcbiancoenero/, accessed 17 March 2017.
Treves, Lotte, 'Ricominciare sempre da capo', *Rivista di Storia dell'Università di Torino*, 63 (2012), www.ojs.unito.it/index.php/RSUT/article/view/280, accessed 15 October 2016.

Index

Note: 'n' after a page indicates the number of a note on that page

Acerbo, Giacomo 100
Agostinetti, Ermanno 107
Alexandra Palace 107
Amendola, Giorgio 55
AMGOT 11, 142
ANPI (National Association of Italian Partisans) 2
Ansaldo, Giovanni 73
Anzani, Decio 82, 83
Arandora Star 60, 83, 84, 85
Atlantic Charter 136, 184
audience research 7, 9
average British 42, 169, 170
average Italian 141, 168, 170, 171
Axis 73, 88, 103, 112, 117, 122, 133, 137, 141, 143, 146, 164, 176, 191, 192
Axis Conversation 45, 115, 130n.63

Badoglio, Pietro 93, 120, 121, 122, 126, 133, 134
Banfi, Alessandro 107
Battino, Raffaello 63–64
BBC Monitoring Service 32, 100
BBC Written Archives Centre 3, 9, 112, 179
Bergamasco, Aldo 146
'black' propaganda 32–33
bolshevism 126, 173
bombing 2, 8, 29, 45, 61, 103, 115, 127, 132, 137, 138, 143, 153, 166, 167, 176, 182

Borgioli, Dino 48
Bottai, Giuseppe 72
Bracken, Brendan 31
Braithwaite, Henry 107
Braybrook 84
Briggs, Asa 2, 5
  see also 'war of words'
Broadcasting House 29, 61, 68
Bury (camp) 84, 85, 86
Bush House 8, 29, 32, 61, 62, 68, 80
Byron, George Gordon 66

Calosso, Umberto 12, 43, 62–66, 75, 81, 89, 90, 91, 92, 93, 95, 122, 134–137, 142, 153, 180
Candidus (Marus, Joseph John) 45, 69–70, 149, 180
Casablanca conference 11, 113
Cassuto, Aldo 42, 46, 172
Catholic Church 40
  see also Christian identity; religion
censorship 13, 32, 33, 49, 50, 70, 87, 108, 175
Centro Sperimentale di Radiofonia 102
Cetra Parlophon 106
Chamberlain, Neville 1, 29, 40
Christian identity 109
  see also religion
Churchill, Winston 26, 31, 93, 109, 113, 133, 134, 136, 164
Ciano, Costanzo 101
Ciano, Galeazzo 121

civil war 60, 145
class 13, 20, 33, 73, 75, 161, 162, 164–166, 170, 171, 173, 174, 175, 176, 179, 184
Commenti ai fatti del giorno 102, 111
Committee for Refugees from Italy 84, 90
Commonwealth 5, 28, 180
communism 22, 30, 173
    Communist 55, 64, 173
        Communist Party 63
Comunità Israelitica di Roma 73
Connecting the Wireless World 4
Crespi, Angelo 89–90
Croce, Benedetto 56, 59, 63, 71–73
Czechoslovakia 30

Daily Telegraph 48
Dalton, Hugh 31
dance music 105
D'Annunzio, Gabriele 69
Deakin, Arthur 171
Delius, Frederick 48
Delmer, Sefton 32–33
Dennis, Geoffrey 43, 66, 73, 87, 93
Department for Enemy Propaganda 31
De Sanctis, Gaetano 58, 72, 76n.12
Deutsches Haus 118, 119
Donaldson's Internment Camp 84
Donati, Giuseppe 55, 63

Eastern Front 118
Eden, Anthony 31, 83, 93
Egypt 63, 64
EIAR 8, 24, 74, 98–108, 111, 127, 132, 158–161, 192
Eisenhower, Dwight D. 113, 133
El Alamein 99, 112, 114, 116–117, 127, 138, 156
Electra House 31, 42
Elgar, Edward 48
Empire Service 28, 160, 194–195
enemy alien 66, 81, 86, 192
Entangled Media History network 4
entangled media history 6, 7
Ente Radio Guerra 103
Ente Radio Rurale 24
European identity 5, 151
exile 1, 3, 8, 10, 12, 13, 14, 30, 33–34, 43, 46, 54–59, 63–64, 66, 68, 72–73, 75–76, 92–95, 146, 147, 169, 192
    see also Italian emigration; refugee

Fabian Society 63
family 22, 165, 167
Fano, Pier Paolo 74
Farquhar, Harold 82
fascist police 13, 57, 157, 159, 186
fashion 67, 165–166
First World War 20–22, 71, 163
Foa, George 48, 114
food 23, 84, 86, 87, 118, 137, 138, 140, 141–143, 150
Foreign Office 3, 11, 12, 23, 28, 29, 31, 33, 49–50, 80–83, 85, 87–99, 91–95, 104, 134, 136, 153, 169, 192
'Fortress Europe' 118
forty-five days 122, 131n.75, 132–134
'fourth front' 20, 23
    'fourth arm' 21
France 1, 29, 55–56, 60, 81, 93, 104, 109, 112–113, 150, 164, 178, 192
Fraenkel, Eduard 73
Free Italy Movement 12, 65, 81, 88–93, 134, 136, 171
Free Italy Talks 63, 81, 89, 91–92, 134
French Service 31, 48, 164, 167
Fronte dell'Uomo Qualunque 46
fuorusciti 56, 83

Garibaldi, Giuseppe 93, 146, 147–148, 150
Garosci, Aldo 56, 72
Gatti, Giuseppe 89
George V 28
German Service 30, 32
Germany 1, 2, 11, 21, 24, 29, 31–32, 40, 73, 81, 102, 104, 109, 112–113, 115–122, 133–134, 136, 139, 141, 145, 149
Giannini, Guglielmo 46
Giglio, Giovanni 89
Gillies, William 82, 84, 89, 90
Glorious Revolution 109
Gobetti, Piero 55, 63, 72–73
Goebbels, Josef 21
Gorini, Mario 106

heritage 2, 12, 137, 144
    see also monuments
Hitler, Adolf 21–22, 25, 40, 73,
    115–116, 121

informant 9, 49, 80, 141, 158, 174,
    175–176, 178, 180, 184
International Broadcasting Union
    25
internment 12, 14, 60, 66, 68, 74, 80,
    82–90, 92, 95, 98, 174,
    177–178, 192
Isle of Man 66, 68, 87
Italian emigration 55
    see also *refugee*
Italian Risorgimento 66, 73, 91, 123,
    148, 152, 171
Italian Round Up 45, 126
Italian Soldiers Programme 46, 167
Italian War Correspondent 45

Jacoby, Felix 72
Jeaffreson 47–48
Jews 30, 66, 72
    Jewish 50, 54, 60, 71, 72, 75

Kempton Park 85
Kirkpatrick, Ivone 31, 92

La Politica in Pantofole 45, 117
Labour Party 12–13, 14, 74, 81–82,
    84, 88–89, 92, 95
Lajolo, Clelia 63
Lawrence, Anthony 43, 47
leaflets 19, 23–24
League of Nations 25
Lebensraum 116
legend 2, 127, 176, 177, 193
    see also myth, rumour and 'word of
        mouth'
leggi fascistissime 55
Limentani, Uberto 43, 47, 60–62
Lingfield (camp) 83–84
Little Italy 82
Lockhart, Bruce 21, 23, 31, 92, 134,
    136, 153
Lodge, Oliver 26
London Diary 45
long armistice 133
    short armistice 133

Magri, Alessandro 74, 88
Man in the Street 46, 68, 151
Manchester Guardian 40–41, 44
March on Rome 55, 57, 63, 82, 99
Marconi, Guglielmo 26, 99–100
Margesson, David 90
Marinetti, Filippo Tommaso 101
Masia, Massenzio 70
mass society 19–20
Mazzini, Giuseppe 136, 146–147
Mazzini Society 91
Mechanical Workers' Union 171
Mendelssohn 48
Middle East 29–30, 104, 127, 192,
    194
Military Intelligence 5 (MI5) 82, 89
Military Intelligence 7 (MI7) 42
MinCulPop 21, 45, 103, 117, 119
Minio, Lorenzo 74
Ministry of Economic Warfare 31, 89
Ministry of Information 31, 41–42, 47,
    87
Momigliano, Arnaldo 44, 71–75, 87
Monologue of the Little Man 46, 68,
    120
Montgomery, Bernard Law 112
monuments 143–144
Moran, H.M. 163
Morse-code signal 26
Moscow conference 93
mother 13, 22, 142, 167, 179
Mr Smith 139–40, 169–170
Munro, Ion 163–174
music 13, 31, 39, 47, 48, 100, 103,
    105–108, 160, 162–163
    see also song
Mussolini 11, 13, 22, 29, 54–57, 82,
    85, 87–88, 90–93, 99–100,
    102, 104, 108, 110–111, 113,
    115–116, 120–122, 126, 133,
    137–138, 146, 164, 172, 178,
    183
myth 1, 2, 12, 61, 76, 81, 114, 127,
    157, 187, 191–193
    see also rumour; 'word of mouth'

Nissim, Elio 29, 43, 46, 66–69, 75,
    87–88, 121, 126, 150, 168,
    193
Nitti, Francesco Saverio 55

Noel-Baker, Philip 94
North Africa 104, 111–113, 116–117, 142, 160, 168, 192, 194, 104

occupation/liberation 14, 133, 145
Ogilvie, Frederick 107
Operation Barbarossa 22
Operation Giant 2 133
Operation Husky 2, 11, 113, 140
Orlando, Ruggero 69, 75, 83, 86–87
Overseas News Department 43
OVRA 81, 90

Pact of Steel 121
Pallotta, Gino 46
Pankhurst, Sylvia 90
Parri, Ferruccio 55
Pavese, Cesare 72
Pertini, Sandro 55, 146
partisan 1, 39, 123, 126, 145–146, 148–151, 153
patriota 152, 122, 123
   patriots 145
Petralia, Tito 106
Petrone, Carlo 80–82, 88–90, 92–93, 95
Pettoello, Decio 88
Pfeiffer, Rudolf 73
Piccialuti Caprioli, Maura 3, 9, 12, 62, 69, 134, 157–159, 175, 186
Piccola Posta della Voce di Londra 46, 168, 182, 186
Poland 30
Political Warfare Executive 12, 21, 31
Portuguese Service 30
prisoner (of war) 4, 13, 32, 46, 74, 80, 83, 86–87, 95, 106, 141, 167–168, 174–176, 179, 183, 186, 194
Pritchard, Bertha 84, 90
Programme Division 42
Progress of Fascist Propaganda 45, 111
proletarian internationalism 171
propaganda 19–26, 28–34, 40–41, 45, 59, 163, 165, 167–168, 175, 178, 186, 193–194
Propaganda Policy Committee 91
'psychological war' 21, 137
Psychological Warfare Department 32
Purcell, Henry 48

racial laws 54, 66, 72
radio balilla 102
Radio Bari 104, 108, 151, 160, 192
Radio Cairo 63
Radio Italia 74
Radio Milano 100, 160
Radio Monaco 149
Radio Moscow 163
Radio Napoli 100, 160
Radio Nations 25
radio referendum 106–107
Radio Rome 40, 108, 112, 149
radio surveys 160
radio transcripts 8–10, 13–14, 46, 48
radio set 5–6, 13, 27, 102, 159–161, 167, 193
   see also transmitter
Radiofono 100
Radiorario 160
Radio Audizioni Italiane (RAI) 75
Rathbone, Eleanor 83
recordings 9
refugee 14, 42, 50, 54, 56, 76, 80, 82–90, 93, 94–95, 153, 167, 169, 192
Reith, John 25–28, 61, 174
relays 107
religion 109, 148–149
repubblichino 62, 123–124, 126
Resistance 2–3, 11, 14, 54–56, 81, 88, 99, 123, 133, 145–148, 150–151, 153, 164, 192, 195
Ribbentrop, von Joachim 121
Ritz 67–68
Rommel, Erwin 113, 192
Ronald, Nigel 82
Roosevelt, Franlin Delano 22, 133–134, 136
Rosselli, Carlo 55, 57, 63
Rosselli, Nello 63
RSI 11, 71, 120, 122–123, 147, 173
rumour 1, 61, 70, 104, 167, 178, 192
   see also 'word of mouth'

Salazar, António de Oliviera 30
Salvemini, Gaetano 55, 65, 90–91
Saragat, Giuseppe 55, 146
Saunders, Sylvia 41
Sceneggiati 45, 48, 120

Scott, Charles Prestwich 40, 44
Setta, Sandro 46
Sforza, Carlo 65
Sharp, Gerald 163
shelter 23, 138, 139
Shelley, Percy Bysshe 66
Shepley, Leon 47, 69
Snell, Lord 83
socialism 126
   Socialist 13, 43, 55, 57, 59, 90, 93–94, 126, 171
      Socialist Party 57, 59, 75, 90
Società Italiana per le Radioaudizioni Circolari (SIRAC) 100
Soldati, Mario 72
song 9, 48, 86, 105, 167
sound effect 9, 48
Sovrintendenza alle Belle Arti 144
Spanish Civil War 63, 93
Special Operations Executive 21, 31, 89
Sprigge, Cecil Jackson Squire 14, 40–42, 45, 50, 66
stereotypes 13, 67, 163, 164–165, 186
Stevens, Harold Raphael 1, 14, 42–43, 45–46, 50, 69, 92, 108–109, 110–111, 116, 121, 134, 136, 143, 153, 157, 168, 177–178, 180–186, 195
Strauss, George 83
Stuart, Campbell 41
Sturzo, Luigi 55, 89–90
surveys 7, 9, 13, 157, 159–160, 174–176, 178, 186, 193
Switzerland 55, 93, 183, 184
Symons, Federico 63

Tarchiani, Alberto 55
Taylor, Maxwell 134
Tchaikovsky, Pëtr Il'ič Čajkovskij 48
telegraph 23, 26, 32, 100
   telegraphy 20, 99
Third Reich 21
Thomas, Ivor 74, 88
Thornhill 63–65
Toscanini, Arturo 48
totalitarian regime 21, 108–109, 151, 157, 191
translation 30, 38, 46–47
transmitter 24, 27, 102, 110

transnational 4–8, 10, 12, 14, 19–20, 23, 25, 33, 192, 194
transnationalism 4
   Transnational Radio Encounters 4
Transport and General Workers Union 171
Trentin, Silvio 55
Treves, Claudio 43, 55, 57–58
Treves, Lotte Dann 84–85
Treves, Paolo 43, 45, 55, 57–60, 62, 72, 83–88, 92, 94, 148, 169–170, 172, 193
   brothers 75, 80, 81–82, 89–90, 93, 95
Treves, Piero 43, 57, 58, 60, 72–73, 83, 87, 94
   brothers 75, 80, 81–82, 89–90, 93, 95
Treves, Renato 72
Turati, Filippo 55, 57, 59

Ullswater Report 27
unconditional surrender 3, 11, 14, 30, 62, 88, 91, 93, 99, 104, 115, 120, 122, 127, 132–134, 136, 142, 153, 158, 172, 192
Undertone 45, 116
United States 2, 22, 48, 64–65, 72, 75, 91–94, 99, 106, 113, 134
Unione Radiofonica Italiana (URI) 99
United Nations 49, 121
USSR 21–22
   Russians 173, 177
      Soviet Union 22, 30, 93, 173

'V' for victory 30
Venturi, Lionello 65, 76n.12

'war of nerves' 137
'war of words' 4, 15n.13
Whittal, Cecil Frederick 14, 41–42, 50, 91
Wilson, Maitland 144
Women's Voluntary Service (WVS) 165
'wop' 106
word of mouth 175–176, 193

Yugoslavia 150, 184

Zencovich, Livio Zino 89, 151

EU authorised representative for GPSR:
Easy Access System Europe, Mustamäe tee 50,
10621 Tallinn, Estonia
gpsr.requests@easproject.com

www.ingramcontent.com/pod-product-compliance
Lightning Source LLC
Chambersburg PA
CBHW071204240426
43668CB00032B/2077